Interface Patterns

ADAPTER (page 19) Provide the interface that a client expects, using the services of a class with a different interface.

FACADE (page 35) Provide an interface that makes a subsystem easy to use.

COMPOSITE (page 49) Allow clients to treat individual objects and compositions of objects uniformly.

BRIDGE (page 65) Decouple an abstraction (a class that relies on abstract operations) from the implementation of its abstract operations so that the abstraction and its implementation can vary independently.

Responsibility Patterns

SINGLETON (page 83) Ensure that a class has only one instance, and provide a global point of access to it.

OBSERVER (page 89) Define a one-to-many dependency among objects so that when one object changes state, all of its dependents are notified and updated automatically.

MEDIATOR (page 109) Define an object that encapsulates the way a set of objects interact. This keeps the objects from referring to each other explicitly and lets you vary their interaction independently.

PROXY (page 123) Provide a placeholder for another object to control access to it.

CHAIN OF RESPONSIBILITY (page 139) Avoid coupling the sender of a request to its receiver by giving more than one object a chance to handle the request.

FLYWEIGHT (page 147) Use sharing to support large numbers of fine-grained objects efficiently.

Construction Patterns

BUILDER (page 163) Move the construction logic for an object outside the class to instantiate.

FACTORY METHOD (page 171) Define the interface for creating an object while retaining control of which class to instantiate.

ABSTRACT FACTORY (page 179) Provide for the creation of a family of related or dependent objects.

PROTOTYPE (page 191) Provide new objects by copying an example.

MEMENTO (page 197) Provide for the storage and restoration of an object's state.

Operation Patterns

TEMPLATE METHOD (page 223) Implement an algorithm in a method, deferring the definition of some steps of the algorithm so that other classes can supply them.

STATE (page 235) Distribute state-specific logic across classes that represents an object's state.

STRATEGY (page 247) Encapsulate alternative strategies (or approaches) in separate classes that each implement a common operation.

COMMAND (page 257) Encapsulate a request as an object so that you can parameterize clients with different requests; you can queue, time, or log requests; and you can allow a client to prepare a special context in which to invoke the request.

INTERPRETER (page 267) Let developers compose executable objects according to a set of composition rules.

Extension Patterns

DECORATOR (page 291) Let developers compose an object's behavior dynamically.

ITERATOR (page 311) Provide a way to access the elements of a collection sequentially.

VISITOR (page 329) Let developers define a new operation for a hierarchy without changing the hierarchy's classes.

Back Matter

Design Patterns
in C#

The Software Patterns Series

Series Editor: John M. Vlissides

The Software Patterns Series (SPS) comprises pattern literature of lasting significance to software developers. Software patterns document general solutions to recurring problems in all software-related spheres, from the technology itself, to the organizations that develop and distribute it, to the people who use it. Books in the series distill experience from one or more of these areas into a form that software professionals can apply immediately.

Relevance and *impact* are the tenets of the SPS. Relevance means each book presents patterns that solve real problems. Patterns worthy of the name are intrinsically relevant; they are borne of practitioners' experiences, not theory or speculation. Patterns have impact when they change how people work for the better. A book becomes a part of the series not just because it embraces these tenets, but because it has demonstrated it fulfills them for its audience.

Titles in the series:

Data Access Patterns: Database Interactions in Object-Oriented Applications; Clifton Nock

Design Patterns Explained, Second Edition: A New Perspective on Object-Oriented Design; Alan Shalloway and James Trott

Design Patterns in C#; Steven John Metsker

Design Patterns in Java™; Steven John Metsker and William C. Wake

Design Patterns Java™ Workbook; Steven John Metsker

.NET Patterns: Architecture, Design, and Process; Christian Thilmany

Pattern Hatching: Design Patterns Applied; John M. Vlissides

Pattern Languages of Program Design; James O. Coplien and Douglas C. Schmidt

Pattern Languages of Program Design 2; John M. Vlissides, James O. Coplien, and Norman L. Kerth

Pattern Languages of Program Design 3; Robert C. Martin, Dirk Riehle, and Frank Buschmann

Pattern Languages of Program Design 5; Dragos Manolescu, Markus Voelter, and James Noble

Patterns for Parallel Programming; Timothy G. Mattson, Beverly A. Sanders, and Berna L. Massingill

Software Configuration Management Patterns: Effective Teamwork, Practical Integration; Stephen P. Berczuk and Brad Appleton

The Design Patterns Smalltalk Companion; Sherman Alpert, Kyle Brown, and Bobby Woolf

Use Cases: Patterns and Blueprints; Gunnar Övergaard and Karin Palmkvist

For more information, check out the series web site at www.awprofessional.com/series/swpatterns

Design Patterns in C#

Steven John Metsker

 **ADDISON–WESLEY**

Boston, San Francisco, New York, Toronto, Montreal
London, Munich, Paris, Madrid
Capetown, Sydney, Tokyo, Singapore, Mexico City

The publisher offers discounts on this book when ordered in quantity for special sales. For more information, please contact:

U.S. Corporate and Government Sales: (800)581-3419
corpsales@pearsontechgroup.com

For sales outside the U.S., please contact:
International Sales: (317)581-3793
international@pearsontechgroup.com

Visit Addison-Wesley on the Web: www.awprofessional.com

Library of Congress Cataloging-in-Publication Data

A catalog record for this book can be obtained from the Library of Congress

Text printed in the United States on recycled paper at Courier Westford, Massachusetts.

ISBN 0321126971

4 5 6 7 CRW 07 06

4th Printing   May 2006

To Emma-Kate and Sarah-Jane,
Two cherubim aswirl
To Alison, the nurturing heart
To heartstring-strumming girls.

Contents

PREFACE

It seems a long time ago (two years!) that I received the initial encouragement for this book from Paul Becker, an editor at the time with Addison-Wesley. I remain grateful to Paul for his help, and to his successor, John Neidhart, who took over as editor when Paul left. I am also grateful for the encouragement of John Vlissides, who is the Patterns Series editor and who has been a supporter of mine for all three of my books.

John Vlissides is also, of course, one of the four authors of *Design Patterns*. John and his co-authors—Erich Gamma, Ralph Johnson, and Richard Helm—produced the work that not only established a list of important patterns that every developer should know, but also set a standard for quality and clarity that I have aspired to attain in my own writing.

In addition to relying heavily on *Design Patterns*, I have benefited from the use of many other books; see Bibliography on 439. In particular, I have depended on *The Unified Modeling Language User Guide* [Booch] for its clear explanations of UML. For concise and accurate help on C# topics, I have consulted *C# Essentials* [Albahari] almost daily. I have also repeatedly drawn on the insights of *C# and the .NET Platform* [Troelsen], and for realistic fireworks examples, I have consistently consulted *The Chemistry of Fireworks* [Russell].

As the present book began to take shape, several excellent reviewers helped to guide its progress. I would like to thank Bill Wake for his early reviews. Bill never ceases to amaze me in his ability to catch the subtlest errors while simultaneously providing advice on overall direction, content, and style. I would also like to thank Steve Berczuk and Neil Harrison. In particular, they hit on the same key point that the book needed more introductory material for each pattern. Their comments drove me to rework the entire book. It is much stronger now because of their advice.

With the help of editors and reviewers, I was able to write this book; but, the text of a book is just the beginning. I would like to thank Nick Radhuber and the entire production staff for their hard work and dedication. Their work renders text into what is to this day its most usable form—a book!

Steve Metsker (Steve.Metsker@acm.org)

CHAPTER 1

INTRODUCTION

This book is for developers who know C# and want to improve their skills as designers. This book covers the same list of techniques as the classic book *Design Patterns*, written by Erich Gamma, Richard Helm, Ralph Johnson, and John Vlissides. This book (*Design Patterns in C#*) provides examples in C# and in a .NET setting. This book also includes many "challenges," exercises designed to help strengthen your ability to apply design patterns in your own C# programs.

Why Patterns?

A *pattern* is a way of doing something, a way of pursuing an intent, a technique. The idea of capturing effective techniques applies to many endeavors: making food, making fireworks, making software, and to other crafts. In any new craft that is starting to mature, the people working on it will begin to find common, effective methods for achieving aims and solving problems in various contexts. The community of people that practice a craft usually invent jargon that helps them talk about their craft. Some of this jargon will refer to patterns, established techniques for achieving certain aims. As a craft and its jargon grows, writers begin to play an important role. Writers document a craft's patterns, helping to standardize the jargon and publicize effective techniques.

Christopher Alexander was one of the first writers to encapsulate a craft's best practices by documenting its patterns. His work relates to architecture—of buildings, not software. In *A Pattern Language: Towns, Buildings, Construction*, Alexander provides patterns for architecting successful buildings and towns. His writing is powerful and has influenced the software community, partially because of the way he looks at intent.

You might state the intent of architectural patterns as something like "to design buildings." But Alexander makes it clear that the intent of architectural patterns is to serve and inspire the people who will occupy buildings and towns. Alexander's work showed that patterns are an excellent way to capture and convey the wisdom of a craft. He also established that properly perceiving and documenting the intent of a craft is a critical, philosophical, and elusive challenge.

The software community has resonated with the patterns approach and has created many books that document patterns of software development. These books record best practices for software process, software analysis, high-level architecture, and class-level design, and new patterns books appear every year. If you are choosing a book to read about patterns, you should spend some time reading reviews of available books and try to select the book that will help you the most.

Why Design Patterns?

A *design pattern* is a pattern—a way to pursue an intent—that uses classes and their methods in an object-oriented (OO) language. Developers often start thinking about design after learning a programming language and writing code for a while. You might notice that someone else's code seems simpler and works better than yours does and you might wonder how that developer achieves such simplicity. Design patterns are a level up from code and typically show how to achieve a goal using a few classes. Other people have discovered how to program effectively in OO languages. If you want to become a powerful C# programmer, then you should study design patterns, especially those in this book—the same patterns that *Design Patterns* explains.

Design Patterns describes 23 design patterns. Many other books on design patterns have followed, so that there are at least 100 design patterns worth knowing. The 23 design patterns that Gamma, Helm, Johnson, and Vlissides placed in *Design Patterns* are probably not absolutely the most useful 23 design patterns to know. On the other hand, these patterns are probably among the 100 most useful patterns. Unfortunately, there is no set of criteria that establishes the value of a pattern, and so the identity of the other 77 patterns in the top 100 is not yet established. Fortunately, the authors of *Design Patterns* chose well, and the patterns they documented are certainly worth learning. Learning these patterns will also serve as a foundation as you branch out and begin learning patterns from other sources.

GoF

You may have noted the potential confusion between "design patterns" the topic and *Design Patterns* the book. The topic and the book title *sound* alike, so to distinguish them, many speakers and some writers refer to the book as the "Gang of Four" book, or the "GoF" book, referring to the number of its authors. In print, it is not so confusing that *Design Patterns* refers to the book and "design patterns" refers to the topic. Accordingly, this book avoids using the term "GoF."

Why C#?

This book gives its examples in C#, the OO language at the center of Microsoft's .NET framework. The .NET framework is a suite of products for developing and managing systems with tiered, OO architectures.

The .NET framework is important simply because of Microsoft's size. Also, .NET aligns at a high level with industry thinking about how to compose an architecture. You can compare most .NET components with competing products from vendors that implement software according to the Java™ 2 Platform, Enterprise Edition (J2EE) specification. But note that J2EE is a specification, not a product, while .NET is the product lineup of one company and its partners.

At a superficial level, C# is important because it is the central OO language for developing in .NET. C# is also important because, like Java, it is a *consolidation language,* designed to absorb the strengths of earlier languages. This consolidation has fueled the popularity of Java and C# and helps ensure that future languages will evolve from these languages rather than depart radically from them. Your investment in C# will almost surely yield value in any language that supplants C#.

The patterns in *Design Patterns* apply to C# because, like Smalltalk, C++, and Java, C# follows a class/instance paradigm. C# is much more similar to Smalltalk and C++ than it is to, say, Prolog or Self. Although competing paradigms are important, the class/instance paradigm appears to be the most practical next step in applied computing. This book uses C# because of the popularity of C# and .NET, and because C# appears to lie along the evolutionary path of languages that we will use for decades ahead.

UML

Where this book's challenges (exercises) have solutions in code, this book uses C#. Many of the challenges ask you to draw a diagram of how classes, packages, and other elements relate. You can use any notation you like, but this book uses Unified Modeling Language (UML) notation. Even if you are familiar with UML, it is a good idea to have a reference handy. Two good choices are *The Unified Modeling Language User Guide* [Booch] and *UML Distilled* [Fowler]. The bare minimum of UML knowledge that you need for this book is provided in Appendix D, "UML at a Glance."

Challenges

No matter how much you read about doing something, you won't feel like you know it until you do it. This is true partially because until you exercise the knowledge you gain from a book, you won't encounter subtleties and you won't grapple with alternative approaches. You won't feel confident about design patterns until you apply them to some real challenges.

The problem with learning through experience is that you can do damage as you learn. You can't apply patterns in production code before you are confident in your own skills. But you need to start applying patterns to gain confidence. What a conundrum! The solution is to practice on example problems where mistakes are valuable but painless.

Each chapter in this book begins with a short introduction and then sets up a series of challenges for you to solve. After you come up with a solution you can compare your solution with one given in Appendix B, "Solutions." The solution in the book may take a different slant from your solution, or may provide some other insight.

You probably can't go overboard in how hard you work to come up with answers to the challenges in this book. If you consult other books, work with a colleague, or write sample code to check out your solution, terrific! You will never regret investing your time and energy in learning how to apply design patterns.

A danger lurks in the solutions that this book provides. If you flip to the solution immediately after reading a challenge, you will not gain much from this book. The solutions in this book can do you more harm than good if you don't first create your own solutions.

The Organization of this Book

There are many ways to organize and categorize patterns. You might organize them according to similarities in structure, or you might follow the order in *Design Patterns*. The most important aspect of any pattern is its intent, that is, the potential value of applying the pattern. This book organizes the 23 patterns of *Design Patterns* according to their intent.

Having decided to organize patterns by intent raises the question of how to categorize intent. This book adopts the notion that the intent of a design pattern is usually easily expressed as the need to go beyond the ordinary facilities that are built into C#. For example, C# has plentiful support for defining the interfaces that a class implements. But if you want to adapt a class's interface to meet the needs of a client, you need to apply the ADAPTER pattern. The intent of the ADAPTER pattern goes beyond the interface facilities built into C#.

This book places design pattern intent in five categories as follows:

- Interfaces
- Responsibility
- Construction
- Operations
- Extensions

These five categories account for the five parts of this book. Each part begins with a chapter that discusses and presents challenges related to features built into C#. For example, the "Interface Patterns" part begins with a chapter on ordinary C# interfaces. This chapter will challenge your understanding of the C# interface construct, especially in comparison to abstract classes. The remaining chapters of the "Interface Patterns" part address patterns whose primary intent involves the definition of an interface, the set of methods that a client can call from a service provider. Each of these patterns addresses a need that cannot be addressed solely with C# interfaces.

Categorizing patterns by intent does not result in each pattern supporting just one type of intent. When a pattern supports more than one type of intent, it appears as a full chapter in the first part to which it applies, and gets a brief mention in subsequent parts. Table 1.1 shows the categorization behind the organization of this book.

Table 1.1: A Categorization of Patterns by Intent.

Intent	Patterns
Interfaces	ADAPTER, FACADE, COMPOSITE, BRIDGE
Responsibility	SINGLETON, OBSERVER, MEDIATOR, PROXY, CHAIN OF RESPONSIBILITY, FLYWEIGHT
Construction	BUILDER, FACTORY METHOD, ABSTRACT FACTORY, PROTOTYPE, MEMENTO
Operations	TEMPLATE METHOD, STATE, STRATEGY, COMMAND, INTERPRETER
Extensions	DECORATOR, ITERATOR, VISITOR

I hope you will question the categorization in Table 1.1. Will you agree that SINGLETON is about responsibility, not construction? Is COMPOSITE an interface pattern? Categorizing patterns is somewhat subjective. But I hope you will agree that thinking about the intent behind patterns and thinking about how you will apply patterns are very useful exercises.

Welcome to Oozinoz!

The challenges in this book all cite examples from Oozinoz Fireworks, a fictional company that manufactures and sells fireworks and puts on fireworks displays. (Oozinoz takes its name from the sounds heard at Oozinoz exhibitions.) You can acquire the code from www.oozinoz.com. For more information about building and testing the source code, see Appendix C, "Oozinoz Source."

Summary

Patterns are distillations of accumulated wisdom that provide a standard jargon, naming the concepts that experienced practitioners apply. The patterns in the classic book *Design Patterns* are among the most useful class-level patterns and are certainly worth learning. This book explains the same patterns as those documented in *Design Patterns*, but gives examples and challenges using C# and the .NET Framework Class Libraries (FCL). By working through the challenges in this book, you will learn to recognize and apply a large portion of the accumulated wisdom of the software community.

PART 1

INTERFACE PATTERNS

CHAPTER 2

INTRODUCING INTERFACES

A class's *interface*, speaking abstractly, is the collection of methods and fields that a class permits objects of other classes to access. This interface usually represents a commitment that the methods will perform the operation implied by their names and as specified by code comments and other documentation. A class's *implementation* is the code that lies within its methods.

C# elevates the notion of interface to be a separate construct, expressly separating interface (what an object must do) from implementation (how an object fulfills this commitment). C# interfaces allow several classes to provide the same functionality, and they open up the possibility that a class can implement more than one interface.

Several design patterns use the features that C# builds in. For example, you might use an interface to adapt a class's interface to meet a client's needs by applying the ADAPTER pattern. But before going beyond the basics built into C#, it's worthwhile ensuring that you are comfortable with how C# features work, starting with C# interfaces.

Interfaces and Abstract Classes

The original book *Design Patterns* [Gamma et al. 1990] frequently mentions the use of abstract classes, but does not describe the use of interfaces. This is because the C++ and Smalltalk languages, which *Design Patterns* uses for its examples, do not have an interface construct. This has a minor impact on the utility of the book for C# developers because C# interfaces are quite similar to abstract classes.

Challenge 2.1

Write down three differences between abstract classes and interfaces in C#.

A solution appears on page 347.

If you had to live without interfaces, you could get by with abstract classes (as C++ does). Interfaces, however, play a critical role in n-tier development and certainly warrant first-rate status as a separate construct. Similarly, if you had to live without delegates, you could make due with interfaces (as Java does.) However, delegates consolidate the common task of registering a method for callback, and as such, delegates are a useful addition to C#.

Interfaces and Delegates

Delegates are similar to interfaces in that they define expectations. Learning to use delegates can be confusing, partly because the word "delegate" may be used to refer to slightly different concepts. Before comparing interfaces with delegates, it is useful to review how delegates work in C#.

The keyword `delegate` in C# introduces a new delegate type. The delegate type establishes which sort of methods can be used to instantiate the delegate type. The delegate type does *not* specify the name of the method, but it does specify the argument types and return type of the method. Consider the following declaration:

```
public delegate object BorrowReader(IDataReader reader);
```

This statement declares a new delegate type. The name of the delegate type is `BorrowReader`. The declaration specifies that this delegate type can be instantiated with any method that accepts an `IDataReader` object as a parameter and that has a return type of `object`. Suppose that you have a class that contains the following method:

```
private static object GetNames(IDataReader reader)
{
    //...
}
```

The `GetNames()` method has the parameter types and return type that the `BorrowReader` delegate type specifies. You can use this method's name to instantiate the delegate type, as in the following statement:

```
BorrowReader b = new BorrowReader(GetNames);
```

The variable b contains an instance of the BorrowReader delegate type. Any code that has access to this delegate instance can invoke it; the delegate instance will then invoke its contained method. The power of the b object is that another method can invoke it and its contained method at an opportune moment. For example, a data services class can obtain a database reader, invoke a BorrowReader delegate instance (passing it the reader), and then release the reader as a resource. The Oozinoz DataLayer namespace provides exactly this set of services.

In the Oozinoz codebase, the BorrowReader delegate type is part of the DataLayer namespace:

```
namespace DataLayer
{
    // ...
    public delegate object BorrowReader(IDataReader reader);
    // ...
}
```

The idea behind this delegate type is to divide the responsibility between classes that work with an IDataReader object. (The IDataReader interface is part of the .NET System.Data namespace.)

The DataLayer namespace includes a DataServices class that supplies a LendReader() method that lends out a reader. The code for LendReader() is as follows:

```
public static object LendReader(
    string sql, BorrowReader borrower)
{
    using (OleDbConnection conn = CreateConnection())
    {
        conn.Open();
        OleDbCommand c = new OleDbCommand(sql, conn);
        OleDbDataReader r = c.ExecuteReader();
        return borrower(r);
    }
}
```

This code uses a database connection that comes from the CreateConnection() method, whose code is as follows:

```
public static OleDbConnection CreateConnection()
{
    String dbName =
        FileFinder.GetFileName("db", "oozinoz.mdb");
    OleDbConnection c = new OleDbConnection();
    c.ConnectionString =
        "Provider=Microsoft.Jet.OLEDB.4.0;" +
        "Data Source=" + dbName;
    return c;
}
```

The CreateConnection() method uses the FileFinder utility class (from the Oozinoz Utilities namespace) to find an Access database in a neighboring db directory. The code uses the database filename to configure the database connection and returns. The `LendReader()` method uses this connection for a database reader it creates, lends out, and closes.

The `LendReader()` method accepts a `select` statement and an instance of the `BorrowReader` delegate type. The code creates a database connection, creates a data reader from that connection, and invokes the `borrower` delegate instance. The `borrower` delegate contains a method; it can contain any method that accepts an `IDataReader` argument and that returns an object. When `LendReader()` invokes the `borrower` delegate, the delegate invokes its contained method and passes along the database reader. The invoked method can use the reader for any purpose. When the invoked method completes, program control returns to the `LendReader()` method.

Note that the `LendReader()` code wraps its delegate invocation inside a `using` statement. The `using` statement will call the `Dispose()` method for the connection after the body of the statement completes (or if an exception is thrown.) The connection will also dispose of the associated reader the body of the `using` statement creates. The design of the `LendReader()` method lets code that creates and releases a database reader run before and after the code of a client that uses the reader.

The following `ShowBorrowing` class provides an example of borrowing a database reader:

```
using System;
using System.Data;
using DataLayer;
public class ShowBorrowing
{
    public static void Main()
    {
        string sel = "SELECT * FROM ROCKET";
        DataServices.LendReader(
            sel, new BorrowReader(GetNames));
    }
    private static object GetNames(IDataReader reader)
    {
        while (reader.Read())
        {
            Console.WriteLine(reader["Name"]);
        }
        return null;
    }
}
```

Running this class prints the names of rockets in the Oozinoz database:

```
Shooter
Orbit
Biggie
...
```

To run this code on your machine, Appendix C, "Oozinoz Source," explains how to acquire and use the Oozinoz code.

The ShowBorrowing class includes a GetNames() method that has the same parameters and return type as the BorrowReader delegate type. This allows the Main() method to instantiate the BorrowReader delegate and use this object as a parameter to the LendReader() method. The GetNames() method returns null, although a more typical borrower method would return the results of having used the reader.

By using a delegate, our design lets the GetNames() method execute at an opportune moment—after creation and before disposal of the reader. We could accomplish the same effect with an interface that defines the method to call back. Suppose that a new method, LendReader2(), accepts an interface instead of a delegate:

```
public static object LendReader2(
    string sel, IBorrower borrower)
{
    using (OleDbConnection conn =
        DataServices.CreateConnection())
    {
        conn.Open();
        OleDbCommand c = new OleDbCommand(sel, conn);
        OleDbDataReader r = c.ExecuteReader();
        return borrower.BorrowReader(r);
    }
}
```

Challenge 2.2

An implementation of the IBorrower interface must supply the method that LendReader2() will call after creating a reader and before disposing of the reader. Write the code for IBorrower.cs.

A solution appears on page 347.

When your design uses a delegate to call back a single method, an interface-based design may be equally effective. The strength of delegates shows more clearly when your design requires a delegate to hold and invoke multiple methods. This occurs most frequently when an object uses a delegate to let multiple clients register an interest in an event, such as the click of a button. As the *C# Language Specification* [Wiltamuth] says in Section 17.5: "An event is a member that enables an object or class to provide notifications."

Challenge 2.3

A C# interface can contain methods, properties, and indexers. An interface can also contain events, but not delegates. Why is that?

A solution appears on page 348.

Understanding delegates in C# can be difficult, especially because we overload the meaning of the word "delegate." For example, we might use the word "delegate" to indicate a delegate declaration, the resulting delegate type, or an instance of a delegate. In particular, it is common to refer to "invoking a delegate," but an object can only invoke an instance of a delegate, not a delegate type. If you find this topic confusing, you are not alone. But it is well worth studying how delegates work in C#, as they form a critical part of how typical applications operate and how classes interface with each other.

Interfaces and Properties

C# interfaces can specify that implementers must provide indexers or properties. The need to specify an indexer may occur when you are defining a new type of collection. The need to specify a property occurs more commonly, specifically when you want to declare that an implementer must have methods for getting and/or setting an attribute.

Consider the following interface that does not use C# properties, but that requires implementers to provide access to attributes of an advertisement object:

```
public interface IAdvertisement
{
    int GetID();
    string GetAdCopy();
    void SetAdCopy (string text);
}
```

This interface is part of the Oozinoz ShowProperties class library. Loosely speaking, this interface specifies two properties for its implementers; but strictly speaking, these are not C# properties. There are advantages to using the C# syntax for specifying properties. The syntax is somewhat more elegant, and more important, unforeseen clients can detect the presence of C# properties through reflection. For example, a DataGrid object will display the properties of objects in an ArrayList collection, so long as the properties are truly C# properties.

Challenge 2.4

Rewrite the code for the IAdvertisement interface to specify C# properties for the ID and ad copy attributes of implementers.

A solution appears on page 348.

The presence of properties in an interface relies on syntactic subtleties and makes a difference in how implementers will perform. As with most aspects of programming languages, it is important to understand both the conceptual value and the details of using C# interface features.

Interface Details

An essential benefit of C# interfaces is that they limit the interaction between objects. This limitation turns out to be a liberation. A class that implements an interface can undergo dramatic change in how it fulfills an interface, while the class's clients remain unaffected. The idea of using interfaces is easy enough to understand, but in practice, details emerge that can send you hunting for reference books.

If you don't like quizzes, then skip to the summary. But if you'd like to test your knowledge of C# interface specifics, then take the following challenge.

Challenge 2.5

The following statements were taken from the C# *Language Specification* [Wiltamuth]. In two of the statements, a word or two has been changed, making the statements false. Which statements are false?

1. An interface defines a contract.

2. Interfaces can contain methods, properties, delegates, and indexers.

3. An interface declaration must declare one or more members.

4. All interface members implicitly have public access.

5. It is a compile-time error for interface member declarations to include any modifiers.

6. Like a non-abstract class, an abstract class must provide implementations of all members of the interfaces that are listed in the base class list of the class.

A solution appears on page 349.

Summary

The power of interfaces is that they delineate what is and isn't expected in how classes collaborate. Interfaces are similar to purely abstract classes, defining expectations, but not implementing them. Interfaces are also similar to delegates, although delegates specify only the parameters and return type of a single method.

Delegates are types, so an interface cannot contain a delegate as a member. However, variables that have a delegate type and that are marked with the event keyword may appear in interfaces.

In addition to methods and events, interfaces can contain indexers and properties. The syntax for these members is interesting, and using these member types makes it easier for clients to use reflection to detect the behavior of implementing classes. Mastering both the concepts and details of applying C# interfaces is well worth the investment of your time. This powerful construct is at the heart of many strong designs and several design patterns.

Beyond Ordinary Interfaces

You can simplify and strengthen your designs with the appropriate application of C# interfaces. Sometimes, though, the design of an interface has to go beyond the ordinary definition and use of an interface.

If you intend to:	Then apply the pattern:
• Adapt a class's interface to match the interface a client expects,	ADAPTER
• Provide a simple interface into a collection of classes,	FACADE
• Define an interface that applies to individual objects and groups of objects,	COMPOSITE
• Decouple an abstraction from its implementation so that the two can vary independently,	BRIDGE

The intent of each design pattern is to solve a problem in a context. Interface-oriented patterns address contexts where you need to define or redefine access to the methods of a class or group of classes. For example, when you have a class that performs a service you need, but with method names that do not match a client's expectations, you can apply the ADAPTER pattern.

CHAPTER 3

ADAPTER

An object is a *client* if it needs to call your code. In some cases, client code will be written after your code exists and the developer can mold the client to use the interfaces of the objects that you provide. In other cases, clients may be developed independently of your code. For example, a rocket simulation program might be designed to use rocket information that you supply, but such a simulation will have its own definition of how a rocket should behave. In such circumstances, you may find that an existing class performs the services that a client needs but with different method names. In this situation, you can apply the ADAPTER pattern. The intent of ADAPTER is to provide the interface that a client expects while using the services of a class with a different interface.

Adapting to an Interface

When you need to adapt your code, you may find that the client developer planned well for such circumstances. This is evident when the developer provides an interface that defines the services that the client code needs, as the example in Figure 3.1 shows. A client class makes calls to a `RequiredMethod()` method that is declared in an interface. You may have found an existing class with a method that can fulfill the client's needs, with a name such as `UsefulMethod()`. You can adapt the existing class to meet the client's needs by writing a class that extends `Existing-Class`, implements `RequiredInterface`, and overrides `RequiredMethod()` so that it delegates its requests to `UsefulMethod()`.

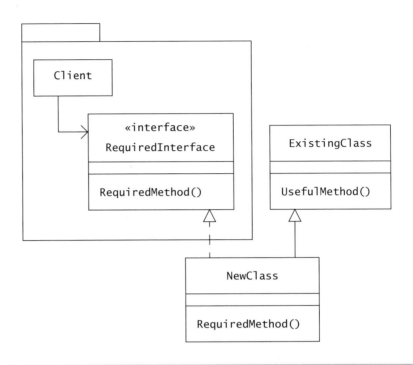

Figure 3.1   When a developer of client code thoughtfully defines the
               client's needs, you may be able to fulfill the interface by
               adapting existing code.

The NewClass class in Figure 3.1 is an example of ADAPTER. An instance of
this class is an instance of RequiredInterface. In other words, the New-
Class class meets the needs of the client.

For a more concrete example, suppose you are working with a package
that simulates the flight and timing of rockets such as those you manufacture at Oozinoz. The simulation package includes an event simulator that
explores the effects of launching several rockets, along with an interface
that specifies a rocket's behavior. Figure 3.2 shows this package.

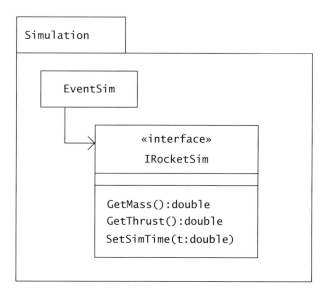

Figure 3.2   The Simulation package clearly defines its requirements for simulating the flight of a rocket.

Suppose that at Oozinoz you have a PhysicalRocket class that you want to plug into the simulation. This class has methods that supply, approximately, the behavior that the simulator needs. In this situation, you can apply ADAPTER, creating a subclass of PhysicalRocket that implements the IRocketSim interface. Figure 3.3 partially shows this design.

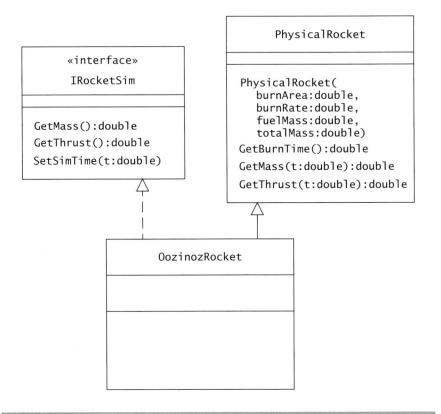

Figure 3.3   When complete, this diagram shows the design of a class that
              adapts the Rocket class to meet the needs of the IRocketSim
              interface.

The PhysicalRocket class has the information that the simulator needs,
but its methods do not exactly match those that the simulation declares in
the IRocketSim interface. Most of the differences occur because the simulator keeps an internal clock and occasionally updates simulated objects
by calling a SetSimTime() method. To adapt the PhysicalRocket class to
meet the simulator's needs, an OozinozRocket object can maintain a _time
instance variable that it can pass to the methods of the PhysicalRocket
class as needed.

Challenge 3.1

Complete the class diagram in Figure 3.3 to show the design of an
OozinozRocket class that lets a PhysicalRocket object participate in a
simulation as an IRocketSim object.

A solution appears on page 350.

The code for PhysicalRocket is somewhat complex as it embodies the
physics that Oozinoz uses to model a rocket. However, it is exactly that
logic we want to reuse without reimplementing. The OozinozRocket class
simply translates calls to use its superclass's methods. The code for this
new subclass will look something like:

```
public class OozinozRocket : PhysicalRocket, IRocketSim
{
    private double _time;
    public OozinozRocket(
        double burnArea, double burnRate,
        double fuelMass, double totalMass)
        : base (burnArea, burnRate, fuelMass, totalMass)
    {
    }
    public double GetMass()
    {
        // challenge!
    }
    public double Thrust()
    {
        // challenge!
    }
    public void SetSimTime (double time)
    {
        _time = time;
    }
}
```

Challenge 3.2

Complete the code for the OozinozRocket class, including methods
GetMass() and GetThrust().

A solution appears on page 351.

When a client defines its expectations in an interface, you can apply
ADAPTER by supplying a class that implements a provided interface and
that subclasses an existing class. You may also be able to apply ADAPTER

even if no interface exists to define a client's expectations. In this situation, you must use an "object adapter."

Class and Object Adapters

The designs in Figures 3.1 and 3.3 show *class adapters* that adapt through subclassing. In a class adapter design, the new adapter class implements the desired interface and subclasses an existing class. This approach will not always work, particularly when the set of methods that you need to adapt is not specified in a C# interface. In such a case, you can create an *object adapter,* an adapter that uses delegation rather than subclassing. Figure 3.4 shows this design.

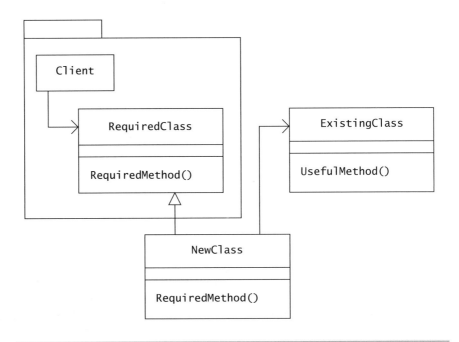

Figure 3.4   You can create an object adapter by subclassing the class that you need, fulfilling the required methods by relying on an object of an existing class.

The NewClass class in Figure 3.4 is an example of ADAPTER. An instance of this class is an instance of the RequiredClass class. In other words, the NewClass class meets the needs of the client. The NewClass class can adapt the ExistingClass class to meet the client's needs by using an instance of ExistingClass.

For a more concrete example, suppose that the simulation package worked directly with a Skyrocket class, without specifying an interface to define the behaviors the simulation needs. Figure 3.5 shows this class.

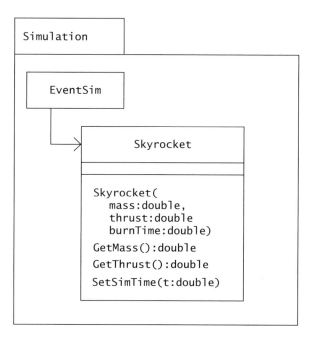

Figure 3.5   In this alternative design, the Simulation package does not specify the interface it needs for modeling a rocket.

The Skyrocket class uses a fairly primitive model of the physics of a rocket. For example, it assumes that the rocket is entirely consumed as its fuel burns. Suppose that you want to apply the more sophisticated physical model that the Oozinoz PhysicalRocket class uses. To adapt the logic in the PhysicalRocket class to the needs of the simulation, you can create an OozinozSkyrocket class as an object adapter that subclasses Skyrocket and that uses a PhysicalRocket object, as Figure 3.6 shows.

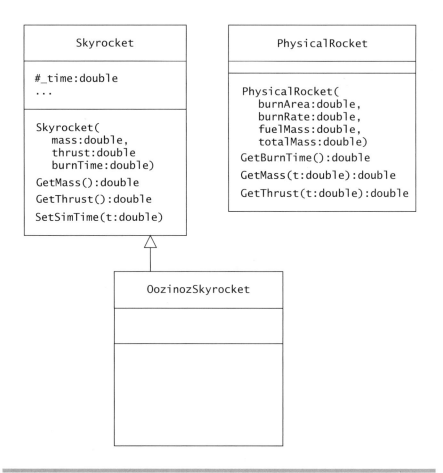

Figure 3.6   When complete, this diagram shows an object adapter design
              that uses information from an existing class to meet the needs
              that a client has of a Skyrocket object.

Notice that the OozinozSkyrocket class subclasses from Skyrocket, not
PhysicalRocket. This will allow an OozinozSkyrocket object to serve as a
substitute wherever the simulation client needs a Skyrocket object. The
Skyrocket class supports subclassing by making its _time variable protected (as shown in the UML diagram) and by making its methods virtual (not shown in the diagram).

The code for the OozinozSkyrocket class might be as follows:

```
public class OozinozSkyrocket : Skyrocket
{
    private PhysicalRocket _rocket;
    public OozinozSkyrocket(PhysicalRocket r) :
        base (r.GetMass(0), r.GetThrust(0), r.GetBurnTime())
    {
        _rocket = r;
    }
    public override double GetMass()
    {
        return _rocket.GetMass(_simTime);
    }
    public override double GetThrust()
    {
        return _rocket.GetThrust(_simTime);
    }
}
```

The OozinozSkyrocket class lets you supply an OozinozSkyrocket object anywhere the simulation package requires a Skyrocket object. In general, object adapters partially overcome the problem of adapting an object to an interface that is not expressly defined.

The object adapter for the Skyrocket class is a more dangerous design than the class adapter that implements the IRocketSim interface. But we should not complain too much. At least the Skyrocket designer marked the methods as virtual. Suppose that this were not the case. Then the OozinozSkyrocket class could not override the GetMass() or GetThrust() methods. A subclass cannot force adaptability onto its superclass.

The best way to plan for adaptation is to define the needs of a client program in an interface. If you do not foresee a specific type of adaptation, you may still want other developers to be able to create object adapters for your class. In this case, place a `virtual` modifier on any methods that you want to let subclasses override.

Adapting Data in .NET

If you search for "adapter" in the online help for Visual Studio .NET, you will find that almost all the results relate to adapting database data. This is not too surprising, because a major goal of an n-tier architecture is to define how data is represented in each tier: in persistent storage, in business objects, and in visual presentations. An architecture must also supply mechanisms for transforming data between these representations, as we will have frequent need to adapt data in one tier to the meet the needs of another tier.

Although the .NET Framework Class Libraries provide ample support for adapting data to the needs of different architectural layers, not all data adapters are examples of the ADAPTER pattern. It is useful to look at a data adapter example and then ask whether ADAPTER plays a role or could play a role. Using the .NET FCL, it is easy to create an adapter that can take a structured query language (SQL) query and extract database data. The Oozinoz `DataServices` class encapsulates this adaptation as a service as follows:

```
using System;
using System.Data;
using System.Data.OleDb;
//...
namespace DataLayer
{
    public class DataServices
    {
        //...
        public static OleDbDataAdapter
            CreateAdapter (string select)
        {
            return new OleDbDataAdapter(
                select, CreateConnection());
        }
        //...
    }
}
```

The static `CreateAdapter()` method returns an "adapter" of type `OleDbDataAdapter` that contains the results of a SQL select statement. One of the most useful methods that the `OleDbDataAdapter` class supports is `Fill()`, a method that pushes database data from the adapter object into a `DataSet` object. An instance of the `DataSet` class is essentially an in-memory relational database (sans engine) that houses tables and their relationships. Several graphical control classes, such as the `DataGrid` class, can extract data from a `DataSet` object. The `OldDbDataAdapter`, `DataSet`, and `DataGrid` classes collaborate to make it easy to wire together applications that whisk data along from a database, through a dataset, and into a visual representation.

To see a data adapter in action at Oozinoz, we need first to take a quick look at the Oozinoz `UI` utility class. This class provides several standard graphical user interface (GUI) objects, including a standard font and a standard `DataGrid` object, as the following code shows:

```
using System;
using System.Drawing;
using System.Windows.Forms;
namespace UserInterface
{
    public class UI
    {
        public static readonly UI NORMAL = new UI();
        protected Font _font =
            new Font("Book Antiqua", 18F);
        public virtual Font Font
        {
            get
            {
                return _font;
            }
        }
        //...
        public virtual DataGrid CreateGrid()
        {
            DataGrid g = new DataGrid();
            g.Dock = DockStyle.Fill;
            g.CaptionVisible = false;
            return g;
        }
    }
}
```

Using the `UI` class along with the `OldDbDataAdapter`, `DataSet`, and `DataGrid` classes, a short program can marry a database adapter to a data grid to display a database table as follows:

```
using System.Windows.Forms;
using System.Data;
using System.Data.OleDb;
using DataLayer;
using UserInterface;
public class ShowAdapter : Form
{
    public ShowAdapter()
    {
        DataSet d = new DataSet();
```

```
            string s = "SELECT * FROM Rocket";
            OleDbDataAdapter a = DataServices.CreateAdapter(s);
            a.Fill(d, "Rocket");
            a.Dispose();

            DataGrid g = UI.NORMAL.CreateGrid();
            g.SetDataBinding(d, "Rocket");
            Controls.Add(g);

            Text = "All My Rockets";
            Font = UI.NORMAL.Font;
        }
        static void Main()
        {
            Application.Run(new ShowAdapter());
        }
    }
```

This program creates an OleDbDataAdapter object that reads all the data in the Rocket table in the database. (The Rocket table is actually a "query" in the oozinoz.mdb Microsoft Access database. You can download this database and all the files that go with this book from www.oozinoz.com. See Appendix C, "Oozinoz Source," for help with obtaining the source.)

The adapter's Fill() method creates a DataTable object within the dataset and names the table "Rocket". The program then releases its database resources with a call to Dispose() and creates a DataGrid object as the only control in the form. The SetDataBinding() method causes the grid to display data from the Rocket table within the supplied dataset.

Running this program produces the display shown in Figure 3.7.

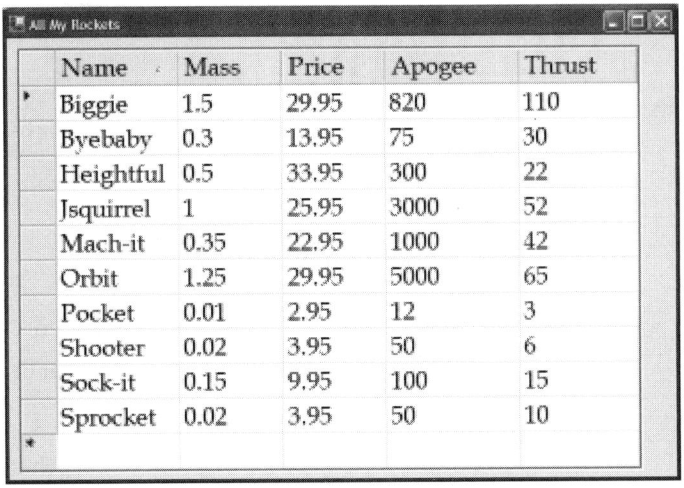
All My Rockets

Name	Mass	Price	Apogee	Thrust
Biggie	1.5	29.95	820	110
Byebaby	0.3	13.95	75	30
Heightful	0.5	33.95	300	22
Jsquirrel	1	25.95	3000	52
Mach-it	0.35	22.95	1000	42
Orbit	1.25	29.95	5000	65
Pocket	0.01	2.95	12	3
Shooter	0.02	3.95	50	6
Sock-it	0.15	9.95	100	15
Sprocket	0.02	3.95	50	10

Figure 3.7 A few lines of C# code can produce this presentation of a database table's contents.

This example shows a flow of data from database through to presentation, but does not show the ADAPTER pattern at play. If ADAPTER were present, we would see an interface that defines the `DataGrid` class's needs (for a class adapter) or we would see subclasses of `DataGrid` (for an object adapter).

The lack of ADAPTER in this example does not imply that the design is inflexible. In fact, the logic in the `SetDataBinding()` method accepts many different types of arguments. A program can pass this method a `DataSet` instance, a `DataTable` instance, a `DataView` instance, a `DataViewManager` instance, or an instance of any class that implements the `IListSource` or `IList` interfaces. The method can also accept a one-dimensional array. Flexible indeed! But, rather than handling so many different sources of data, the `DataGrid` class might actually be more flexible if it defined its expectations in an interface. Figure 3.8 shows this approach, along with a class that adapts the interface to an instance of `IList`.

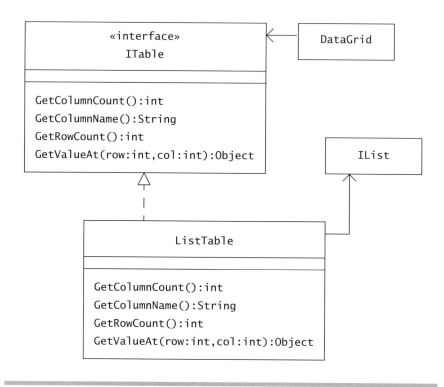

Figure 3.8   This design uses an adapter to adapt a source object's data to
              the needs of a DataGrid object.

Note that the design in Figure 3.8 is merely a proposal: The existing FCL
classes are not laid out this way and there is no ITable interface in the
FCL. The design suggests that the developers of the DataGrid class might
supply an ITable interface to define the DataGrid class's needs. Then,
instead of building support for IList objects into the DataGrid class's Set-
DataBinding() method, a ListTable class could adapt a list's data to
appear as a table.

Challenge 3.5

The DataGrid class accepts many different data types as its data source
instead of specifying its requirements in an interface. List two benefits of
an ADAPTER design that would specify an ITable interface and that
would provide adapter classes for different data sources.

A solution appears on page 353.

As data flows from persistent storage through business layers and into presentation code, there are often opportunities to adapt a data source to meet the needs of a data consumer. The ADAPTER pattern is not too prevalent in .NET, and a greater presence would arguably slim down control classes and provide more flexibility in how adaptation occurs.

Summary

The ADAPTER pattern lets you use an existing class to meet a client class's needs. When a client specifies its requirements in an interface, you can usually create a new class that implements the interface and subclasses an existing class. This approach creates a *class adapter* that translates a client's calls into calls to the existing class's methods.

When a client does not specify the interface it requires, you may still be able to apply ADAPTER, creating a new subclass class of the client that uses an instance of the existing class. This approach creates an *object adapter* that forwards a client's calls to an instance of the existing class. This approach can be dangerous, especially if you don't (or perhaps can't) override all the methods that the client might call.

Data flow in the .NET architecture provides many examples of adaptation, but few examples of the ADAPTER pattern. This is arguably a missed opportunity that occurs when a class such as DataGrid does not define its needs in an interface. When you architect your own systems, consider the power and flexibility that you and other developers can derive from an architecture that uses ADAPTER to advantage.

CHAPTER **4**

FACADE

A great advantage of OO programming is that it helps keep applications from becoming monolithic programs with hopelessly interwoven pieces. An "application" in an OO system is, ideally, a minimal class that knits together the behaviors from reusable toolkits of other classes. A toolkit or subsystem developer often creates packages of well-designed classes without providing any applications that tie the classes together. The packages in the .NET FCL are generally like this; they are toolkits from which you can weave an endless variety of domain-specific applications.

The reusability of toolkits comes with a problem: The diverse applicability of classes in an OO subsystem may offer an oppressive variety of options. A developer who wants to use a toolkit may not know where to begin. An Integrated Development Environment (IDE) such as Visual Studio .NET can isolate a developer from a toolkit's complexity, but IDEs often create large amounts of code that a developer may not want to own. Another approach to simplifying the use of a toolkit is to supply a facade, a small amount of code that provides a typical, no-frills usage of the classes in a class library. A facade is a class with a level of functionality that lies between a toolkit and a complete application, offering a simplified usage of the classes in a package or subsystem. The intent of the FACADE pattern is to provide an interface that makes a subsystem easy to use.

An Ordinary Facade

The .NET classes that provide data access services to .NET programmers are collectively called ADO.NET. Data access is a book-length topic, but oftentimes you will just want to fetch a little data from a well-known location. This is where the FACADE pattern can help, supplying a simplified interface to a complex subsystem. For example, the Oozinoz DataServices class applies FACADE, providing a simplified interface to the ADO.NET, as shown in Figure 4.1.

35

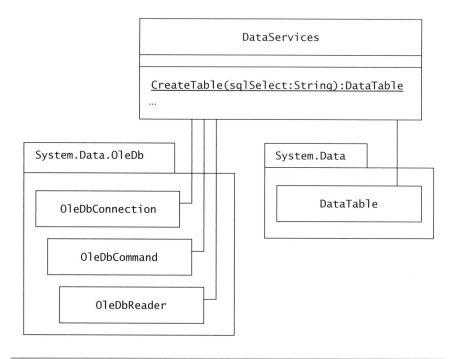

Figure 4.1   The `DataServices` class applies the FACADE pattern, isolating developers from the complexity of ADO.NET.

The `DataServices` class's `CreateTable()` method accepts a SQL select statement and returns a corresponding `DataTable` object, ready for display in a user interface. The examples in this book get their data from a Microsoft Access database named `oozinoz.mdb` (downloadable from www.oozinoz.com, as described in Appendix C, "Oozinoz Source"). The `CreateTable()` method finds this database, connects to it, and uses `OleDb-Command` and `OleDbReader` objects to produce a `DataTable` object.

A developer who just wants to display some data from a specific table can ignore the underlying complexity of ADO.NET and use the facade, as in the following code:

```
using System.Windows.Forms;
using DataLayer;
using UserInterface;
public class ShowRocketsFromTable : Form
{
    public ShowRocketsFromTable()
    {
        DataGrid g = UI.NORMAL.CreateGrid();
        g.DataSource = DataServices.CreateTable(
          "SELECT Name, Apogee, Price, Thrust FROM Rocket");
        Controls.Add(g);
```

```
            Text = "Show Facade";
            Font = UI.NORMAL.Font;
        }
        public static void Main()
        {
            Application.Run(new ShowRocketsFromTable());
        }
    }
```

Running this program produces the window shown in Figure 4.2.

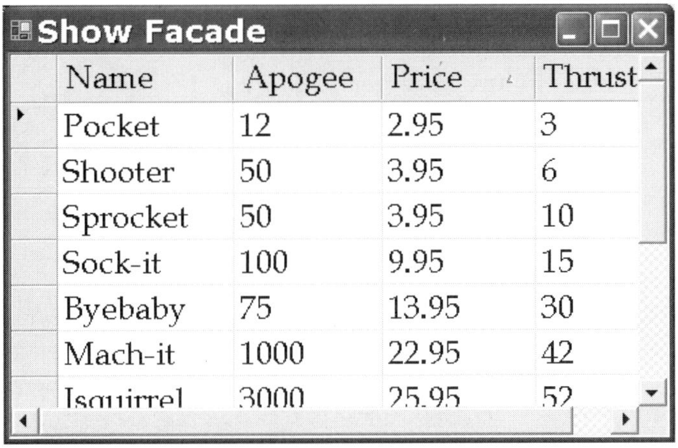

Name	Apogee	Price	Thrust
Pocket	12	2.95	3
Shooter	50	3.95	6
Sprocket	50	3.95	10
Sock-it	100	9.95	15
Byebaby	75	13.95	30
Mach-it	1000	22.95	42
Isquirrel	3000	25.95	52

Figure 4.2   This window results from the ShowRocketsFromTable class's use of the DataServices facade.

Like an IDE, the FACADE pattern can make the power of the .NET FCL accessible, while shielding developers from the libraries' complexity.

Challenge 4.1

State two advantages that a facade has over an IDE (or that an IDE has over a facade.)

A solution appears on page 353.

You may find that you need more than one facade for a subsystem, and you may improve your facades over time. In addition, you may find that facades will begin to appear as you *refactor* (or reorganize) your code.

Refactoring to FACADE

Facades often arise out of normal application development. As you separate your code's concerns into different classes, you may refactor out a class whose primary job is to provide simplified access to a subsystem. Consider an example from the early days at Oozinoz, when there were not yet standards for GUI development. Suppose you come across an application that a developer has created to show the flight path of an unexploded shell. Figure 4.3 shows this class.

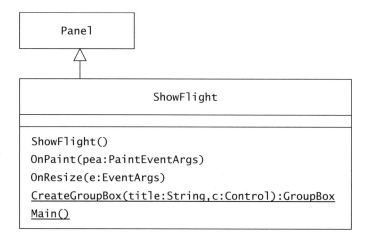

Figure 4.3   The ShowFlight class displays the flight path of an unexploded shell.

Aerial shells are designed to explode high in the sky with spectacular results. But occasionally a shell does not explode at all (it is a *dud*). If a shell does not explode, its return to earth becomes interesting. A shell, unlike a rocket, is unpowered, so if you ignore the effects of wind and air resistance, the flight path of a dud is a simple parabola. Figure 4.4 shows a screen shot of the window that appears when you execute Show-Flight.Main().

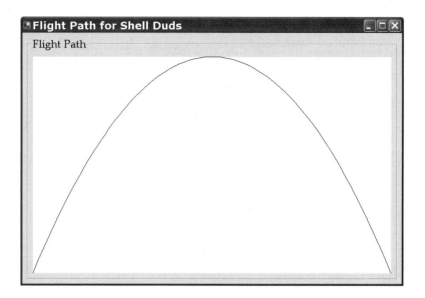

Figure 4.4   The ShowFlight application shows where a dud may land.

There is a problem with the ShowFlight class: It intermingles three purposes. Its primary purpose is to act as a panel that displays a flight path. A secondary purpose is to act as a complete application, wrapping the flight path panel in a titled border and displaying it. A final purpose of this class is to calculate a parabolic flight path. The ShowFlight class currently performs this calculation in its OnPaint() code:

```
protected override void OnPaint(PaintEventArgs pea)
{
    int nPoint = 101;
    double w = Width - 1;
    double h = Height - 1;
    Point[] points = new Point[nPoint];
    for (int i = 0; i < nPoint; i++)
    {
        double t = ((double) i) / (nPoint - 1);
        points[i].X = (int) (t * w);
        points[i].Y = (int) (4 * h * (t - .5) * (t - .5));
    }

    Pen p = new Pen(ForeColor);
    Graphics g = pea.Graphics;
    g.DrawLines(p, points);
}
```

See the sidebar titled "Parametric Equations" in this chapter for an explanation of how this code establishes the x and y values of the dud's path.

The ShowFlight class has an OnResize() method that repaints the panel when its size changes:

```
protected override void OnResize(System.EventArgs e)
{
    base.OnResize(e);
    Refresh();
}
```

The class constructor sets up initial properties for the panel, and a static utility method wraps a group box around a panel.

```
public ShowFlight()
{
    BackColor = Color.White;
    Dock = DockStyle.Fill;
}
public static GroupBox CreateGroupBox(
    String title, Control control)
{
    GroupBox gb = new GroupBox();
    gb.Text = title;
    gb.Dock = DockStyle.Fill;

    Panel p = new Panel();
    p.Dock = DockStyle.Fill;
    p.DockPadding.All = 10;
    p.Controls.Add(control);

    gb.Controls.Add(p);
    return gb;
}
```

Note that the CreateGroupBox() method tucks the provided control inside a padding panel. (The GroupBox class does not provide a DockPadding property, unlike the Panel class and Form class.) The padding keeps the flight path curve from touching the sides of the group box. The Main() method also adds padding to the Form object that it uses to contain the application's controls.

```
public static void Main()
{
    ShowFlight sf = new ShowFlight();
    GroupBox gb = CreateGroupBox("Flight Path", sf);
    Form f = new Form();
    f.DockPadding.All = 10;
    f.Text = "Flight Path for Shell Duds";
    f.Font = UI.NORMAL.Font;
    f.Controls.Add(gb);

    Application.Run(f);
}
```

Executing this program produces the display shown in Figure 4.4.

Parametric Equations

When you need to plot a curve, it can be difficult to describe the y values as functions of x values. *Parametric equations* let you define both x and y in terms of a third parameter that you introduce. Specifically, you can define that time t goes from 0 to 1 as the curve is drawn, and define x and y as functions of the parameter t.

    x = w * t

Note that as t goes from 0 to 1, x goes from 0 to w.

The y values for a parabola must vary with the square of the value of t, and y values increase going down the screen. For a parabolic flight, y should be 0 at time t = .5, so we can write an initial equation as follows:

    y = k * (t - .5) * (t - .5)

Here k represents a constant that we still need to determine. The equation provides for y to be 0 at t = .5, and provides for y to have the same value at t = 0 and t = 1. At those two times, y should be h, the height of the display area. With a little algebraic manipulation, you can find the complete equation for y as follows:

    y = 4 * h * (t - .5) * (t - .5)

Figure 4.4 shows the equations for a parabola in action.

Another advantage of parametric equations is that there is no problem drawing curves that have more than one y value for a given x value. Consider drawing a circle. The equation for a circle with a radius of 1 is:

    $x^2 + y^2 = r^2$

or

    $y = +- sqrt (r^2 - x^2)$

Handling the fact that two y values emerge for every x value is complicated. It's also difficult to adjust these values to plot correctly within a Graphics object's height and width. Polar coordinates make the function for a circle simpler.

    x = r * cos(theta)
    y = r * sin(theta)

These formulas are parametric equations that show x and y as functions of a new parameter, theta. The variable theta represents the sweep of an arc that varies from 0 to 2*pi as a circle is drawn. You can set the radius of a circle so that it will fit within the height h and width w of a Graphics object. A handful of parametric equations suffice to plot a circle within the bounds of a Graphics object as follows:

    theta = 2 * pi * t
    r = min(w, h)/2
    x = w/2 + r * cos(theta)
    y = h/2 - r * sin(theta)

Translating these equations into C# produces the circle in Figure 4.5. (The code that produced this display is in the ShowCircle application in the code from oozinoz.com.)

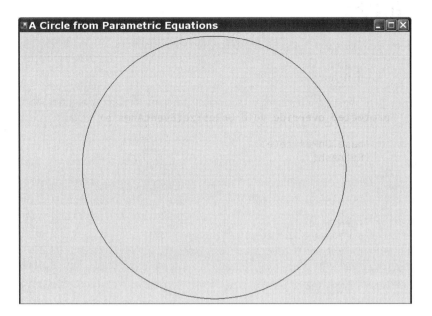

Figure 4.5   Parametric equations simplify the modeling of curves where y is not a
                  single-valued function of x.

The code that draws a circle is a fairly direct translation of the mathematical formulas. One
subtlety is that the code reduces the height and width of the Graphics object because the pixels
are numbered from 0 to Height-1 and from 0 to Width-1.

```
using System;
using System.Drawing;
using System.Windows.Forms;
public class ShowCircle : Form
{
    protected override void OnPaint(PaintEventArgs pea)
    {
        int nPoint = 101;
        double w = ClientSize.Width - 1;
        double h = ClientSize.Height - 1;
        double r = Math.Min(w, h) / 2.0 - 10.0;
        Point[] points = new Point[nPoint];
        for (int i = 0; i < nPoint; i++)
        {
            double t = ((double) i) / (nPoint - 1);
            double theta = Math.PI * 2.0 * t;
```

```
            points[i].X = (int) (w / 2 + r * Math.Cos(theta));
            points[i].Y = (int) (h / 2 - r * Math.Sin(theta));
        }
        Pen p = new Pen(ForeColor);
        Graphics g = pea.Graphics;
        g.DrawLines(p, points);
    }

    protected override void OnResize(EventArgs e)
    {
        base.OnResize(e);
        Refresh();
    }

    public static void Main()
    {
        Form f = new ShowCircle();
        f.ClientSize = new Size(500, 500);
        f.Text = "A Circle from Parametric Equations";
        Application.Run(f);
    }
}
```

Defining x and y functions in terms of t lets you divide the tasks of determining x values and y values. This is often simpler than defining y in terms of x and often facilitates the mapping of x and y onto a Graphics object's coordinates. Parametric equations also simplify the plotting of curves where y is not a single-valued function of x.

The code in the ShowFlight class is effective, but you can make it more maintainable and reusable by refactoring it into classes that have separate concerns. Suppose that you hold a design review and decide to make the following changes:

- Introduce a Function delegate that accepts a double (the value of time) and returns a double (the function's value).

- Move the plotting code of the ShowFlight class into a PlotPanel class, but adjust it to use Function delegates for x and y values. Define the PlotPanel constructor to accept two Function delegate instances and the number of points to plot.

- Add a CreatePlotPanel() method to the existing UI utility class to manufacture a standard PlotPanel object, setting the anchor and color values as the ShowFlight class does currently.

Challenge 4.2

Complete the diagram in Figure 4.6 to show the code for `ShowFlight` refactored into three types: a `Function` delegate, a `PlotPanel` class that plots two parametric functions, and a `UI` facade class. In your redesign, create a `ShowFlight` class to contain `X()` and `Y()` methods and a `Main()` method to launch the application.

A solution appears on page 354.

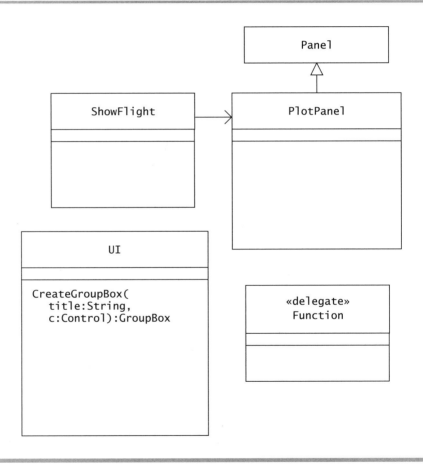

Figure 4.6   This diagram shows the flight path application refactored into classes that each have one job.

After refactoring, the `Function` delegate defines how a parametric equation looks. Suppose that you create a `Functions` namespace to contain the `Function` delegate and possibly other types. Then the contents of `Function.cs` might be:

```
namespace Functions
{
    public delegate double Function (double t);
}
```

The `PlotPanel` class emerges from the refactoring as a class that has just one job: displaying a pair of parametric equations.

```
using System;
using System.Drawing;
using System.Windows.Forms;
using Functions;
namespace UserInterface
{
    public class PlotPanel : Panel
    {
        private int _nPoint;
        private Point[] points;
        private Function _xFunc;
        private Function _yFunc;
        public PlotPanel(
            int nPoint, Function xFunc, Function yFunc)
        {
            _nPoint = nPoint;
            points = new Point[_nPoint];
            _xFunc = xFunc;
            _yFunc = yFunc;
            BackColor = Color.White;
            Dock = DockStyle.Fill;
        }
        protected override void OnPaint(PaintEventArgs pea)
        {
            double w = Width - 1;
            double h = Height - 1;
            for (int i = 0; i < _nPoint; i++)
            {
                double t = ((double) i) / (_nPoint - 1);
                points[i].X = (int) (_xFunc(t) * w);
                points[i].Y = (int) (h * (1 - _yFunc(t)));
            }

            Pen p = new Pen(ForeColor);
            Graphics g = pea.Graphics;

            g.DrawLines(p, points);
        }
        protected override void OnResize(EventArgs e)
        {
            base.OnResize(e);
            Refresh();
        }
    }
}
```

Notice that the `PlotPanel` class is now part of the `UserInterface` namespace, the same namespace in which the `UI` class resides. You may recall from Chapter 3, "Adapter," that the UI class already had a Create-Grid() method. After refactoring the ShowFlight class, the UI class also has CreateGroupBox() and CreatePlotPanel() methods. The UI class is growing into a facade that makes it easy to use .NET controls.

An application that uses these controls may be a small class whose only job is to lay out the controls and display them. For example, the code for the ShowFlight2 class is as follows:

```
using System;
using System.Windows.Forms;
using Functions;
using UserInterface;
public class ShowFlight2
{
    private static double X(double t)
    {
        return t;
    }
    private static double Y(double t)
    {
        // y is 0 at t = 0, 1; y is 1 at t = .5
        return 4 * t * (1 - t);
    }
    public static void Main()
    {
        PlotPanel p = new PlotPanel(
            101, new Function(X), new Function(Y));
        Panel p2 = UI.NORMAL.CreatePaddedPanel(p);
        GroupBox gb =
            UI.NORMAL.CreateGroupBox("Flight Path", p2);
        Form f = new Form();
        f.DockPadding.All = 10;
        f.Font = UI.NORMAL.Font;
        f.Text = "Flight Path for Shell Duds";
        f.Controls.Add(gb);

        Application.Run(f);
    }
}
```

The ShowFlight2 class provides the X and Y functions for the flight path of a dud. The Main() method lays out the user interface and displays it. Running this class produces the same results as running the original Show-Flight class, but now you have a reusable facade that simplifies the creation of a GUIs in .NET applications.

Facades, Utilities, and Demos

A facade class may have all static methods, in which case it is called a *utility* in UML [Booch]. We could make the UI class's methods static, although doing so would prevent overriding these methods in future subclasses.

A *demo* is an example that shows how to use a class or subsystem. As such, demos provide much of the same value as facades.

Challenge 4.3

Write down two differences between a demo and a facade.

A solution appears on page 355.

The `System.Windows.Forms` package contains `MessageBox`, a class that makes it easy to pop up a standard dialog box. For example, the following code displays and re-displays a dialog until the user clicks the Yes button, as Figure 4.7 shows.

```
using System.Windows.Forms;
public class ShowMessageBox
{
    public static void Main()
    {
        DialogResult dr;
        do
        {
          dr = MessageBox.Show(

            "Had enough?",
            " A Stubborn Dialog",
            MessageBoxButtons.YesNo,
            MessageBoxIcon.Question);

        }
        while (dr == DialogResult.No);
    }
}
```

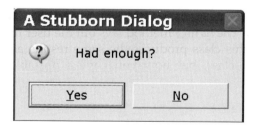

Figure 4.7   The `MessageBox` class makes it easy to display dialogs such as this one.

Challenge 4.4

The `MessageBox` class makes it easy to display a dialog. Say whether this class is a facade, a utility, or a demo, and justify your answer.

A solution appears on page 355.

Challenge 4.5

Few facades appear in the .NET FCL. Why is that?

A solution appears on page 355.

Summary

Ordinarily you should refactor the classes in a subsystem until each class has a well-defined purpose. This will make your code easier to maintain, but it can also make it difficult for a user of your subsystem to know where to begin. To help the developer who is using your code, you can supplies demos or facades that go with your subsystem. A demo is usually a standalone, nonreusable application that shows one way to apply a subsystem. A facade is usually a configurable, reusable class with a higher level interface that makes the subsystem easier to use.

CHAPTER 5

COMPOSITE

A *composite* is a group of objects in which some objects may contain others, so that some objects represent groups and others represent individual items, or *leaves*. When you model a composite, two powerful concepts emerge. One important modeling idea is to design groups so that they can contain either individual items or other groups. (A common error is to define groups so that they can contain only leaves.) A second powerful concept is to define common behaviors for individual objects and for compositions. You can bring these ideas together by defining a common type for groups and items, and modeling groups as containing a collection of objects of this type. This fulfills the intent of the COMPOSITE pattern: COMPOSITE lets clients treat individual objects and compositions of objects uniformly.

An Ordinary Composite

Figure 5.1 shows an ordinary composite structure. The Leaf and Composite classes share a common interface that Component abstracts, and a Composite object retains a collection of other Composite and Leaf objects.

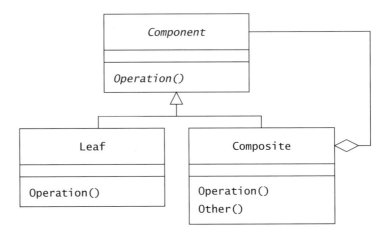

Figure 5.1   The key ideas of COMPOSITE are that composites can contain other composites (not just leaves), and that composite and leaf nodes share a common interface.

Note that the Component class in Figure 5.1 is an abstract class with no concrete operations, so you could define it as an interface that Leaf and Composite implement.

Challenge 5.1

Why does the Composite class in Figure 5.1 maintain a collection of Component objects instead of just maintaining a collection of leaves?

A solution appears on page 356.

Recursive Behavior in Composites

Engineers at Oozinoz perceive a natural composition in the processing machines they use to produce fireworks. The factory is composed of bays; each bay has one or more manufacturing lines; a line is a collection of machines that collaboratively produce material to meet a schedule. The developers at Oozinoz have modeled this domain by treating factories, bays, and lines as composite "machines," using the class structure shown in Figure 5.2.

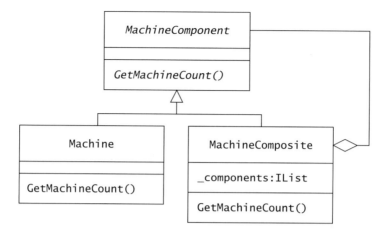

Figure 5.2   The GetMachineCount() method is an appropriate behavior for both individual machines and composites.

As Figure 5.2 shows, one behavior that applies to both individual machines and to collections of machines is GetMachineCount(), which returns the number of machines in any given component.

Challenge 5.2

Write the code for the GetMachineCount() methods implemented by Machine and by MachineComposite.

Example solutions appear on page 356.

Suppose that MachineComponent also needs the following methods:

Method	Behavior
IsCompletelyUp()	Says whether all the machines in a component are in an "up" state.
StopAll()	Directs all the machines in a component to stop processing.
GetOwners()	Returns a set of process engineers responsible for the machines in a component.
GetMaterial()	Return all of the in-process material in a machine component.

The definition and operation of each method in MachineComponent is recursive. For example, the count of machines in a composite is the sum of the counts of machines in its components.

Challenge 5.3

For each method declared by MachineComponent, give recursive definitions for MachineComposite and nonrecursive definitions for Machine.

Method	Class	Definition
GetMachineCount()	MachineComposite	Returns the sum of the counts for each component in components.
	Machine	Returns 1.
IsCompletelyUp()	MachineComposite	??
	Machine	??
StopAll()	MachineComposite	??
	Machine	??
GetOwners()	MachineComposite	??
	Machine	??
GetMaterial()	MachineComposite	??
	Machine	??

A solution appears on page 356.

Composites, Trees, and Cycles

In a composite structure, we can say that a node is a tree if it holds references to other nodes. However, this definition is a bit loose. To be more precise, we can apply a few terms from graph theory to object modeling. We can start by drawing an object model as a *graph* (a collection of nodes and edges) with objects as nodes and object references as edges.

Consider an object model of an *assay* (an analysis) of a batch of a chemical. The Assay class has a batch attribute of type Batch, and the Batch class has a chemical attribute of type Chemical. Suppose there is a particular Assay object a whose batch attribute refers to a Batch object b. Suppose too that the chemical attribute of the Batch object b refers to a Chemical c.

Figure 5.3 shows two alternative diagrams of this object model. (For information on how to depict object models using UML, see "Appendix D: UML at a Glance.")

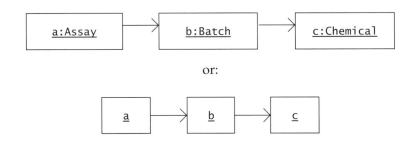

Figure 5.3   The two UML diagrams show alternative representations of the same information: Object a refers to object b, and object b refers to object c.

There is a *path* (a series of object references) from a to c because a refers to b and b refers to c. A *cycle* is a path in which a node appears twice. There would be a cycle of references in this object model if the c Chemical object referred back to the a Assay object.

Object models are *directed graphs*: An object reference has a direction. Graph theory usually applies the term *tree* to refer to undirected graphs. However, a directed graph may be called a *tree* if:

- It has a *root* node that has no references to it.

- Every other node has exactly one *parent,* the node that refers to it.

The object model that Figure 5.3 depicts is a tree. For larger object models, it can be difficult to tell whether the model is a tree. Figure 5.4 shows the object model of a factory (called plant) that is a MachineComposite object. This plant contains a bay that has three machines: m, n, and o. The object model also shows that the plant object's list of machine components contains a direct reference to machine m.

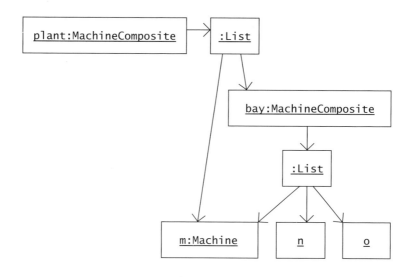

Figure 5.4   An object model that forms a graph that is neither cyclic nor a tree.

The object graph in Figure 5.4 does not contain a cycle, but note that the object graph is not a tree because two objects refer to the Machine object m. If we remove (or disregard) the plant object and its list, the bay object *is* the root of a tree.

Methods that work on composites may have defects if they assume all composites are trees. Challenge 5.2 asked for a definition of a GetMachineCount() operation. The Machine class implementation of this operation as given in the solution to this challenge is arguably correct.

```
public override int GetMachineCount()
{
    return 1;
}
```

The MachineComposite class also correctly implements GetMachineCount(), returning the sum of the counts for each of a composite's components.

```
public override int GetMachineCount()
{
    int count = 0;
    foreach (MachineComponent mc in _components)
    {
        count += mc.GetMachineCount();
    }
    return count;
}
```

These methods are correct so long as MachineComponent objects are trees. It can happen, though, that a composite you suppose is a tree suddenly is not a tree. This is especially likely to occur when users can edit the composition. Consider an example that might occur at Oozinoz.

The fireworks engineers at Oozinoz use a GUI application to record and update the composition of machinery in the factory. One day, they report a defect regarding the number of machines reported to exist in the factory. You can reproduce their object model with the `Plant()` method of the `ExampleMachine` class (in namespace `Machines`).

```
public static MachineComposite Plant()
{
    MachineComposite plant = new MachineComposite(100);
    MachineComposite bay = new MachineComposite(101);
    Machine m = new Mixer(102);
    Machine n = new StarPress(103);
    Machine o = new ShellAssembler(104);
    bay.Add(m);
    bay.Add(n);
    bay.Add(o);
    plant.Add(m);
    plant.Add(bay);
    return plant;
}
```

This code produces the `plant` object in Figure 5.4.

Challenge 5.4

What does the following program print out?

```
using System;
using Machines;
public class ShowPlant
{
    public static void Main()
    {
        MachineComponent c = ExampleMachine.Plant();
        Console.WriteLine(c.GetMachineCount());
    }
}
```

A solution appears on page 357.

The GUI application that Oozinoz uses to let engineers build object models of a factory's machinery should check whether a node already exists in a component tree before adding it a second time. A simple way to do this is to maintain a set of existing nodes. You may not, however, always have control over how a composite is formed. In this case, you can write an `IsTree()` method to check whether a composite is a tree.

An object model is a tree if an algorithm can traverse its references without encountering the same node twice. You can implement an `IsTree()` method on the abstract class `MachineComponent` so that it delegates to an `IsTree()` method that maintains a collection of visited nodes. The `MachineComponent` class can leave the implementation of the parameterized IsTree(h:Hashtable) method abstract. Figure 5.5 shows the placement of the IsTree() methods.

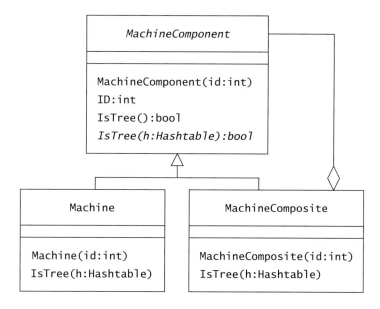

Figure 5.5   An IsTree() method can detect whether a composite is in fact a tree.

The MachineComponent code delegates an IsTree() call to its abstract IsTree(h:Hashtable) method.

```
public bool IsTree()
{
    return IsTree(new Hashtable());
}

public abstract bool IsTree(Hashtable visited);
```

These methods use the Hashtable class because (at this writing) there is no Set class in the .NET System.Collections library. Chapter 16, "Factory Method," introduces a Set class that relies on an underlying Hashtable object.

The Machine and MachineComposite classes must implement the abstract IsTree(h:Hashtable) method. The implementation of IsTree() for Machine is simple, reflecting the fact that individual machines are always trees.

```
public override bool IsTree(Hashtable visited)
{
    visited.Add(ID, this);
    return true;
}
```

The MachineComposite implementation of IsTree() must add the receiving object to the visited collection and then iterate over the composite's components. The method can return false if any component has been previously visited, or if any component is not itself a tree. Otherwise, the method can return true.

Challenge 5.5

Write the code for MachineComposite.IsTree(Hashtable visited).

A solution appears on page 357.

With some care, you can guarantee that an object model is a tree by refusing changes that would make IsTree() false. On the other hand, you may need to allow composites that are not trees, particularly when the problem domain you are modeling contains cycles.

Composites with Cycles

The non-tree composite that Challenge 5.4 referred to was an accident that stemmed from a user marking a machine as both part of a plant and part of a bay. For physical objects, you may want to disallow the notion that an object is contained by more than one other object. However, a problem domain can have nonphysical elements where cycles of containment make sense. This occurs frequently when modeling process flows.

Consider the construction of aerial shells such as the one that Figure 5.6 depicts. We launch a shell from a *mortar* (a tube) by igniting the lifting charge of black powder that is seated beneath the core charge. The secondary fuses burn while the shell in the air, eventually reaching the core. When the shell core explodes, its stars ignite, creating the visual effects of aerial fireworks.

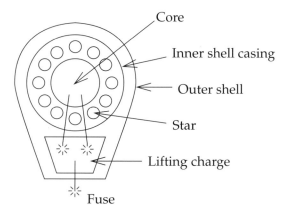

Core

Inner shell casing

Outer shell

Star

Lifting charge

Fuse

Figure 5.6   An aerial shell uses two charges: one for initial lift, and one to expel explosive stars when the shell is at its peak.

The process flow for making an aerial shell consists of building an inner shell, having it inspected, and then either reworking it or finishing its assembly.

To make the inner shell, an operator uses a shell assembler that places stars in a hemispherical casing, inserts a black powder core, attaches more stars on top of the core, and seals this subassembly with another hemispherical casing.

An inspector verifies that the inner shell meets safety and quality standards. If it doesn't, the operator disassembles the inner shell and makes it again (grumbling). When an inner shell passes inspection, the operator finishes the shell, using a fuser that connects a lifting charge to the inner shell with fusing. Finally, the operator manually wraps the complete aerial shell.

As with machine composites, Oozinoz engineers have a GUI that lets them describe the composition of a process. Figure 5.7 shows the class structure that supports process modeling.

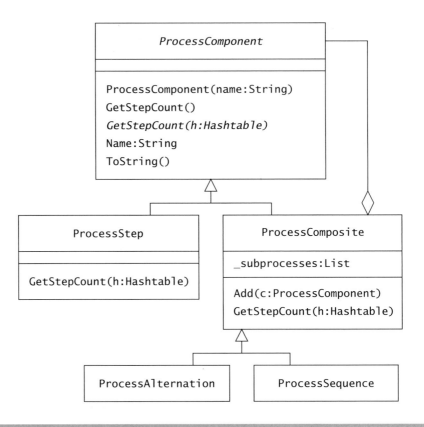

Figure 5.7   The process for manufacturing fireworks includes some steps
              that are alternations or sequences of other steps.

Figure 5.8 shows the objects that represent the process flow for making an
aerial shell. The make process is a sequence of the buildInner step, the
inspect step, and the reworkOrFinish subprocess. The reworkOrFinish
subprocess takes one of two alternate paths. It may require a disassemble
step followed by the make process, or it may require just the finish step.

Challenge 5.6

Figure 5.8 shows the objects in a model of the shell assembly process. A
complete object diagram would show links between any objects that
refer to each other. For example, the diagram shows the references that
the make object retains. Your challenge is to fill in the missing links in the
diagram.

A solution appears on page 358.

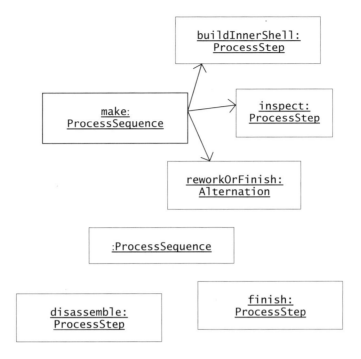

Figure 5.8   This diagram, when completed, will show an object model of
the Oozinoz process for making aerial shells.

The GetStepCount() operation in the ProcessComponent hierarchy counts
the number of individual processing steps in a process flow. Note that
this count is not the "length" of the process, but rather the number of leaf
node processing steps in the process's object graph. The GetStepCount()
method has to be careful to count each step only once, and to not enter an
infinite loop when a process contains a cycle. The ProcessComponent class
implements the GetStepCount() method so that it relies on a comanion
method that passes along a set of visited nodes.

```
public int GetStepCount()
{
    return GetStepCount(new Hashtable());
}

internal abstract int GetStepCount(Hashtable visited);
```

The ProcessComposite class takes care in its implementation of the
GetStepCount() method not to visit a previously visited node.

```
public override int GetStepCount(Hashtable visited)
{
    visited.Add(Name, this);
    int count = 0;
    foreach (ProcessComponent pc in _subprocesses)
    {
        if (!visited.Contains(pc.Name))
        {
            count += pc.GetStepCount(visited);
        }
    }
    return count;
}
```

The ProcessStep class implementation of GetStepCount() is simple.

```
public override int GetStepCount(Hashtable visited)
{
    visited.Add(_name, this);
    return 1;
}
```

The Oozinoz Processes namespace contains a ShellProcess class that has a Make() method that returns the make object that Figure 5.8 depicts. The Testing namespace has a TestProcess class that provides automated tests of various types of process graphs. For example, the TestProcess class includes a method that tests that the GetStepCount() operation correctly counts the number of steps in the cyclic make process.

```
public void TestShell()
{
    AssertEquals(4, ShellProcess.Make().GetStepCount());
}
```

This test runs (and passes) within the NUnit testing framework. See www.nunit.org for more information about NUnit.

Consequences of Cycles

Most operations on a composite, such as counting the number of leaf nodes, make sense even if the composite is not a tree. Usually, the only difference that non-tree composites introduce is that you have to be careful to not operate on a given node twice. However, some operations become meaningless if the composite contains a cycle. For example, we can't algorithmically determine the maximum number of steps that might be required to make an aerial shell at Oozinoz, because the rework step may be repeated an arbitrarily large number of times. Any operation that depends on the length of a path in a composite won't make sense if the composite contains a cycle. So, while we can talk about the *height* of a tree (the longest path from the root to a leaf), there is no maximum-length path in a cyclic graph.

Another result of allowing composites that are not trees is that you lose the ability to assume that each node has a single parent. If a composite is not a tree, then a node may have more than one parent. For example, the process that Figure 5.8 models might have several composite steps that use the `inspect` step, giving the `inspect` object multiple parents. There is no inherent problem in a node having multiple parents, but a problem may arise if you create a model that insists otherwise.

Summary

COMPOSITE contains two powerful, related concepts. One concept is that a group can contain either individual items or other groups. Related to this concept is the idea that groups and individual items may share a common interface. These ideas come together in object modeling, where you can create an abstract class or a C# interface that defines the behaviors that are common to groups and to individual objects.

Modeling composites often leads to recursive definition of methods on composite nodes. When recursion is present, there is a danger of writing code that produces an infinite loop. To avoid such problems, you can take steps to guarantee that your composites are always trees. Alternatively, you can allow cycles to occur in a composite, but you have to modify your algorithms to watch for recursion.

CHAPTER 6

BRIDGE

The BRIDGE pattern focuses on the design of an abstraction. The word *abstraction* refers to a class that relies on a set of abstract operations, where there are several possible implementations of the set of abstract operations.

The ordinary way to implement an abstraction is to create a class hierarchy with an abstract class at the top that defines the abstract operations; each subclass in the hierarchy provides a different implementation of the set of abstract operations. However, this approach becomes insufficient when you need to subclass the hierarchy for some other reason.

You can create a *bridge* by moving the set of abstract operations to an interface, so that an abstraction will depend on an implementation of the interface. The intent of the BRIDGE pattern is to decouple an abstraction from the implementation of its abstract operations so that the abstraction and its implementation can vary independently.

An Ordinary Abstraction

Nearly every C# class is an abstraction, in the sense that each class is an approximation, an idealization, or a simplification of the class of real objects that it models. When discussing BRIDGE, though, we specifically use the word abstraction to mean a class that relies on a set of abstract operations.

Suppose that you have machine control classes that interact with some of the physical machines at Oozinoz that produce fireworks. The classes reflect differences in how the machines operate. However, you might want to create some abstract operations that would achieve the same result on any machine. Figure 6.1 shows the current control classes.

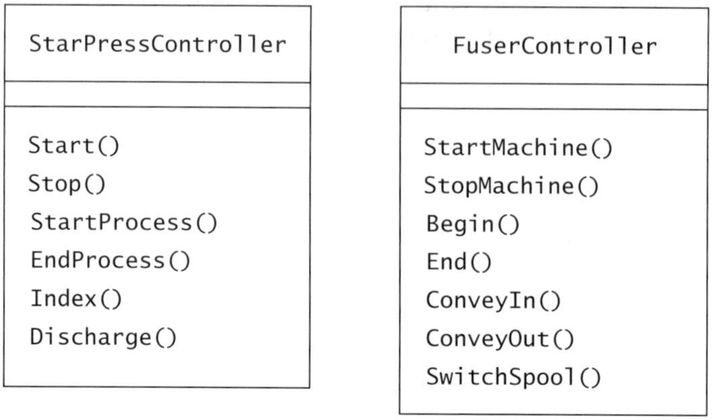

StarPressController
Start()
Stop()
StartProcess()
EndProcess()
Index()
Discharge()

FuserController
StartMachine()
StopMachine()
Begin()
End()
ConveyIn()
ConveyOut()
SwitchSpool()

Figure 6.1   These two classes have similar methods that you might abstract into a common model for driving machines.

Both controller classes in Figure 6.1 have methods to start and stop the machines they control, although the StarPressController class names these methods Start() and Stop(), while the FuserController class names them StartMachine() and StopMachine(). Both controllers also have methods for moving a bin into the processing area (Index() and ConveyIn()), for beginning and ending the processing of a bin, and for removing a bin (Discharge() and ConveyOut()). The FuserController class also has a method that can switch in a backup spool of fuse.

Now suppose that you want to create a Shutdown() method that ensures an orderly shutdown, performing the same steps on both machines. To simplify the writing of a Shutdown() method, you would like to standardize the names for common operations, such as StartMachine(), StopMachine(), StartProcess(), StopProcess(), ConveyIn(), and ConveyOut(). Now suppose that you can't change the controller classes because one of them comes from the machine supplier.

Challenge 6.1

State how you can apply a design pattern to allow controlling various machines with a common interface.

A solution appears on page 359.

Figure 6.2 shows the introduction of an abstract MachineManager class with subclasses that forward machine control calls, adapting them into methods that FuserController and StarPressController support.

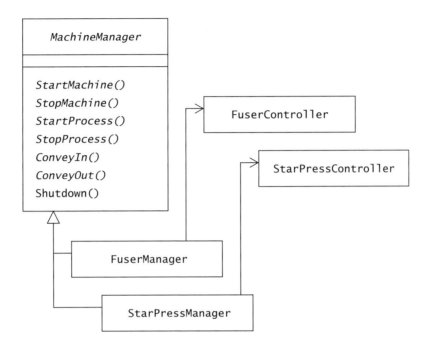

Figure 6.2   The FuserManager and StarPressManager classes implement the abstract methods of MachineManager by passing through the calls to corresponding methods of FuserController and StarPressController objects.

There is no problem if a machine controller has some operations that are unique to a particular machine type. For example, although Figure 6.2 doesn't show it, the FuserManager class also has a SwitchSpool() method that it forwards to the same method of a FuserController object.

Challenge 6.2

Write a Shutdown() method for the MachineManager class that will stop processing, discharge the bin that was in process, and stop the machine.

A solution appears on page 359.

The `MachineManager` class's `Shutdown()` method is concrete, not abstract. However, we can say it is an *abstraction* because the method universalizes (or *abstracts*) the definition of what steps are taken to shut down a piece of equipment.

From Abstraction to Bridge

The `MachineManager` hierarchy is factored along the lines of different equipment, so that each machine type requires a different subclass of the `MachineManager` class. What happens if you need to organize the hierarchy along another line? For example, suppose that you work on the machines themselves so that they provide acknowledgement of the steps they complete. Correspondingly, you want to create a handshaking `MachineManager` subclass with methods that let you parameterize the interaction with the machine, such as setting a timeout value. However, you still need different machine managers for star presses and fusers. If you don't reorganize the `MachineManager` hierarchy first, your new hierarchy might look like Figure 6.3.

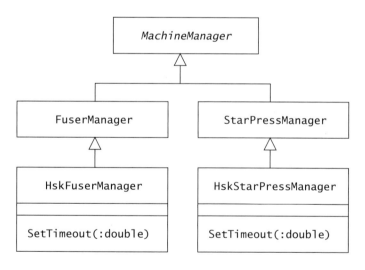

Figure 6.3   The handshaking (Hsk) subclasses add parameterization of how long to wait for acknowledgement from a real machine.

The hierarchy in Figure 6.3 factors classes along two lines: according to machine type and according to whether handshaking is supported. This dual principle for factoring creates problems. In particular, a method such as `SetTimeout()` may contain identical code in two places, but we cannot factor it up in the hierarchy because the superclasses do not support the handshaking idea.

In general, there is no way for the handshaking classes to share code, since there is no handshaking superclass. As we add more classes to the hierarchy, the problem gets worse. If we eventually have controllers for five machines and then we decide to change the SetTimeout() method, we may have to change code in five places.

In this situation, we need to apply BRIDGE. We can decouple the Machine-Manager abstraction from the implementation of its abstract operations by moving its abstract methods to a separate hierarchy. The MachineManager class remains an abstraction. The effect of calling its methods will depend on whether we are controlling a star press or a fuser.

Separating the abstraction from the implementation of its abstract methods lets the two hierarchies vary independently. We can add support for new machines without affecting the MachineManager hierarchy. We can also extend the MachineManager hierarchy without changing any of the machine controllers. Figure 6.4 suggests the desired separation.

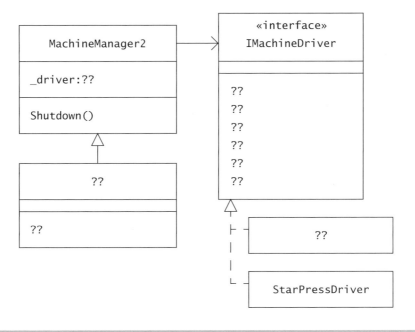

Figure 6.4   When complete, this diagram shows a separation of the MachineManager abstraction from the implementation of its abstract operations.

The goal of the new design is to separate the `MachineManager` hierarchy from the implementation of the hierarchy's abstract operations.

Challenge 6.3

Figure 6.4 shows the `MachineManager` hierarchy refactored into a bridge. Fill in the missing labels.

A solution appears on page 359.

Note in Figure 6.4 that the `MachineManager` class becomes concrete, although it is still an abstraction. The abstract methods that `MachineManager` depends on now reside in the `IMachineDriver` interface. The name of this interface suggests that the classes that adapt `MachineManager` requests to specific machines have become drivers. A *driver* is an object that operates a computer system or an external device according to a well-specified interface. Drivers provide the most common example of the BRIDGE pattern in practice.

Drivers as Bridges

Applications that use drivers are abstractions. The effect of running the application depends on which driver is in place. Each driver is an instance of the ADAPTER pattern, providing the interface a client expects using the services of a class with a different interface. An overall design that uses drivers is an instance of BRIDGE. The design separates application development from the development of the drivers that implement the abstract operations on which the applications rely.

A driver-based design forces you to create a common, abstract model of the machine or system that will be driven. This has the advantage of letting code on the abstraction side apply to any of the drivers that it might execute against. Defining a common set of methods for the drivers may also incur the disadvantage of eliminating behavior that one driven entity might support. Recall from Figure 6.1 that a fuser controller has a `Switch-Spool()` method. Looking at the refactoring in Figure 6.4, where did this method go? The answer is that we abstracted it out. You can include the `SwitchSpool()` method in the new `FuserDriver` class. However, this can lead to code on the abstraction side that checks to see if its driver is a `FuserDriver` instance.

To avoid losing the `SwitchSpool()` method, we could have required every driver to implement this method, understanding that some drivers will simply ignore the call. When choosing an abstract model of the operations that a driver will support, you will often have this choice. You can include methods that some drivers cannot support, or you can exclude methods that will either reduce what abstractions can do with the driver or that force the abstractions to include special-case code.

Database Drivers

These tradeoffs in having a broad or narrow interface in an implementation of BRIDGE also appear in database drivers. For example, in .NET, you can use the `OleDbDataReader` class to work with almost any database, including SQL Server. However, .NET also provides the `SqlDataReader` class that works only with SQL Server and is (or should be) faster than the `OleDbDataReader`. In addition, the `SqlDataReader` class offers methods that the `OleDbDataReader` class does not, such as the `GetSqlMoney()` method.

Challenge 6.4

Suppose that at Oozinoz we currently have only SQL Server databases. Provide an argument that we should use readers and adapters that are specific to SQL Sever. Provide another argument that we should *not* do this.

A solution appears on page 360.

Summary

An *abstraction* is a class that depends on abstract methods. The simplest example of an abstraction is an abstract hierarchy where concrete methods in the superclass depend on other abstract methods. You may be forced to move these abstract methods to another hierarchy if you want to factor the original hierarchy along another line. In this case, you would apply BRIDGE, separating an abstraction from the implementation of its abstract methods.

The most common example of BRIDGE occurs in drivers, specifically database drivers. Database drivers provide good examples of the tradeoffs that are inherent in a BRIDGE structure. A driver may require methods that an implementer cannot support. On the other hand, a driver may neglect useful methods that would apply to a particular database. This can push you back into writing code that is specific to an implementation instead of being abstract. It is not always clear whether you should value abstraction over specificity, but it is important to make these decisions consciously.

PART 2

RESPONSIBILITY PATTERNS

CHAPTER 7

INTRODUCING RESPONSIBILITY

The responsibility of an object is comparable to the responsibility of a representative in the Oozinoz call center. When you order fireworks from Oozinoz, the person you speak to is a representative for the company—a proxy. He or she performs foreseeable tasks, usually by delegating those tasks to other systems and people. Sometimes the representative will delegate a request to a single, central authority who will mediate the situation or escalate problems up a chain of responsibility.

Like call center representatives, ordinary objects have the information and methods they need to operate independently. There are times, though, when you need to centralize responsibility, diverting from the normal, independent operation of objects. Several design patterns address this need. There are also patterns that let objects escalate requests and that isolate an object from other objects that depend on it. Responsibility-oriented patterns provide techniques for centralizing, escalating, and limiting ordinary object responsibility.

Ordinary Responsibility

You probably have a strong sense of how attributes and responsibilities should come together in a well-formed class, although it can be challengng to explain your views.

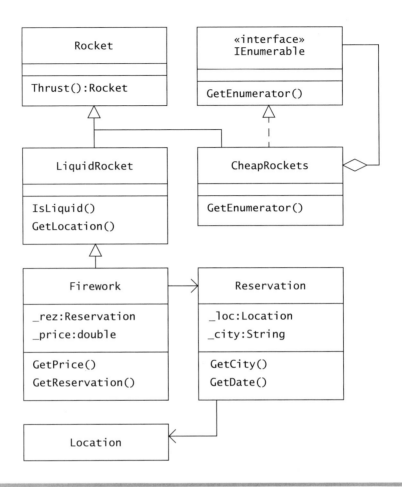

Figure 7.1   What's wrong with this picture?

Challenge 7.1

The class structure shown in Figure 7.1 has at least ten questionable assignments of responsibility. Circle as many problems as you can find, and for four of these points, write a statement describing what is wrong.

Solutions appear on page 360.

Looking at all the oddities in Figure 7.1 may loosen up your thinking about appropriate object modeling. This is a good frame of mind to be in when you set out to define terms, such as what is a *class*. The value of defining terms increases as it helps people communicate and decreases as it becomes a goal in itself and a source of conflict. In this spirit, take the following difficult challenge:

Challenge 7.2

Define the qualities of an effective, useful class.

Points to consider appear on page 361.

One feature that makes a class easier to use is that its method names suggest, accurately, what the methods do. There are times, though, when a method's name does not contain enough information for you to predict the exact effects of calling a method.

Challenge 7.3

Give an example where, for good reason, the effect of calling a method cannot be predicted from the method's name.

Some solutions appear on page 362.

Establishing principles for the proper assignment of responsibility in OO systems seems to be an area ripe for progress in computer science. A system in which every class and method clearly defines its responsibilities and bears them correctly is a strong system, probably stronger than most systems we encounter today.

Controlling Responsibility with Accessibility

It is common to speak of classes and methods bearing various responsibilities. In practice, this usually translates into *you* bearing responsibility for the solid design and proper functioning of your code. Fortunately, C# offers some relief. You can limit the accessibility of your classes, fields, and methods, and thereby limit your responsibility to developers that use your code. Table 7.1 gives informal definitions of the effects of access modifiers. Knowing the informal definitions of the effects of access modifiers may help you concentrate on the subtleties.

Table 7.1: Access Modifiers in C#

Access	Informal Definition
`public`	access not limited
`protected internal`	access limited to this program or types derived from the containing class
`protected`	access limited to te containing class or types derived from the containing class
`internal`	access limited to this program
`private`	access limited to the containing type

The *C# Language Specification* [Wiltamuth] gives the definitions in Table 7.1, referring to them as "intuitive meanings," and following them with detailed specifications. Several subtleties arise in practice that will require you to consider the formal definition (rather than an intuitive definition) of these modifiers. One area of subtlety to consider is whether access affects objects or classes.

Challenge 7.4

Can an object refer to a private member of another instance of the same class? Specifically, will the following code compile?

```
public class Firework
{
    private double _price = 0;
    /// ...
    private double Compare(Firework f)
    {
        return _price - f._price;
    }
}
```

A solution appears on page 362.

Some of the details regarding access to `protected` and `protected internal` members can be difficult to grasp. In particular, the *C# Language Specification* [Wiltamuth] says:

> When a `protected` instance member is accessed outside the program text of the class in which it is declared, and when a `protected internal` instance member is accessed outside the program text of the program in which it is declared, the access is required to take place through an instance of the derived class type in which the access occurs.

It may take more then one reading to understand that sentence, but try to apply it to the following challenge:

Challenge 7.5

The following code will not compile. Can you say why?

```
public class Machine
{
    protected void Unload() {}
}
public class Hopper : Machine
{
    public void Show()
    {
        Hopper h = new Hopper();
        h.Unload();
        Machine m = new Machine();
        m.Unload();
    }
}
```

A solution appears on page 363.

The intuitive meaning of `internal` access, according to the *C# Language Specification* [Wiltamuth], is "access limited to this program." The following challenge depends on whether "program" means namespace, assembly, or something else:

Challenge 7.6

The following code is in the file named `ShowInternal.cs` in the
`ShowAccessibility` directory. In this code, the `Bin` class accesses an
internal member of the `Process` class. Say whether or not this code
will compile and explain your answer.

```
namespace Processes
{
    public class Process
    {
        internal string _name = "";
    }
}

namespace Materials
{
    public class Bin
    {
        private string _current;
        public void setCurrentStep(Processes.Process p)
        {
            _current = p._name;
        }
    }
}
```

A solution appears on page 363.

Access modifiers help you limit your responsibility by limiting the services that you provide to other developers. For example, if you don't
want other developers to be able to manipulate one of your class's fields,
you can mark the field `private`. On the other hand, you will provide
future developers more flexibility if you mark your fields `protected`. You
should make a conscious decision and perhaps establish a group policy
about how you want to limit access to restrict your current responsibilities while permitting future extensions.

Summary

As a C# developer, you take on responsibility for creating classes that
form a logical collection of attributes and associated behaviors. Composing a good class is an art, but we can establish certain characteristics of
well-designed classes. In the classes you write, you are also responsible
for ensuring that your methods perform the services implied by their
names. You can limit this responsibility with the proper use of accessibil-

ity, but you should consider tradeoffs between security and flexibility in the accessibility of your code.

Beyond Ordinary Responsibility

Regardless of how a class limits access to its members, OO development normally distributes responsibility to individual objects. In other words, OO development promotes encapsulation, the idea that an object works on its own data.

Distributed responsibility is the norm, but several design patterns oppose this norm and move responsibility to an intermediary or central object. For example, the SINGLETON pattern concentrates responsibility in a single object and provides global access to this object. One way to remember the intent of SINGLETON and several other patterns is as exceptions to the ordinary rule of distributed responsibility.

If you intend to:	Then apply the pattern:
• Centralize responsibility in a single instance of a class,	SINGLETON
• Decouple an object from awareness of which other objects depend on it,	OBSERVER
• Centralize responsibility in a class that oversees how a set of other objects interact,	MEDIATOR
• Let an object act on behalf of another object,	PROXY
• Allow a request to escalate up a chain of objects until one handles it,	CHAIN OF RESPONSIBILITY
• Centralize responsibility in shared, fine-grained objects,	FLYWEIGHT

The intent of each design pattern is to solve a problem in a context. Responsibility-oriented patterns address contexts where you need to deviate from the normal rule that responsibility should be distributed as far as possible.

CHAPTER 8

SINGLETON

Objects can usually act responsibly just by performing their own work on their own attributes, without incurring obligations beyond self-consistency. Some objects, though, take on increased responsibilities, such as modeling real-world entities, coordinating work, or modeling the overall state of a system. When a particular object in a system bears a responsibility on which other objects rely, you need some way of finding the responsible object. For example, you might need to find an object that represents a particular machine, or a customer object that can construct itself from data in a database, or an object that initiates system memory recovery.

When you need to find a responsible object, in some cases, the object that you need will be the only instance of its class. For example, a fireworks factory might need exactly one Factory object. In this case, you can use SINGLETON. The intent of the SINGLETON pattern is to ensure that a class has only one instance, and to provide a global point of access to it.

SINGLETON Mechanics

The mechanics of SINGLETON are more memorable than its intent. It is easier to explain *how* to ensure that a class has only one instance than it is to say *why* you might want this restriction. You might categorize SINGLETON as a "creational" pattern, as *Design Patterns* does. You should, of course, think of patterns in whatever way helps you remember, recognize, and apply them. But the *intent* of the SINGLETON pattern implies that a specific object bears a responsibility on which other objects rely.

You have some options regarding how you create an object that takes on a unique role. But, regardless of how you create a singleton, you have to ensure that other developers don't create new instances of the class you intend to limit.

83

Challenge 8.1

How can you prevent other developers from constructing new instances of your class?

A solution appears on page 363.

When you design a singleton class, you need to decide when to instantiate the single object that will represent the class. One choice is to create this instance as a static field in the class. For example, a SystemStartup class might include the line:

```
private static Factory _factory = new Factory();
```

This class could make its unique instance available through a public, static GetFactory() method.

Rather than creating a singleton instance ahead of time, you might wait until the instance is first needed, lazy-initializing it. For example, the SystemStartup class might make its single instance available with:

```
public static Factory GetFactory()
{
    if (_factory == null)
    {
        _factory = new Factory();
        // ...
    }
    return _factory;
}
```

Challenge 8.2

Why might you decide to lazy-initialize a singleton instance rather than initializing it in its field declaration?

A solution appears on page 363.

Singletons and Threads

To lazy-initialize a singleton in a multi-threaded environment, you must prevent multiple threads from initializing the singleton.

In a multi-threaded environment, there is no guarantee that a method will run to completion before a method in another thread starts running. This opens the possibility, for example, that two threads will try to initialize a singleton at roughly the same time. Suppose that a method finds that a singleton is null. If another thread begins executing at that moment, it will also find that the singleton is null. Then both methods will proceed to initialize the singleton. To prevent this sort of contention, you need a locking facility to help coordinate methods running in different threads.

The C# language and .NET FCL include good support for multi-threaded development. In particular, C# supplies every object with a *lock*, an exclusive resource that represents possession of the object by a thread. To ensure that only one thread initializes a singleton, you can synchronize the initialization on the lock of a suitable object. Other methods that require exclusive access to the singleton can synchronize on the same lock. For advice on concurrent OO programming, *Concurrent Programming in Java* [Lea] is an excellent resource. This book suggests synchronizing on the lock that belongs to the class itself, as in the following code:

```csharp
using System;
namespace BusinessCore
{
    public class Factory
    {
        private static Factory _factory;
        private static Object _classLock = typeof(Factory);
        private long _wipMoves;
        private Factory()
        {
            _wipMoves = 0;
        }
        public static Factory GetFactory()
        {
            lock (_classLock)
            {
                if (_factory == null)
                {
                    _factory = new Factory();
                }
                return _factory;
            }
        }
        public void RecordWipMove()
        {
            // challenge!
        }
    }
}
```

The GetFactory() code ensures that if a second thread begins to lazy-initialize the singleton after another thread has begun the same initialization, the second thread will wait to obtain the _classLock object's lock. When it obtains the lock, the second thread will find that the singleton is no longer null.

The _wipMoves variable records the number of times that work in process (WIP) advances. Every time a bin moves onto a new machine, the subsystem that causes or records the move must call the factory singleton's `RecordWipMove()` method.

Challenge 8.3

Write the code for the `RecordWipMove()` method of the `Factory` class.

A solution appears on page 363.

Recognizing SINGLETON

Unique objects are not uncommon. In fact, most objects in an application bear a unique responsibility—why would you create two objects with identical responsibilities? Similarly, nearly every class has a unique role—why would you develop the same class twice? On the other hand, singleton classes—classes that allow only a single instance—are relatively rare. The fact that an object or class is unique does not imply that the SINGLETON pattern is at work. Consider the classes in Figure 8.1.

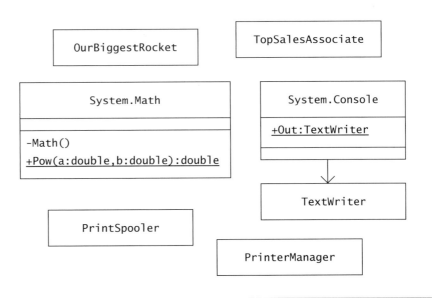

Figure 8.1   Which classes appear to apply SINGLETON?

Challenge 8.4

For each class in Figure 8.1, say whether it appears to be a singleton class and why.

Solutions appear on page 364.

Summary

Code that supports SINGLETON ensures that a class has only one instance and provides a global point of access to it. A common way to achieve this is through lazy-initialization of a singleton object, instantiating it only when the singleton is first needed. In a multi-threaded environment, you must take care to manage the collaboration of threads that may access a singleton's methods and data at approximately the same time.

Uniqueness of a class's or an object's role does not imply that the SINGLETON pattern is in use. The SINGLETON pattern centralizes authority in a single instance of a class.

CHAPTER 9

OBSERVER

Clients ordinarily gather information from an interesting object by calling its methods. But when an interesting object changes, a problem arises: How do clients that depend on the object's information know that the information has changed?

You may encounter designs that make an object responsible for informing clients when an interesting aspect of the object changes. The problem with this is that the knowledge of which attributes about an object are interesting lies with the client. The interesting object shouldn't accept responsibility for updating the client.

One solution is to arrange for clients to be informed when the object changes, and leave it to the clients to follow up with interrogations about the object's new state. The intent of the OBSERVER pattern is to define a one-to-many dependency between objects so that when one object changes state, all its dependents are notified so that they can react to the change.

C# Support for Observer

The OBSERVER pattern lets an object ask to be notified when another object changes. C# has built-in support for this common requirement. Delegates and events in C# simplify (or at least compact) implementations of the OBSERVER pattern. Suppose that a program needs to have its AssignTub() method called when a user clicks a certain button. The program can set up observation of the button with the following line of code:

```
_button.Click += new EventHandler(AssignTub);
```

In this statement,

- _button is an instance of the Button class.
- EventHandler is a delegate type.
- Click, an instance variable of the Button class, is of type EventHandler.
- AssignTub is a local method with parameter types and a return type that match those specified by EventHandler.

The beauty of the built-in support for OBSERVER shows in this single, simple line of code that sets up observation of a GUI control. You can emulate this code in your own programs without understanding much about delegates or the OBSERVER pattern. However, it is well worth going beyond emulating existing code and developing a deeper understanding of how delegates in C# work.

Delegate Mechanics

Delegates let you define how classes that we might call Interesting and Curious interact. Declaring a delegate type lets you specify the signature of a method that you want to be called back. The delegate type specifies the return value and parameters, but not the name of a method to call back. For example, you might want to define a minimal delegate type that specifies a method signature with a void return value and no parameters. The following code shows such a delegate:

```
public delegate void ChangeHandler();
```

This declaration is as simple as possible. It allows an interesting object to notify observers of change without taking on responsibility for passing any other information about the change. We can use a design diagram to shows the relationships between an Interesting class, a Curious class, and a ChangeHandler delegate type, as Figure 9.1 shows.

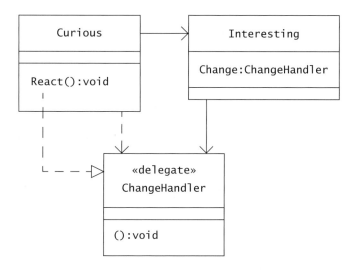

Figure 9.1   The Curious class has a method that matches the signature of
the ChangeHandler delegate type. The Interesting class has
an instance of the ChangeHandler delegate type.

The method in the ChangeHandler delegate in Figure 9.1 specifies the arguments (none) and the return type void, but does not provide a method name. This is how delegate types work: A program can instantiate the ChangeHandler delegate type with any method whose parameters and return type match the delegate type declaration.

Figure 9.1 uses three types of arrows to show three relationships for the Curious class:

- The non-dashed, open arrowhead means that the Curious class has a reference to an Interesting object.

- The dashed line with a closed, hollow arrowhead means that the Curious class's React() method matches the delegate type. That is, the React() method has the same arguments (none) and return type (void) as the ChangeHandler delegate type.

- The dashed line and open arrowhead means a Curious instance may depend on an instance of the ChangeHandler delegate type. Specifically, instances of the Curious class will depend on Change-Handler delegates for notification of changes in instances of the Interesting class.

The Interesting class has a field named Change whose type is the Change-Handler delegate type. The code for the Interesting class might look as follows:

```
class Interesting
{
    public ChangeHandler Change;
    public void Wiggle()
    {
        if (Change != null) Change();
    }
}
```

This code lets an interested class arrange to be notified whenever the Interesting class's Wiggle() method executes. Now the question is, how can code in the Curious class instantiate the ChangeHandler delegate type with a method to call back, and add this delegate instance into the Change variable? To understand this, it is important to note that, although the only way to declare a delegate type is with a delegate declaration, a delegate type is a class type that derives from the System.Delegate class. Figure 9.2 shows this relationship.

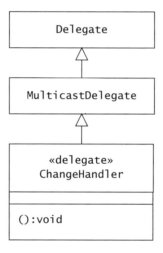

Figure 9.2   The ChangeHandler delegate type (and all other delegate types) inherits the behavior of the Delegate and MulticastDelegate classes.

A useful behavior that delegate types inherit is the ability to combine delegate instances. For example, the Curious class's constructor instantiates the ChangeHandler delegate type and combines this new delegate instance with an Interesting object's Change delegate.

```
class Curious
{
    public Curious(Interesting i)
    {
        i.Change += new ChangeHandler(React);
    }
    public void React()
    {
        Console.WriteLine("Something happened!");
    }
}
```

The Interesting object's Change delegate may be null when the Curious constructor executes. In this case, the Change delegate will simply assume the value of the delegate that the Curious object adds in. A delegate variable such as Change can hold multiple delegate instances, although in this example, we will only use one.

The delegate instance that the Curious constructor creates encapsulates a Curious object's React() method. The following example creates an Interesting object and a Curious object, and invokes the Interesting object's Wiggle() method:

```
class ShowDelegate
{
    static void Main(string[] args)
    {
        Interesting i = new Interesting();
        Curious c = new Curious(i);
        i.Wiggle();
    }
}
```

Running this application prints out the following:

```
Something happened!
```

Challenge 9.1

Draw a sequence diagram that illustrates the flow of messages from the application's Wiggle() call, through the Change delegate, and to the Curious object.

A solution appears on page 365.

We have not yet used the event keyword in this example, but we probably should now. The Interesting class declares its Change delegate with the following line:

```
public ChangeHandler Change;
```

We can amend this line to read as follows:

```
public event ChangeHandler Change;
```

The advantage of marking Change as an event is that C# will limit access to the event. Without this restriction, any method with access to an Interesting object could invoke the Change delegate as follows:

```
i.Change();
```

We can now say that Change is "an event," although such a loose description may be confusing to developers who are still learning how events and delegates work.

A Classic Example—OBSERVER in GUIs

The most prevalent example of the use of delegates and events occurs in GUIs. Whenever a user clicks a button or adjusts a slider, many objects in the application may need to react to the change. The .NET FCL anticipates that you will be interested to know when a user changes a GUI component, and the OBSERVER pattern is evident throughout the GUI libraries, especially in the System.Windows.Forms library. GUI components such as sliders (or "track bars," in .NET) contain events that let you register local methods to activate when the event occurs.

Consider a typical Oozinoz GUI application, such as the one that Figure 9.3 shows. This application lets a fireworks engineer experiment visually with parameters that determine the relationship between a rocket's thrust and the burn rate and surface area of its fuel.

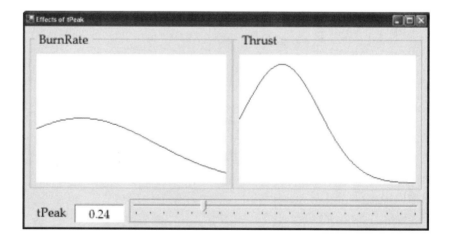

Figure 9.3   The curves shown change in real time as the user adjusts the tPeak variable with the slider.

When a solid rocket engine ignites, the part of its fuel that is exposed to air burns, producing thrust. From ignition to maximum burn rate, the burn area increases from the initial ignition area to the full surface area of the fuel. This maximum burn rate occurs at time t_{peak}. The ballistics application normalizes time so that time is 0 at ignition and time is 1 when burning stops, so t_{peak} is a number between 0 and 1.

One set of burn rate and thrust equations that Oozinoz uses is:

$$rate = 0.5\left(25^{-(t-t_{peak})^2}\right)$$

$$thrust = 1.7 \cdot \left(\frac{rate}{0.6}\right)^{1/0.3}$$

The ShowBallistics application produces the plots in Figure 9.3, which shows how t_{peak} affects the burn rate and thrust of a rocket. As a user moves the slider, the value of t_{peak} changes and the curves take on new shapes. Figure 9.4 shows the GUI layout of the application.

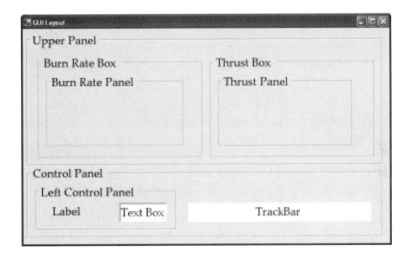

Figure 9.4   The layout of the ShowBallistics application.

When the slider moves, the burn rate panel, thrust panel, and text box must update. The panels are instances of PlotPanel, a class introduced in Chapter 4, Facade. This class's constructor requires an instance of the Function delegate type (also introduced in Chapter 4), which will contain a method that provides a function of time, the burn rate or thrust function in this example. The ShowBallistics application uses two auxiliary classes to represent the burn rate and thrust equations. Figure 9.5 shows these classes.

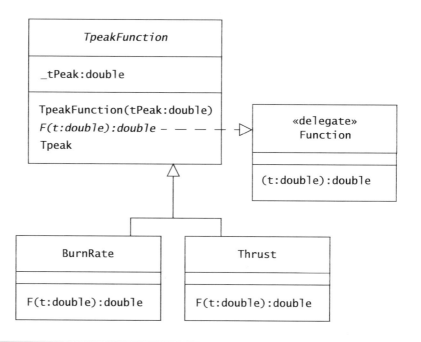

Figure 9.5   The BurnRate and Thrust classes have methods that match the
              Function delegate, and have access to an inherited Tpeak
              property.

The BurnRate and Thrust classes inherit a Tpeak property that they use in
calculating their functions of time. For example, the code for BurnRate is
as follows:

```
public class BurnRate : TpeakFunction
{
    public BurnRate(double tPeak) : base(tPeak)
    {
    }
    public override double F(double t)
    {
        return F(t, Tpeak);
    }
    public static double F(double t, double tPeak)
    {
        return .5 * Math.Pow(25, -Math.Pow((t - tPeak), 2));
    }
}
```

The BurnRate class's constructor passes an initial tPeak value to its superclass TpeakFunction, where the value is stored in a Tpeak property. The
BurnRate class's F() method matches the Function delegate so that the
application can plot a BurnRate object in a PlotPanel. The F() instance
method relies on a second, static method that takes tPeak into account.
The C# idiom here is as follows: We have a function that has more param-

eters than a delegate expects. To match the delegate, we save the extra parameters as instance variables to which the method refers. Then to instantiate the delegate, we provide an instance of the class that contains the extra variables. For example, the ShowBallistics class contains the lines:

```
private BurnRate _burnRate = new BurnRate(0);
// ...
_burnRatePanel = UI.NORMAL.CreatePaddedPanel(
    new PlotPanel(NPOINT, new Function(_burnRate.F)));
```

Observe that the code instantiates the Function delegate with an instance method of a BurnRate object that contains a tPeak value.

When the slider moves, the application calculates a new peak time value and updates the burn rate and thrust function. It also updates the text box that shows the tPeak value and redisplays the plot panels. To register a callback method for slider events, the ShowBallistics application uses the following statement:

```
_slider.Scroll += new EventHandler(SliderScroll);
```

Figure 9.6 shows the classes of the objects that the ShowBallistics class updates as the slider moves.

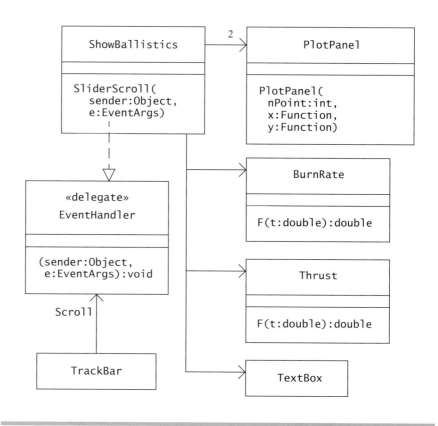

Figure 9.6   The ShowBallistics application depends on a TrackBar
              object's Scroll event to know when to update its function
              objects and graphical components.

The code that executes when the slider moves is as follows:

```
private void SliderScroll(object sender, EventArgs e)
{
    double val = Slider().Value;
    double tp =
        (val - Slider().Minimum) /
        (Slider().Maximum - Slider().Minimum);
    ValueTextBox().Text = tp.ToString();
    _burnRate.Tpeak = tp;
    BurnRatePanel().Refresh();
    _thrust.Tpeak = tp;
    ThrustPanel().Refresh();
}
```

This code is not necessarily bad, but note that it undoes the intent of
OBSERVER. The point of OBSERVER is to free the observed object from
responsibility for updating other objects interested in its state. For example, we don't want a slider to have to know which objects to update when
the slider moves. The .NET libraries support this idea, reducing the

responsibility of components such as sliders to mere notification of change. But the ShowBallistics application puts us back in the situation we had hoped to avoid: A single object (the application) knows which objects to update and it takes responsibility for doling out the appropriate invocations.

An alternative design will let each object that is interested in change register its interest and then respond appropriately when the change occurs. In modifying the design, you have to take some care to ensure that the order of events will not create a defect. For example, if your plotting panels and function objects all listen to the slider, the panels might update themselves before the functions do, so that the panels would not reflect the new slider value. To avoid such races, you might decide to differentiate the event of the slider moving from the event of tPeak changing.

Challenge 9.2

Provide a new class diagram showing a design that calls for the text box and the functions to watch for change in the slider, and for the plotting panels to watch for change in the functions.

A solution appears on page 366.

Suppose that you change TpeakFunction, the superclass of BurnRate and Thrust, to listen for changes in the slider and propagate changes in its Tpeak property. The following code shows this approach:

```
public abstract class TpeakFunction
{
    private double _tPeak;
    private TrackBar _slider;
    public event EventHandler Change;

    public TpeakFunction(double tPeak, TrackBar slider)
    {
        Tpeak = tPeak;
        _slider = slider;
        slider.Scroll += new EventHandler(SliderScroll);
    }
    public double Tpeak
    {
        get
        {
            return _tPeak;
        }
        set
        {
            _tPeak = value;
            if (Change != null)
            {
                Change(this, EventArgs.Empty);
```

```
                }
            }
        }
        private void SliderScroll(object sender, EventArgs e)
        {
            double val = _slider.Value;
            Tpeak =
                (val - _slider.Minimum) /
                (_slider.Maximum - _slider.Minimum);
        }
        public abstract double F(double t);
    }
```

A TpeakFunction object listens to a TrackBar object's Scroll event and
invokes its own Change event when the Tpeak value changes. A plotting
class can watch for changes in the Tpeak property with code such as the
following:

```
    public class AlertPlotPanel : PlotPanel
    {
        public AlertPlotPanel(int nPoint, TpeakFunction tf) :
            base (nPoint, new Function(tf.F))
        {
            tf.Change += new EventHandler(FunctionChange);
        }
        private void FunctionChange(object sender, EventArgs e)
        {
            Refresh();
        }
    }
```

This design also requires a TextBox subclass that can listen to the slider
with code such as the following:

```
    public class ValueTextBox : TextBox
    {
        private TrackBar _slider;
        public ValueTextBox(TrackBar slider)
        {
            _slider = slider;
            _slider.Scroll += new EventHandler(SliderScroll);
        }
        private void SliderScroll(object sender, EventArgs e)
        {
            double val = _slider.Value;
            double tp =
                (val - _slider.Minimum) /
                (_slider.Maximum - _slider.Minimum);
            Text = tp.ToString();
        }
    }
```

There is a problem with the ValueTextBox code: It essentially duplicates
the code in the TpeakFunction class that calculates peak time from the
slider value. We might alter the design to have the text box listen to one of
the functions, but the text box doesn't really depend on these functions; it
depends on the peak time value. It's also a bit subtle that the panels

depend on the functions. A simpler approach would be to introduce a class to contain critical peak time value, perhaps a `Tpeak` class. We could let the application listen to the slider and update a `Tpeak` object, and let all other interested components listen to the value of this object. This approach becomes a "Model/View/Controller" design.

Model/View/Controller

As applications and systems grow, it is important to divide and re-divide responsibility so that classes and packages stay small enough to maintain. The phrase *Model/View/Controller* (MVC) refers to separating an interesting object (the model) from GUI elements that portray and manipulate it (the view and controller.) C# can support this separation with delegates and events, but as the previous section showed, not all designs that use events are MVC designs.

The initial versions of the `ShowBallistics` application combine intelligence about an application GUI with information about ballistics. You can refactor this code, following MVC to divide this application's responsibilities. In this refactoring, the revised `ShowBallistics` class should retain the views and controllers in its GUI elements.

The creators of MVC envisioned that the look of a component (its "view") might be separable from its feel (its "controller"). In practice, the appearance of a GUI component and its support for user interaction are tightly coupled, and C# does not divide views from controllers. The value of MVC is to push the "model" out of an application into its own domain.

The "model" in the `ShowBallistics` application is the tPeak value. To refactor to MVC, we might introduce a `Tpeak` class that would hold a peak time value and would allow interested listeners to register for change events. Such a class might look as follows:

```
public class Tpeak
{
    private double _value = 0;
    public event System.EventHandler Change;

    public double Value
    {
        get
        {
            return _value;
        }
        set
        {
```

```
                _value = value;
                if (Change != null)
                {
                    Change(this, System.EventArgs.Empty);
                }
            }
        }
    }
```

If you were to review this code at an Oozinoz code review, two points would likely arise: This code has little to do with burn rates, and there is no reason to send an `EventArgs` argument that is always empty. Let us address the latter point first. Instead of sending meaningless arguments in the `Change` event, we can introduce an argument-free delegate as follows:

```
public delegate void ChangeHandler();

public class Tpeak
{
    private double _value = 0;
    public event ChangeHandler Change;

    public double Value
    {
        get
        {
            return _value;
        }
        set
        {
            _value = value;
            if (Change != null)
            {
                Change();
            }
        }
    }
}
```

This code is simpler, but still almost none of it relates to the time at which a rocket engine's fuel burn rate peaks. In fact, this code looks like a fairly generic utility for holding a value and for alerting listeners when the value changes. We can refactor the code to mine out that genericity, but first it is worth looking at a revised design that uses the `Tpeak` class.

Now we can create a design where the application watches the slider, and everything else watches a `Tpeak` object. When the slider moves, the application sets a new value in the `Tpeak` object. The panels and text box listen to the `Tpeak` object and update themselves when the value changes. The

BurnRate and Thrust classes use the Tpeak object to calculate their functions, but they don't need to listen to (that is, register for) Change events.

Challenge 9.3

Create a class diagram that shows the application depending on the slider and the text box and plotting panels depending on a Tpeak object.

A solution appears on page 367.

This design allows for the work of translating the slider's value into the peak time value to be done once. The application updates a single Tpeak object, and all GUI objects that listen for change can query the Tpeak object for its new value.

However, the Tpeak class does little more than hold a value, so we want to try factoring out a value holder class. In addition, it is likely that an observed number such as peak time is not a standalone value, but rather is the attribute of some domain object. For example, peak time is an attribute of a rocket engine. We might want to improve our design to separate our classes, with a value holding class that lets GUI objects observe domain objects.

Layering

When you divide GUI objects from domain or business objects, you can create layers of code. A *layer* is a group of classes with similar responsibilities, often collected in a single namespace and assembly. Higher layers, such as a GUI layer, usually depend only on classes in equal or lower layers. Layering usually includes a clear definition of the interfaces between layers, such as a GUI and the business objects it represents.

Figure 9.7 shows an Engine class that has a Tpeak property; it also shows a PropertyHolder class that can wrap access to a property, notifying listeners when the property changes. The ShowBallistics class is part of a layer of GUI objects, and the Engine class is part of a layer of business objects. We will also place the PropertyHolder class in the business layer, partially because we want it to be available to other business objects.

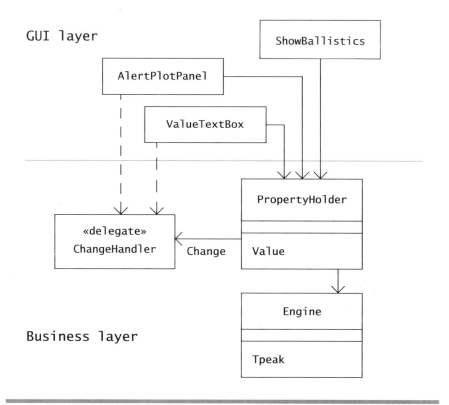

Figure 9.7   The PropertyHolder class relays changes in a business object's
                 property to a GUI application.

The PropertyHolder class contains the logic that supports the OBSERVER
pattern. A PropertyHolder instance holds a property for a business object
and updates listeners when the property changes. How can we implement this class?

We might consider using delegates to represent a property's get and set
methods. However, C# will not, at this writing, allow instantiation of a
delegate with a property. An alternative is to use reflection, as the following code shows:

```
public class PropertyHolder
{
    private Object _obj;
    private PropertyInfo _prop;
    public event ChangeHandler Change;
    public PropertyHolder (Object o, String propertyName)
    {
        _obj = o;
        _prop = _obj.GetType().GetProperty(propertyName);
    }
    public Object Value
    {
        get
```

```
            {
                return _prop.GetValue(_obj, null);
            }
            set
            {
                _prop.SetValue(_obj, value, null);
                Change();
            }
        }
    }
```

The `PropertyHolder` class's constructor takes any object and the name of a property, and provides a generic `Value` property. The application that wants to observe and alter this property can instantiate `PropertyHolder` as follows:

```
private PropertyHolder _ph;
// ...
public ShowBallistics()
{
    Engine e = new Engine();
    _ph = new PropertyHolder(e, "Tpeak");
    InitializeComponent(); // set up and launch GUI
}
//...
private TrackBar Slider()
{
    if (_slider == null)
    {
        _slider = new TrackBar();
        //...
        _slider.Scroll += new EventHandler(SliderScroll);
    }
    return _slider;
}
//...
private void SliderScroll(object sender, EventArgs e)
{
    double val = Slider().Value;
    double tp = (val - Slider().Minimum) /
                (Slider().Maximum - Slider().Minimum);
    _ph.Value = tp;
}
```

Listeners register for change notification by adding a `ChangeHandler` delegate to the `Change` event. For example, the text box code might look as follows:

```
public class ValueTextBox : TextBox
{
    private PropertyHolder _ph;
    public ValueTextBox(PropertyHolder ph)
    {
        _ph = ph;
        _ph.Change += new ChangeHandler(PropertyChange);
    }
    private void PropertyChange()
    {
        Text = _ph.Value.ToString();
    }
}
```

When you apply MVC, the flow of events may seem indirect. The ballistics application listens for changes in a TrackBar object's Scroll event and passes new values of peak time to a PropertyHolder object. This object invokes its Change event, notifying the application's label and panels, and these objects repaint themselves. Change propagates from the GUI layer to the business layer, and back up to the GUI layer.

Challenge 9.4

Fill in the missing labels in Figure 9.8.

A solution appears on page 368.

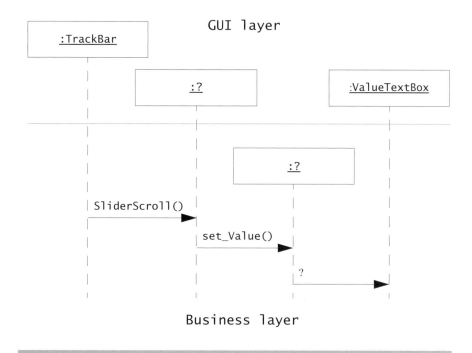

Figure 9.8   MVC causes calls to pass from a GUI layer into a business layer
and back into the GUI layer.

The flow of events in the application now crosses in and out of the business layer. The benefit of this design is in the layering of responsibility, which makes the code easier to maintain. For instance, in the ballistics example, you can add a second GUI, perhaps for a handheld device, without having to change classes in the business object layer. You might also add a new source of change that updates the property holder. In this case, the OBSERVER mechanics you have in place will automatically update objects in the GUI layer.

Layering also opens the possibility of arranging for different layers to execute on different computers. A layer that executes on a computer is a *tier* in an *n-tier* system. An n-tier design can reduce the amount of code that must execute on a user's desktop. It also lets you make changes in business classes without updating software on user machines, greatly simplifying deployment. However, sending messages between computers is not free, and you must make a move to an n-tier deployment judiciously. For example, you probably could not afford for users to wait as scroll events travel back and forth between a user's desktop and a server. In such a case, you would probably have to let scrolling occur on the user's machine, with a decision to commit to a new peak time value left as a separate user action.

Summary

The OBSERVER pattern appears frequently in GUI applications and is a fundamental aspect of .NET's GUI libraries. With these components, you never have to change or subclass a component class just to communicate its events to an interested object. For small applications, a common practice is to register a single object—the application—to receive all the events in a GUI. There is no inherent problem with this, but you should recognize that it reverses the distribution of responsibility that OBSERVER intends. For a large GUI, consider moving to an MVC design, letting each interested object register for events rather than introducing a mediating central object. MVC also lets you create loosely coupled layers that can change independently and that may execute on different machines.

CHAPTER 10

MEDIATOR

Ordinary OO development distributes responsibility as far as it will go, with each object doing its own work independently. The OBSERVER pattern supports this distribution by minimizing the responsibility of an object that other objects find interesting. The SINGLETON pattern also resists the distribution of responsibility and lets you centralize responsibility in particular objects that clients locate and reuse. Like SINGLETON, the MEDIATOR pattern centralizes responsibility, but for a particular set of objects rather than for all the clients in a system.

Providing a central authority for a group of objects is useful when the interactions between the objects gravitate toward the complex condition where every object is aware of every other object in the group. Centralization of responsibility is also useful when the logic surrounding the interactions of the related objects is independent from the other behavior of the objects. The MEDIATOR pattern defines an object that encapsulates how a set of objects interact. This promotes loose coupling, keeping the objects from referring to each other explicitly, and lets you vary their interaction independently.

A Classic Example—GUI Mediators

You will probably most often encounter the MEDIATOR pattern when you develop an application with a GUI. Such applications tend to become *thick*, gathering code that you can refactor into other classes. The Show-Flight class in Chapter 4, "Facade," initially performed three roles. Before you refactored it, this class acted as a display panel, a complete GUI application, and a flight path calculator. After refactoring the application that launches the flight panel display became simple, containing just a few lines of code. Large applications, however, can remain complex after this type of refactoring, even when they contain just the logic that creates components and arranges for the components' interaction. Consider the application in Figure 10.1.

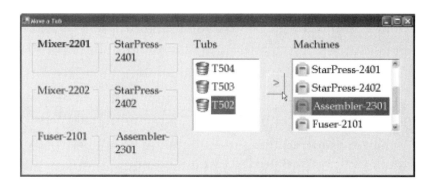

Figure 10.1   This application lets its user manually update the location of a
              tub of chemicals.

Oozinoz stores chemical batches in rubber tubs. Machines at Oozinoz
read bar codes on the tubs to keep track of where tubs are in the factory.
Sometimes a manual override is necessary, particularly when humans
move a tub instead of waiting for a robot to transfer it. Figure 10.1 shows
a new, partially developed application that lets a user specify the machine
at which a tub is located.

In the MoveATub application, when the user lets the cursor hover over one
of the machines, the machine name becomes bold and the list of tubs
changes to show the tubs at that machine. The user can then select one of
these tubs, select a target machine, and click the ">" button to update the
location of the tub. Figure 10.2 shows the application class.

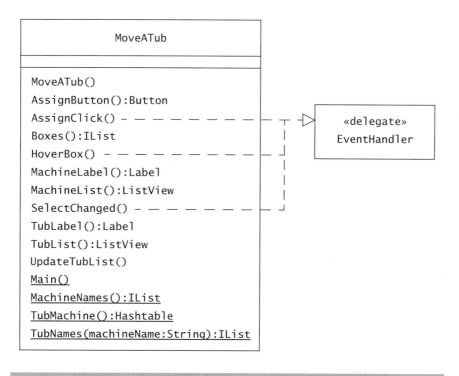

Figure 10.2   The MoveATub class has a mix of component-building, event-handling, and mock database methods.

The developer working on this application created it initially with a wizard and has begun refactoring it. About half the methods in MoveATub exist to lazy-initialize variables that contain the application's GUI components. The AssignButton() method is typical.

```
private Button AssignButton()
{
    if (_assignButton == null)
    {
        _assignButton = new Button();
        _assignButton.Enabled = false;
        _assignButton.Location = new Point(552, 104);
        _assignButton.Size = new Size(40, 48);
        _assignButton.Text = ">";
        _assignButton.Click +=
            new System.EventHandler(AssignClick);
    }
    return _assignButton;
}
```

The existence of hard-coded numbers that specify the button's location and size reflect the fact that this code came from a wizard. The developer will eventually remove these literal values by moving to a docking strategy for the GUI layout. But the immediate problem is that the MoveATub class has a high number of methods.

Most of the static methods provide a mock database of tub names and machine names. The developer will eventually drop this approach of working with just names and upgrade the application to work with Tub objects and Machine objects. Most of the remaining methods in the application contain logic that handles the application's events. For example, the SelectChanged() method manages whether or not the assign button is enabled.

```
private void SelectChanged(object sender, EventArgs e)
{
    //...
    AssignButton().Enabled =
        MachineList().SelectedItems.Count > 0 &&
        TubList().SelectedItems.Count > 0;
}
```

We might consider moving SelectChanged() and the other event handling methods into a separate mediator class. We should first note that the MEDIATOR pattern is already at work in this class—components do not update each other directly. For example, it is not the case that the machine and list components update the assign button directly. Rather, the Move-ATub application registers for the lists' select events and updates the button based on whether items from both lists are selected. In the tub moving application, a MoveATub object acts as a mediator, receiving events and dispatching corresponding actions.

The mechanics of the .NET FCL nudge you into using a mediator, although there is nothing in the FCL that requires an application to be its own mediator. Instead of mingling component creation methods with event handling methods and with mock database methods all in one class, you can move an application's methods into classes with separate specializations.

Challenge 10.1

Complete the diagram in Figure 10.3 to show a refactoring of MoveATub, introducing a separate mock database class and a mediator class to receive the events of the MoveATub GUI.

A solution appears on page 369.

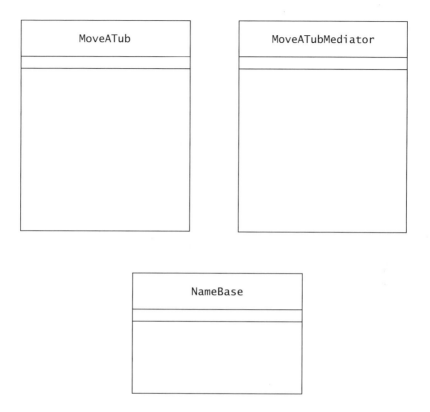

Figure 10.3   Separate the component-building, event-handling. and mock
                database parts of the application.

Refactoring consolidates the mediator into a separate class, letting you
develop it and focus on it separately. Now when the MoveATub application
runs, components pass events to a MoveATubMediator object. The mediator
may take action on non-GUI objects, for example to update the database
when an assignment is made. The mediator object may also call back
components in the GUI, for example to disable the assign button after an
assignment is made.

Challenge 10.2

Draw a diagram that shows what happens when the user clicks the OK
button. Show whichever objects you think are most important and show
the messages that pass among these objects.

A solution appears on page 370.

GUI components in .NET apply the MEDIATOR pattern as a matter of course, notifying a mediator when events occur rather than taking responsibility for updating other components directly. GUI applications give rise to perhaps the most common application of the MEDIATOR pattern, but there are other cases where you may want to introduce a mediator.

Whenever the interaction of a set of objects is complex, you can centralize the responsibility for this interaction in a mediator object that stands outside the interacting group. This promotes *loose coupling*, a reduction in the responsibility that the interacting objects bear to each other. Managing the interaction of objects in an independent class also has the advantage of simplifying and standardizing the interaction rules. One example of the value of a mediator occurs when you need to manage relational integrity.

Relational Integrity Mediators

Part of the strength of the OO paradigm is that it lets you easily map connections between C# objects and objects in the real world. However, there are at least two fundamental deficits in a C# object model's ability to reflect the real world. First, objects in the real world vary with time, but there is no support for this built into C#. For example, assignment statements obliterate any previous value instead of remembering it, as a human would. Second, in the real world, relations are as important as objects, but relations receive little support in today's OO languages, including C#. For example, there is no built-in support for the fact that if Star Press 2402 is in Bay 1, then Bay 1 must contain Star Press 2402. In fact, it is quite possible for such relations to go awry in C#, which in turn invites the application of the MEDIATOR pattern.

Relational Integrity

An object model is *relationally consistent* if every time object **a** points to object **b**, object **b** points to object **a**.

For a more rigorous definition, consider two classes, `Alpha` and `Beta`. Let A represent the set of objects in the model that are instances of class `Alpha`, and let B represent the set of objects that are instances of class `Beta`. Let **a** and **b** denote members of A and B, and let the *ordered pair* (**a**, **b**) denote that object **a** ∈ A has a reference to object **b** ∈ B. This reference may be either a direct reference or one of a set of references, as when object a has a `List` object that includes **b**.

The *Cartesian product* A × B is the set of all possible ordered pairs (**a**, **b**) with **a** ∈ A and **b** ∈ B. The sets A and B allow the two Cartesian products A × B and B × A. An *object model relation* on A and B is the subset of A × B that exists in an object model. Let AB denote this subset, and let BA denote the subset of B × A that exists in the model.

Any binary relation R ⊆ A × B has an *inverse* R^{-1} ⊆ B × A defined by:

(**b**, **a**) ∈ R^{-1} if and only if (**a**, **b**) ∈ R

The inverse of AB provides the set of references that must occur from instances of B to instances of A if the object model is consistent. In other words, instances of classes `Alpha` and `Beta` are relationally consistent if and only if BA is the inverse of AB.

Consider rubber tubs of chemicals at Oozinoz. Tubs are always assigned to a particular machine. You can model this relationship with a table, as Table 10.1 shows.

Table 10.1: A Relationship of Tubs and Machines

TUB	MACHINE
T305	StarPress-2402
T308	StarPress-2402
T377	ShellAssembler-2301
T379	ShellAssembler-2301
T389	ShellAssembler-2301
T001	Fuser-2101
T002	Fuser-2101

Table 10.1 shows the *relation* of tubs and machines, or the way in which they stand with regard to each other. Mathematically, a relation is a subset of all ordered pairs of objects, so there is a relation of tubs to machines, and a relation of machines to tubs. See the sidebar "Relational Consis-

tency" for a more strict definition of relational consistency in an object model.

When you record tub and machine relational information in a table, you can guarantee that each tub is on only one machine by enforcing the restriction that each tub occurs only once in the Tub column. The most common way to do this is to make the Tub column the primary key of the table in a relational database. With this model, as in reality, there is no way a tub can appear on two machines at once.

An object model cannot guarantee relational integrity as easily as a relational model can. Consider the MoveATub application. The developer working on its design will eventually stop working with just names and will begin working with Tub objects and Machine objects. When a real tub is near a real machine, the object representing the tub will have a reference to the object representing the machine. Each Machine object will have a collection of Tub objects representing tubs near the machine. Figure 10.2 shows a typical object model.

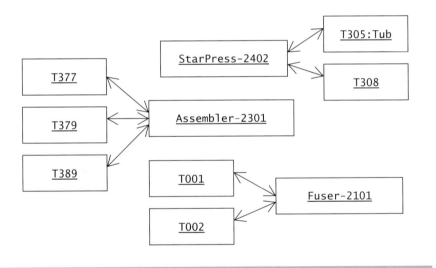

Figure 10.2   An object model distributes information about relations.

The arrowheads in Figure 10.2 emphasize that tubs know about machines, and machines know about tubs. The information about the relationship of tubs and machines is now distributed across many objects, instead of being in a central table. The distribution of the tub/machine relationship makes the management of the relationship more difficult, and makes this management a candidate for application of the MEDIATOR pattern.

Consider a defect that occurred at Oozinoz when a developer began modeling a new machine that included a bar code reader for identifying tubs.

After scanning a tub for its ID, the developer set the location of tub t to machine m with the following code:

```
//tell tub about machine, and machine about tub
t.setMachine(m);
m.addTub(t);
```

Challenge 10.3

Suppose that object t represents tub T308 and object m represents machine Fuser-2101. Complete the object diagram in Figure 10.3, showing the effects of the code that updates the tub's location. What defect does this reveal?

A solution appears on page 371.

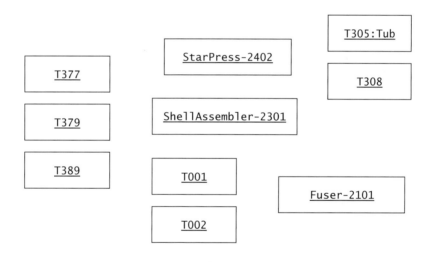

Figure 10.3   When completed, this diagram will show the flaw in a developer's code that updates a tub's location.

The easiest way to guarantee relational consistency is to pull the relational information back into a single table managed by a mediating object. Instead of having tubs know about machines and machines know about tubs, you can give all these objects a reference to a mediator that keeps a single table of tubs and machines. This "table" can be an instance of the Hashtable class (from the System.Collections library). Figure 10.4 shows a class diagram with a mediator in place.

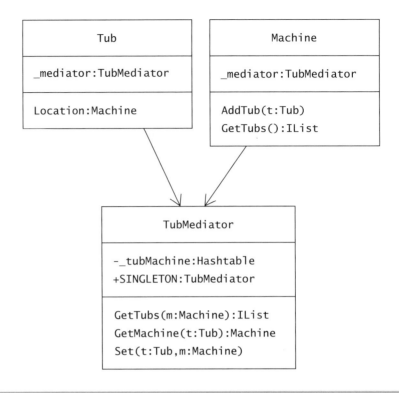

Figure 10.4   Tub and Machine objects rely on a mediator to control the
                relationship between tubs and machines.

The Tub class has a Location property that allows for recording which
machine a tub is near. The code behind this property ensures that a tub
can only be in one place at one time, using a TubMediator singleton object
to manage the tub/machine relation:

```
using System;
namespace Machines
{
    public class Tub
    {
        private String _id;
        private TubMediator _mediator =
            TubMediator.SINGLETON;
        public Tub(String id)
        {
            _id = id;
        }
        public Machine Location
        {
            get
            {
                return _mediator.GetMachine(this);
```

```
            }
            set
            {
                _mediator.Set(this, value);
            }
        }
        public override String ToString()
        {
            return _id;
        }
        public override int GetHashCode()
        {
            //...
        }
        public override bool Equals(Object o)
        {
            //...
        }
    }
}
```

The Tub class's Location property uses a mediator to update a tub's location, delegating responsibility for maintaining relational integrity to the mediator. The Tub class implements the GetHashCode() and Equals() methods so that Tub objects will store properly in a hash table. The detail for this code is as follows:

```
public override int GetHashCode()
{
    return _id.GetHashCode();
}
public override bool Equals(Object o)
{
    if (o == this)
    {
        return true;
    }
    if (!(o is Tub))
    {
        return false;
    }
    Tub t = (Tub) o;
    return _id.Equals(t._id);
}
```

The TubMediator class uses a Hashtable object to store the tub/machine relationship. By storing the relation in a table, the mediator can guarantee that the object model never allows two machines to possess a single tub.

```
public class TubMediator
{
    private Hashtable _tubMachine = new Hashtable();

    public Machine GetMachine(Tub t)
    {
        // challenge!
    }

    public IList GetTubs(Machine m)
    {
        ArrayList al = new ArrayList();
        IDictionaryEnumerator e =
            _tubMachine.GetEnumerator();
        while (e.MoveNext())
        {
            if(e.Value.Equals(m))
            {
                al.Add(e.Key);
            }
        }
        return al;
    }
    public void Set(Tub t, Machine m)
    {
        // challenge!
    }
}
```

Challenge 10.4

Write the code for the `TubMediator` methods `GetMachine()` and `Set()`.

A solution appears on page 371.

Rather than introducing a mediator class, you could place the logic for ensuring that tubs never appear on two machines at once inside the code for the `Tub` and `Machine` classes. However, this logic pertains to relational integrity and has little to do with how chemical tubs and factory machines work. The logic is also error-prone. In particular, a common error would be to move a tub to a new machine, updating the tub and machine, but forgetting to update the machine that was the tub's previous location.

Moving the relation management code to a mediator lets an independent class encapsulate the logic for how this set of objects interact. In the mediator, it is easy to ensure that changing a `Tub` object's `Location` property automatically moves the tub away from its current machine. The following NUnit test code (from `TubTest.cs`) shows this behavior:

```
[Test]
public void TestLocationChange()
{
    // setup
    Tub t = new Tub("T403");
    Machine m1 = new Machine(1001);
    Machine m2 = new Machine(1002);
    // place the tub on m1
    t.Location = m1;
    Assertion.Assert(m1.GetTubs().Contains(t));
    Assertion.Assert(!m2.GetTubs().Contains(t));
    // move the tub
    t.Location = m2;
    Assertion.Assert(!m1.GetTubs().Contains(t));
    Assertion.Assert(m2.GetTubs().Contains(t));
}
```

When you have an object model that is not tied to a relational database, you can use mediators to sustain the relational integrity of your model. Moving the relation management logic into mediators lets these classes specialize in maintaining relational integrity.

Challenge 10.5

With respect to moving logic out of one class and into a new one, MEDIATOR is similar to other patterns. List two other patterns that may involve refactoring an aspect of behavior out of an existing class or hierarchy.

A solution appears on page 372.

Summary

The MEDIATOR pattern promotes loose coupling, keeping related objects from referring to each other explicitly. MEDIATOR shows up most often in GUI application development, where you don't want to manage the complexity of individual widgets updating each other. The architecture of .NET guides you in this direction, encouraging you to define objects that register for GUI events. If you are developing user interfaces with C#, you are probably applying MEDIATOR.

.NET nudges you into using MEDIATOR when creating a GUI, but .NET does not require you to move this mediation outside an application class. Doing so can simplify your code. You can let a mediator class concentrate on the interaction between GUI components, and let an application class concentrate on component construction.

There are other cases where you can benefit from introducing a mediator object. For example, you might need a mediator to centralize responsibility for maintaining the relational integrity in an object model. You can apply MEDIATOR whenever you need to define an object that encapsulates how a set of objects interact.

CHAPTER 11

PROXY

An ordinary object does its own work in support of the public interface that it advertises. It can happen, though, that a legitimate object cannot live up to this ordinary responsibility. This may occur when an object takes a long time to load, when you need to intercept messages to the object, or when the object is running on another computer. In these cases, a proxy object can take the responsibility that a client expects and forward requests appropriately to an underlying target object. The intent of the PROXY pattern is to provide a surrogate or placeholder for another object to control access to it.

A Simple Proxy

A proxy object usually has an interface that is nearly identical to the interface of the object for which it is a proxy or substitute. The proxy does its work by judiciously forwarding requests to the underlying object that the proxy controls access to. A classic example of PROXY relates to avoiding the expense of loading large images into memory. Suppose that images in an application belong in pages or panels that do not initially display. To avoid loading all the images before they are needed, you might let proxies for the images act as placeholders that load the required visual images on demand. This section provides an example of an image proxy, but note: Designs that use PROXY are sometimes questionable because they rely on the forwarding of method calls to underlying objects. This forwarding may create a fragile, high-maintenance design.

Suppose that an Oozinoz engineer tells you he is working on an image proxy that will show a small, temporary image while a larger image is loading. He has a working prototype that appears in Figure 11.1. The code for this application is in the classes ShowProxy and PictureBoxProxy.

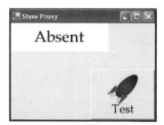

Figure 11.1   These screen shots show a mini-application before and after
               loading a large image.

The application in Figure 11.1 uses a PROXY design. When the application
runs, it initially does not load the large image of the crowd watching a
fireworks display. Instead, it shows a proxy image that shows the word
"Absent." When the user clicks the Test button, the proxy image loads the
real image, and the application resizes itself to show the new, large image.
The developer is using this demonstration program to show that he has
worked out the ideas of letting a proxy image stand in for a (large)
desired image until the application needs the second image.

In .NET, the control normally used for presenting an image is the PictureBox class. The developer has created a PictureBoxProxy class that lets
a proxy stand in for a .NET PictureBox object. The proxy intercepts
requests for the PictureBox object's image, showing a small initial image
until the larger image has loaded. Figure 11.2 shows the design for this
application.

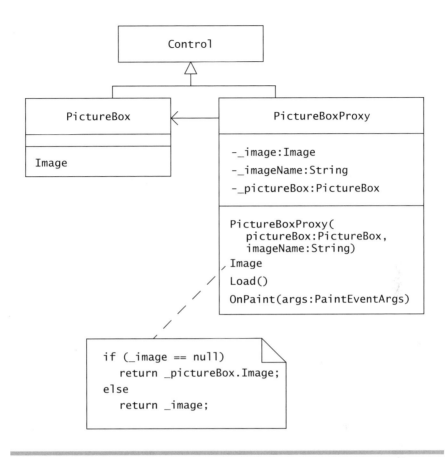

Figure 11.2   A `PictureBoxProxy` object forwards an `Image` property request to an underlying `PictureBox` object if the desired image has been loaded.

The `PictureBoxProxy` class constructor accepts a `PictureBox` object to proxy for and accepts a filename for a large image to load on demand. The class declaration and constructor code are as follows:

```
public class PictureBoxProxy : Control
{
    private PictureBox _pictureBox;
    private string _imageName;
    private Image _image;

    public PictureBoxProxy(
        PictureBox pictureBox, string imageName)
    {
        _pictureBox = pictureBox;
        _imageName = imageName;
    }
    //...
}
```

The constructor code accepts the "subject," the object for which this object is a proxy. The constructor code also accepts the file that contains an image to be loaded on demand.

The remainder of the `PictureBoxProxy` code provides an `Image` property that forwards requests to the underlying `PictureBox` object if the large image is not yet loaded. This code appears as follows:

```
public class PictureBoxProxy : Control
{
    //...
    public Image Image
    {
        get
        {
            if (_image == null)
                return _pictureBox.Image;
            else
                return _image;
        }
    }
    public void Load()
    {
        _image = UI.GetImage(_imageName);
    }
    protected override void OnPaint(PaintEventArgs pea)
    {
        Graphics g = pea.Graphics;
        g.DrawImage(Image, 0, 0);
    }
}
```

The `GetImage()` method of the `UI` class finds the file on disk and loads it as an image. The `OnPaint()` method always displays the proxy object's `Image` property, but that property's logic will forward the request to the `PictureBox` subject if the proxy's `Load()` method has been called.

The developer wants to extend this code to allow for a callback, so that a `PictureBoxProxy` object can alert an application when a large image completes loading. Before investing more time in this design, the developer is asking for your review of the design and code so far.

Challenge 11.1

The `PictureBoxProxy` class is *not* a well-designed, reusable component. Point out two problems with the design.

A solution appears on page 372.

As you review someone's design, you must concurrently form an understanding and opinion of the design. When you encounter a developer who feels he or she is using a specific design pattern, you may disagree about whether the pattern is present. In this example the PROXY pattern is evident, but this does not demonstrate that the design is good—in fact, much better designs exist. When the PROXY pattern appears in a design, its presence should be justified because the use of forwarding can create problems that other designs may avoid. As you read the next section, you should form an opinion about whether PROXY is a desirable choice.

A Data Proxy

Applying the PROXY pattern can create a maintenance burden, so when you use PROXY the context of the problem that you are solving should justify your design. One such context occurs when a subsystem that you do not control supplies you with an object over which you would like to have more control. For example, the .NET `SqlDataReader` and `OleDbDataReader` classes provide "data reader" objects that let you read data from a database table. These classes are sealed so you cannot subclass them. You might ask whether there is any way that you can control the behavior of a data reader object. Here, PROXY provides an answer.

Both the `SqlDataReader` and `OleDbDataReader` classes implement an `IDataReader` interface. You can create a new class that implements this interface. An instance of your class can selectively forward calls to an underlying instance of `SqlDataReader` or `OleDbDataReader`. You can use this technique to improve Oozinoz's `DataLayer` class library.

The `DataLayer` class library at Oozinoz supplies a data reader that programs can use to access the Oozinoz database. The current design "lends" data readers to a calling application, arranging to close the reader when an application's method finishes using the reader. This helps the data layer team ensure that resources are closed when not in use. Now suppose that the team wants further control over how applications use data readers. One way to achieve this control is to hand out a proxy reader rather than the reader itself. This leaves the door open for the data layer team to intercept and control messages, limiting the direct interaction between applications and the database.

Challenge 11.2

Suggest two possible uses where a data layer could benefit from a proxy data reader that intercepts and forwards calls to a .NET-supplied reader.

A solution appears on page 373.

Having decided to create a proxy for the database reader, the design team encounters an immediate obstacle. The `IDataReader` interface requires a large number of members from its implementers, as Figure 11.3 shows.

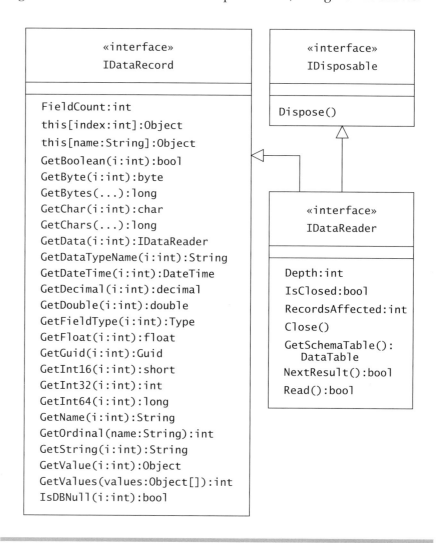

Figure 11.3   The `IDataReader` interface requires many properties, indexers, and methods from its implementers.

In the image loading example, the developer chose not to forward every method call to the `PictureBox` subject. However, in this example, the data layer team has a goal of supporting unforeseen uses of proxies. We don't know how proxy users will be using a proxy, so we have to forward every call. To help simplify the code, the team decides to create a pure proxy class that will forward every call to another data reader class. Subclasses of the proxy can then easily intercept any specific call by overriding that method.

We can create a `DataReaderProxy` class that implements the `IDataReader` interface and that requires another `IDataReader` object in its constructor. The `DataReaderProxy` class can implement every method that `IDataReader` specifies, with each method simply forwarding its call to this subject reader. Figure 11.4 shows the `DataReaderProxy` class.

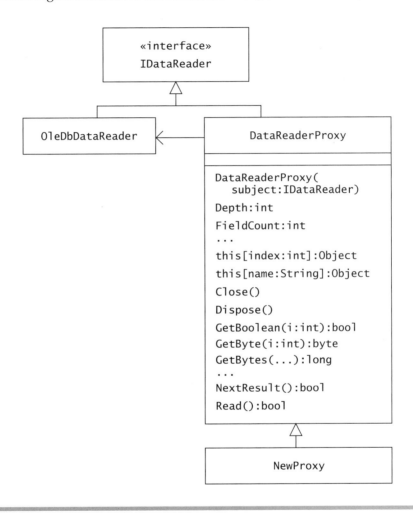

Figure 11.4   A `DataReaderProxy` object has the single job of forwarding its calls to another reader, such as an `OleDbDataReader` object.

The `DataReaderProxy` class is unusual in that its code is completely predictable from its design. You might consider using reflection to read all the members of `IDataRecord` (and the interfaces it inherits from), and to generate the code for `DataReaderProxy.cs` automatically. However, coding the class by hand takes only about an hour. Using a manual approach, the data layer team creates a class that looks like the following:

```
public class DataReaderProxy : IDataReader
{
    private IDataReader _subject;
    public DataReaderProxy(IDataReader subject)
    {
        _subject = subject;
    }
    public virtual int FieldCount
    {
        get
        {
            return _subject.FieldCount;
        }
    }
    public virtual object this [string name]
    {
        get
        {
            return _subject[name];
        }
    }
    public virtual bool GetBoolean(int i)
    {
        return _subject.GetBoolean(i);
    }
    //...
}
```

Every property, indexer, and method in the DataReaderProxy code forwards its request to the IDataReader object the constructor receives. New proxy classes can subclass DataReaderProxy to intercept a subset of these requests.

For example, suppose that you want to create a data reader proxy that blocks access to information about rocket apogees, either because this is trade secret information or because you don't want advertisements to rely on this volatile attribute. You can code a proxy that always returns 0 when asked about an apogee attribute as follows:

```
using System;
using System.Data;
using DataLayer;
public class LimitingReader : DataReaderProxy
{
    public LimitingReader(IDataReader subject) :
        base (subject)
    {
        // challenge!
    }
    public override object this [string name]
    {
        get
        {
            // challenge!
        }
    }
}
```

Challenge 11.3

Fill in the code for the constructor and indexer in `LimitingReader`.

A solution appears on page 373.

The following short program demonstrates a `LimitingReader` object in action:

```
using System;
using System.Data;
using DataLayer;
public class ShowProxyReader
{
    public static void Main()
    {
        string sel = "SELECT * FROM ROCKET";
        DataServices.LendReader(
            sel, new BorrowReader(GetNames));
    }
    private static Object GetNames(IDataReader reader)
    {
        LimitingReader proxy =
            new LimitingReader(reader);
        while (proxy.Read())
        {
            Console.Write("{0,10} ", proxy["Name"]);
            Console.Write("{0,7:C} ", proxy["price"]);
            Console.Write("{0,5}", proxy["apogee"]);
            Console.WriteLine();
        }
        return null;
    }
}
```

The `Main()` method borrows a data reader from the data layer by supplying a delegate that identifies `GetNames()` as the method that will use the reader. The data layer will close the reader after the `GetNames()` method completes. For demonstration purposes, the `GetNames()` method wraps a `LimitingReader` proxy around the supplied reader. The formatting strings in the calls to `WriteLine()` define how the output appears. For example, in "{0,7:C} ", the 0 specifies the first parameter, and 7:C specifies a width of seven characters and a currency format. You can read more about string formatting by searching msdn.microsoft.com for "Standard Numeric Format Strings".

Running the program prints out:

```
 1Shooter    $3.95      0
    Orbit   $29.95      0
   Biggie   $29.95      0
  Mach-it   $22.95      0
   Pocket    $2.95      0
   Sock-it   $9.95      0
  Sprocket   $3.95      0
 Heightful  $33.95      0
  Byebaby   $13.95      0
 Jsquirrel  $25.95      0
```

As the output shows, the code blocks access to the values of rocket apogees.

The PROXY pattern's reliance on forwarding usually creates a maintenance burden. For example, when the .NET readers change, the Oozinoz data layer team will have to update the data reader proxy. To avoid this burden, you should usually consider alternatives to PROXY, but there will be times when PROXY is the right choice. In particular, when the object for which you need to intercept messages is executing on another machine, there may be no substitute for PROXY.

Remote Proxies

When the object whose method you want to call is running on another computer, you must find a way to communicate with the remote object other than calling it directly. You could open a socket on the remote machine and devise some protocol to pass messages to the remote object. Ideally, such a scheme would let you pass messages in almost the same way as if the object were local. You should be able to call methods on a proxy object that forwards the calls to the real object on the remote machine. In fact, such schemes have been realized, notably in the Common Object Request Broker Architecture (CORBA), in Java's Remote Method Invocation (RMI), and in ASP.NET (Active Server Pages for .NET).

ASP.NET makes it about as easy as possible for a client to obtain a proxy object that forwards calls to a desired object that is active on another computer. To experiment with ASP.NET, you will need a good reference on this topic, such as *C# and the .NET Platform* [Troelsen 2001]. The following example is not a tutorial on ASP.NET, but is rather a rapid tour of using ASP.NET to create and use a Web service.

To explore the use of ASP.NET, suppose that you decide to create a server that will provide rocket information from the Oozinoz database, and a client that shows it can retrieve this information. During development, you will run both the server and client on your machine.

This example requires the following steps:

1. Get Internet Information Server (IIS) running on your machine.

2. Associate a disk directory with a Uniform Resource Locator (URL).

3. Create a small Web services file.

4. Test your new service.

5. Obtain a proxy for the Web service by directly querying the Web service.

6. Write and demonstrate a small client.

Figure 11.5 shows these steps laid out as server-side and client-side tasks.

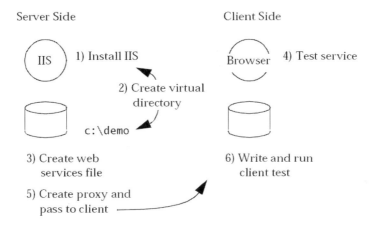

Figure 11.5   By following the steps in this figure, you can experiment with remote proxies in .NET.

Step 1: To get IIS running on your machine, you need the IIS software (it is likely that you have this software even if you haven't yet installed it). Run the Administrative Tools item from the Control Panel. If you don't see Internet Information Services as a tool, go back to the Control Panel, execute Add or Remove Programs, and choose Add/Remove Windows Components (which on some Windows operating systems is a button). A dialog will appear that indicates if IIS is available for installation. If you cannot run IIS on your system, you will not be able to execute the remaining steps, although reading these steps may give you a sense of how an ASP.NET application works.

Step 2: Create a c:\demo directory and a c:\demo\bin directory to store your server pages. (You can name the demo directory something else if you like.) Run Internet Information Services from Control Panel/Administrative Tools. Navigate to the Default Web Site node and add a "virtual directory" with the alias demo associated with c:\demo.

Step 3: If you haven't obtained the Oozinoz code, download it from www.oozinoz.com, unzip it, and create an oozinoz environment variable that points to the top level oozinoz directory (above the db, bin, and other directories). Copy the class libraries DataLayer.dll, Fireworks.dll, and Utilities.dll from the Oozinoz bin directory to c:\demo\bin. Finally, copy the DataWebService.asmx from the Oozinoz config directory into c:\demo. That file's contents are as follows:

```
<%@ WebService Language="c#" Class="DataWebService" %>
using System;
using System.Web.Services;
using DataLayer;
using Fireworks;

[WebService(Namespace="http://localhost/webservices/")]
public class DataWebService
{
    [WebMethod]
    public Rocket RocketHome(string name)
    {
        return (Rocket) DataServices.Find(
            typeof(Rocket), name);
    }
}
```

This file's asmx extension indicates that it contains "Active Server" methods for .NET. The file's contents begin with an ASP directive that specifies the page's language and the class that will provide a service. The remaining code is all C#. The WebService attribute provides a namespace for the service. The WebMethod attribute marks the RocketHome() method as a service that IIS should make available. You might think that RocketHome() should be a static method since it uses no instance variables. However, ASP.NET requires Web service methods to be non-static. Inside RocketHome(), the Find() method looks up a rocket in the Oozinoz database by using the rocket's name.

Step 4: You can test this service by entering http://localhost/demo/DataWebService.asmx in a Web browser. IIS will compile the asmx file on the fly so there is no intermediate build step. However, this test will not work if DataLayer.dll and FireWorks.dll are not in c:\demo\bin, and it will not work if IIS is not running. If you have trouble getting this demonstration running on your system, you may benefit from reviewing a more thorough tutorial on ASP. If this step does work, you will see a Web page like the one in Figure 11.6.

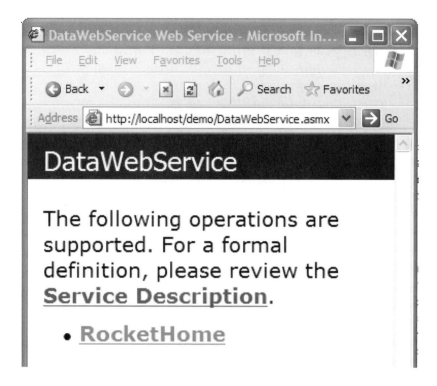

Figure 11.6   This figure shows that IIS is able to find and build the services file.

If you click on the RocketHome link, you can enter the name of a rocket, such as JSquirrel, and retrieve an XML serialization of the rocket. Your Web service is up and running.

Step 5: Once you have a Web service available, you can capture the interface of the service using a Web Services Description Language (WSDL) tool. The file wsdl.exe is part of the .NET Framework software development kit. To execute wsdl, first ensure that the directory in which it resides is part of your execution path—that you can type wsdl and get a response. Then enter the following command:

```
C:\demo>wsdl http://localhost/demo/DataWebService.asmx?wsdl
```

This command will create a DataWebService.cs file that contains a proxy that clients can use. In particular, this file contains a RocketHome() method that operates differently from the RocketHome() method in DataWebService.asmx. When called, the new RocketHome() method creates a corresponding text request following the Simple Object Access Protocol (SOAP), passes this message to the IIS server, decodes the response, and gives the result to the calling client.

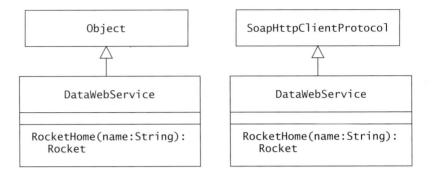

Figure 11.7   The wsdl tool creates a DataWebService proxy class that has
               the same public interface as the original but with internal
               operations that use SOAP to communicate with a server-side
               counterpart.

Step 6: Now you can create a client that uses the proxy. Create a directory
such as c:\democlient, copy DataWebService.cs into it, and create a new
file named ShowClient.cs in this directory with the following contents:

```
using System;
class ShowClient
{
    static void Main()
    {
        Rocket r =
            // challenge!
        Console.WriteLine(
            "Rocket {0}, Thrust: {1} Price: {2:C}",
            r.Name, r.Thrust, r.Price);
    }
}
```

Challenge 11.4

Replace the //challenge! line above with an expression that creates a
proxy for a rocket type named "JSquirrel".

A solution appears on page 374.

The ShowClient program looks up a rocket and displays some of the
rocket's attributes. You can build and execute this program as follows:

```
C:\democlient>dir /b
    DataWebService.cs
    ShowClient.cs

C:\democlient>csc ShowClient.cs DataWebService.cs
    ...

C:\democlient>dir /b
    DataWebService.cs
    ShowClient.cs
    ShowClient.exe

C:\democlient>ShowClient
    Rocket Jsquirrel, Thrust: 52 Price: $25.95

C:\democlient>
```

The instantiation of a rocket in the ShowClient program launches a chain of requests that wind from client to a Web service to a database. This may seem like a lot of work for a meager result, but the beauty is in the architecture. In particular, we can scale and tune the Web services machine to provide rocket information to many clients throughout the Oozinoz enterprise. Client, service, and database are now decoupled, letting us tailor each piece.

A central benefit of ASP.NET is that it lets client programs interact with a local object that is a proxy for a remote object. The interface for the proxy will match the interface of the remote object so client developers hardly need to be aware of the remote calls that take place. ASP.NET supplies the communication mechanics and isolates both server and client from the knowledge that two implementations of DataWebService are collaborating to provide nearly seamless interprocess communication.

Summary

Implementations of the PROXY pattern establish a placeholder object that manages access to a target object. A proxy object can isolate clients from shifts in the state of a desired object, as when loading an image endures a discernible duration. The problem with PROXY is that by its nature, it relies on a tight coupling between the placeholder and the proxied object. Occasionally in practice, you may benefit from the use of PROXY, but alternative designs often offer more stable solutions.

Nowhere is PROXY more justified than in remote computing. Here, the pattern represents the ideal form of inter-computer communication: Rather than relying on some other protocol, distributed computing schemes such as ASP.NET establish communication with remote objects as normal-looking method calls. This lets a client communicate with a remote object through a proxy as if the remote object were local. The role of PROXY in distributed computing appears to be a permanent advance in OO computing.

CHAPTER 12

CHAIN OF RESPONSIBILITY

Object-oriented developers strive to keep objects loosely coupled, keeping the responsibility between objects specific and minimal. This lets you introduce change more easily and with less risk of introducing defects. Decoupling occurs naturally in C#, to a degree. Clients see only an object's visible interface and remain isolated from the details of the object's implementation. This arrangement, however, leaves in place the fundamental coupling that the client knows which object has the method the client needs to call.

You can loosen the restriction that a client must know which object to use when you can arrange a group objects in a kind of hierarchy that allows each object to either perform an operation or to pass the request along to another object. The intent of the CHAIN OF RESPONSIBILITY pattern is to avoid coupling the sender of a request to its receiver by giving more than one object a chance to handle the request.

An Ordinary CHAIN OF RESPONSIBILITY

The CHAIN OF RESPONSIBILITY pattern often emerges in real life when a person who is responsible for a task either does it personally or delegates it to someone else. Such a situation occurs at Oozinoz where engineers are responsible for maintaining the fireworks manufacturing machines.

As described in Chapter 3, "Composite," Oozinoz models machines, lines, bays, and factories all as "machine components." This approach allows simple, recursive implementations of operations, such as shutting down all the machines in a bay. It also simplifies the modeling of engineering responsibility in the factory. At Oozinoz, there is always an engineer who is responsible for any particular machine component, although this responsibility may be assigned at different levels. For example, a complex machine such as a star press may have an engineer directly assigned to it. A simpler machine may not have a directly assigned engineer, in which case, the engineer responsible for the line or bay that the machine occupies will take responsibility for the machine.

We would like to avoid forcing client objects to interrogate several objects when seeking the responsible engineer. We can apply CHAIN OF RESPONSI-BILITY here, giving every machine component a `Responsible` property. Figure 12.1 shows this design.

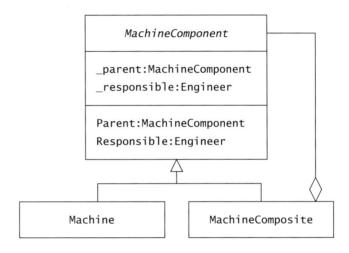

Figure 12.1   Every `Machine` or `MachineComposite` object has `Parent` and `Responsible` properties, inherited from the `MachineComponent` class.

The design reflected in Figure 12.1 allows but does not require each machine component to keep track of its responsible engineer. If a machine does not have a directly assigned engineer, the machine can pass a request asking for its responsible engineer to its "parent." In practice, a machine's parent is a line, a line's parent is a bay, and a bay's parent is a factory. Somewhere in this chain, there is always, at Oozinoz, a responsible engineer.

The advantage of this design is that clients of machine components don't have to determine how engineers are assigned. A client can ask any machine component for its responsible engineer. Machine components isolate their clients from knowledge of how responsibilities are assigned. On the other hand, this design has some possible disadvantages.

Challenge 12.1

Point out two weaknesses of the design shown in Figure 12.1.

A solution appears on page 374.

The CHAIN OF RESPONSIBILITY pattern helps to simplify client code when it's not obvious which object in a group should handle a request. If you do not have CHAIN OF RESPONSIBILITY in place, you may come across areas where it will help you migrate your code to a simpler design.

Refactoring to CHAIN OF RESPONSIBILITY

If you find client code that makes probing calls before issuing the request it really wants to make, you may be able to improve the design through refactoring. To apply CHAIN OF RESPONSIBILITY, determine the operation that objects in a group or class will sometimes be able to support. For example, machine components at Oozinoz can sometimes provide a reference to a responsible engineer. Add the desirable operation to each class in the group, but implement it with a chaining strategy for cases where a specific object needs help in satisfying the request.

Consider the Oozinoz codebase's modeling of tools and tool carts. Tools are not part of the MachineComponent hierarchy, but are similar to machines in some ways. In particular, tools are always assigned to tool carts, and tool carts have a responsible engineer. Suppose that a visualization shows all the tools and machines in a given bay, and has popup help that displays the responsible engineer for any chosen item. Figure 12.2 shows the classes involved in finding the engineers responsible for selected equipment.

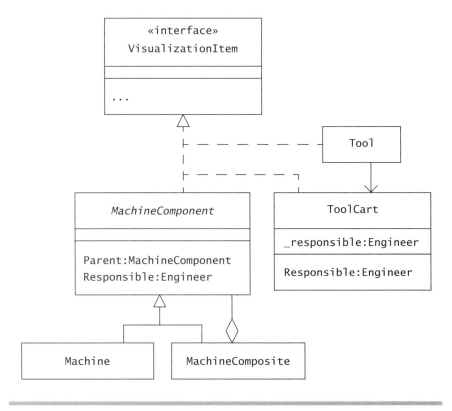

Figure 12.2   Items in a simulation include machines, machine composites,
tools, and tool carts.

The VisualizationItem interface specifies a few behaviors that classes
need to participate in the visualization, but does not have a Responsible
property. In fact, not all items in the visualization have direct knowledge
of which engineer is responsible for them. When the visualization needs
to determine which engineer is responsible for an item, the answer
depends on which kind of item is selected. Machines, machine groups,
and tools have a Responsible property, but tools do not. To see who is
responsible for a tool, the code has to see which cart the tool belongs with
and then determine who is responsible for the cart. To find the responsible engineer for a simulated item, an application's menu code uses a
series of if statements and is operators. These traits are signs that refactoring can improve the code, which is as follows:

```
using System;
namespace Machines
{
    public class AmbitiousMenu
    {
        public Engineer GetResponsible(
            VisualizationItem item)
        {
```

```
        if (item is Tool)
        {
            Tool t = (Tool) item;
            return t.ToolCart.Responsible;
        }
        if (item is ToolCart)
        {
            ToolCart tc = (ToolCart) item;
            return tc.Responsible;
        }
        if (item is MachineComponent)
        {
            MachineComponent c =
                (MachineComponent) item;
            if (c.Responsible != null)
            {
                return c.Responsible;
            }
            if (c.Parent != null)
            {
                return c.Parent.Responsible;
            }
        }
        return null;
    }
  }
}
```

The intent of the CHAIN OF RESPONSIBILITY pattern is to relieve callers from knowing which object can handle a request. In this example, the caller is a menu and the request is to find a responsible engineer. In the current design, the caller has to know which items have a Responsible property. You can clean up this code by applying CHAIN OF RESPONSIBILITY, giving all simulated items a Responsible property. This moves the requirement for knowing which objects know their engineer into the simulated items and away from the menu.

Challenge 12.2

Redraw the diagram in Figure 12.2, moving the Responsible property to VisualizationItem and adding this behavior to Tool.

A solution appears on page 375.

The menu code becomes simpler once it can ask any selectable item for its responsible engineer, as follows:

```
using System;
namespace Machines
{
    public class AmbitiousMenu2
    {
        public Engineer GetResponsible(
            VisualizationItem item)
        {
            return item.Responsible;
        }
    }
}
```

The implementation of the `Responsible` property for each item is simple, too.

Challenge 12.3

Write the code for the `Responsible` property for:

A) `MachineComponent`

B) `Tool`

C) `ToolCart`

Sample solutions appear on page 376.

Anchoring a Chain

When you write the `Responsible` property for `MachineComponent`, you have to consider that a `MachineComponent` object's parent might be `null`. Alternatively, you can tighten up your object model, insisting that `MachineComponent` objects have a parent that is not `null`. To achieve this, you can add a parent argument to the constructor for `MachineComponent`. (You may even want to throw an exception when the supplied object is `null`, so long as you know where this exception will be caught.) Also, consider that some object will be the *root*, a distinguished object that has no parent. A reasonable approach is to create a `MachineRoot` class as a subclass of `MachineComposite` (not `MachineComponent`). Then you can guarantee that a `MachineComponent` object always has a responsible engineer if:

1. The constructor(s) for MachineRoot require an Engineer object.

2. The constructor(s) for MachineComponent require a non-null parent object that is itself a MachineComponent.

Challenge 12.4

Fill in the constructors in Figure 12.3 to support a design that ensures that every MachineComponent object has a responsible engineer.

A solution appears on page 377.

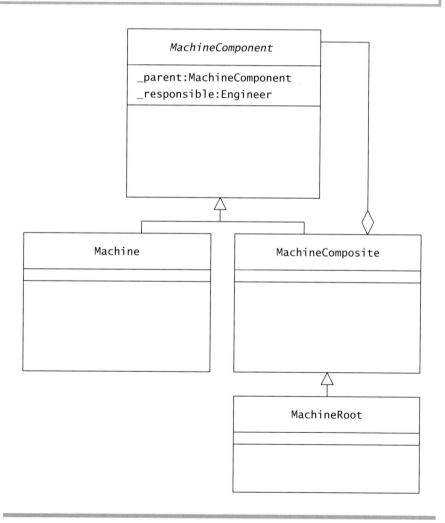

Figure 12.3   How can constructors ensure that every MachineComponent object has a responsible engineer?

By anchoring a chain of responsibility, you strengthen the object model and simplify the code. Now you can implement the `getResponsible()` method of `MachineComponent` as:

```
public Engineer getResponsible()
{
    if (responsible != null)
    {
        return responsible;
    }
    return parent.getResponsible();
}
```

CHAIN OF RESPONSIBILITY without Composite

CHAIN OF RESPONSIBILITY requires a strategy for ordering a search for an object that can handle a request. Usually the order to follow will depend on an underlying aspect in the modeled domain. This frequently occurs when there is some kind of composition, as in the Oozinoz machine hierarchy. However, this pattern can apply outside of object models that are composites.

Challenge 12.5

Cite an example where the CHAIN OF RESPONSIBILITY pattern might occur where chained objects do not form a composite.

A solution appears on page 378.

Summary

When you apply the CHAIN OF RESPONSIBILITY pattern, you relieve a client from having to know which object in a collection supports a given behavior. By setting up the search for responsibility to occur across objects, you decouple the client from any specific object in the chain.

The CHAIN OF RESPONSIBILITY pattern occurs occasionally when an arbitrary chain of objects can apply a series of different strategies to tackling some problem such as parsing a user's input. More frequently, this pattern occurs in aggregations, where a containment hierarchy provides a natural ordering for a chain of objects. CHAIN OF RESPONSIBILITY leads to simpler code in both the hierarchy and the client.

CHAPTER 13

FLYWEIGHT

The FLYWEIGHT pattern provides for sharing an object between clients, creating a responsibility for the shared object that normal objects need not consider. An ordinary object doesn't have to worry much about shared responsibility. Most often, only one client will hold a reference to an object at any one time. When the object's state changes, it's because the client changed it, and the object does not have any responsibility to inform any other clients. Sometimes, though, you will want to arrange for multiple clients to share access to an object.

One incentive for sharing an object among multiple clients occurs when you must manage thousands or tens of thousands of small objects, such as the characters in an online version of a book. In such a case, you may have a performance incentive to share these fine-grained objects among many clients. A book needs only one A object, although it needs some way to model when different As appear.

In any application that has a large number of small objects, you may need to provide a way for clients to safely share the common elements of these objects. The intent of the FLYWEIGHT pattern is to use sharing to support large numbers of fine-grained objects efficiently.

Immutability

The FLYWEIGHT pattern lets multiple clients share access to a limited number of objects—the flyweights. For this to work, you have to consider that when a client changes the state of an object, the state changes for every client that has access to the object. When multiple clients share access to an object, the easiest and most common way to keep clients from affecting each other is to restrict clients from introducing any state changes in the shared object. You can achieve this by making an object *immutable* (that is, unchangeable) so that once created, the object cannot change. The most common immutable objects in C# are instances of the String class. Once you create a string, neither you nor any client with access to the string can change its characters.

Challenge 13.1

Provide a justification of why the creators of C# made `String` objects immutable, or argue that this was an unwise restriction.

A solution appears on page 378.

When you have large numbers of similar objects, you may want to arrange for shared access to these objects, but they may not be immutable. In this case, a preliminary step in applying the FLYWEIGHT pattern is to extract the immutable part of an object so that this part can be shared.

Extracting the Immutable Part of a Flyweight

Around Oozinoz, chemicals are as prevalent as characters in a document. The purchasing, engineering, manufacturing, and safety departments are all concerned with directing the flow of thousands of chemicals through the factory. Batches of chemicals are often modeled with instances of the `Substance` class, shown in Figure 13.1.

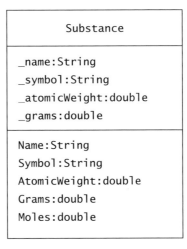

Figure 13.1   A `Substance` object models a physical batch of chemical material.

The Substance class has get- properties for its attributes and also has a Moles property that returns the number of *moles*—a count of molecules—in the substance. A Substance object represents a quantity of a particular molecule. Oozinoz uses a Mixture class to model combinations of substances. For example, Figure 13.2 shows an object diagram of a batch of black powder.

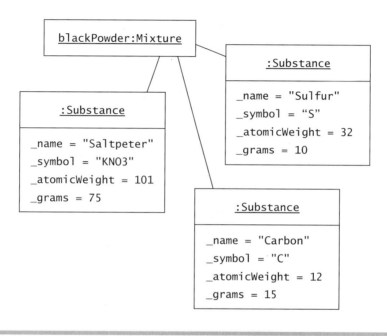

Figure 13.2   A batch of black powder contains saltpeter, sulfur, and carbon.

Suppose that, given the proliferation of chemicals at Oozinoz, you decide to apply FLYWEIGHT to reduce the number of Substance objects in Oozinoz applications. To treat Substance objects as flyweights, a first step is to separate its mutable and immutable parts. Suppose that you decide to refactor the Substance class, extracting its immutable part into a Chemical class.

Challenge 13.2

Complete the class diagram in Figure 13.3 to show a refactored Substance2 class and a new, immutable Chemical class.

A solution appears on page 379.

Substance2
??
. . .
??
. . .

Chemical
??
. . .
??
. . .

Figure 13.3   Complete this diagram to extract the immutable aspects of Substance2 into the Chemical class.

Sharing Flyweights

Extracting the immutable part of an object is half the battle in applying the FLYWEIGHT pattern. The remaining work includes creating a flyweight factory that instantiates flyweights and that arranges for clients to share them. You also have to ensure that clients will use your factory instead of constructing instances of the flyweight class themselves.

To make chemicals flyweights, you need some kind of factory, perhaps a ChemicalFactory class, with a static method that returns a chemical given its name. You might store chemicals in a hash table, creating known chemicals as part of the factory's initialization. Figure 13.4 shows a design for a ChemicalFactory.

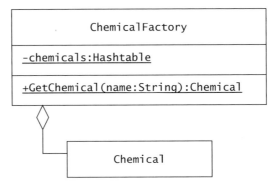

Figure 13.4   The ChemicalFactory class is a flyweight factory that returns Chemical objects.

The code for `ChemicalFactory` can use a static constructor to store `Chemical` objects in a hash map.

```
using System;
using System.Collections;
namespace Chemicals
{
    public class ChemicalFactory
    {
        private static Hashtable _chemicals =
            new Hashtable();
        static ChemicalFactory ()
        {
            _chemicals["carbon"] =
                new Chemical("Carbon", "C", 12);
            _chemicals["sulfur"] =
                new Chemical("Sulfur", "S", 32);
            _chemicals["saltpeter"] =
                new Chemical("Saltpeter", "KNO3", 101);
            //...
        }
        public static Chemical GetChemical(String name)
        {
            return (Chemical) _chemicals[name.ToLower()];
        }
    }
}
```

Having created a factory for chemicals, you now have to take steps to ensure that other developers use this factory instead of instantiating the `Chemical` class themselves. A simple approach is to rely on the accessibility of the `Chemical` class.

Challenge 13.3

How can you use the accessibility of the `Chemical` class to discourage other developers from instantiating `Chemical` objects?

A solution appears on page 380.

Access modifiers do not supply the complete control over instantiation that you might want. You might like to ensure that `ChemicalFactory` is absolutely the only class that can create new `Chemical` instances. To achieve this level of control, you can apply a *nested* class, defining the `Chemical` class within `ChemicalFactory`.

To access a nested type, clients must specify the enclosing type with expressions such as the following:

```
ChemicalFactory.Chemical c =
    ChemicalFactory.GetChemical("saltpeter");
```

You can simplify the use of a nested class by introducing an IChemical interface and making the name of the class ChemicalImpl. The IChemical interface can specify three readable properties as follows:

```
public interface IChemical
{
    string Name { get; }
    string Symbol { get; }
    double AtomicWeight { get; }
}
```

Clients will never reference the inner class directly, so you can make it private, ensuring that only ChemicalFactory2 has access to it.

```
using System;
using System.Collections;
namespace Chemicals
{
    public class ChemicalFactory2
    {
        private static Hashtable _chemicals =
            new Hashtable();
        /* challenge! */ : IChemical
        {
            private String _name;
            private String _symbol;
            private double _atomicWeight;

            internal ChemicalImpl (
                String name,
                String symbol,
                double atomicWeight)
            {
                _name = name;
                _symbol = symbol;
                _atomicWeight = atomicWeight;
            }
            public string Name
            {
                get { return _name; }
            }
            public string Symbol
            {
                get { return _symbol; }
            }
            public double AtomicWeight
            {
                get { return _atomicWeight; }
            }
        }
        /* challenge! */ ChemicalFactory2 ()
        {
            _chemicals["carbon"] =
                new ChemicalImpl("Carbon", "C", 12);
            _chemicals["sulfur"] =
                new ChemicalImpl("Sulfur", "S", 32);
            _chemicals["saltpeter"] =
```

```
                new ChemicalImpl("Saltpeter", "KNO3", 101);
                //...
        }
        public static IChemical GetChemical(String name)
        {
            return /* challenge! */;
        }
    }
}
```

Challenge 13.4

Complete the code for the ChemicalFactory.cs.

A solution appears on page 380.

Summary

The FLYWEIGHT pattern lets you share access to objects such as characters, chemicals, and borders, which may appear in large quantities. The flyweight objects must be immutable, a feature that you can establish by extracting the immutable part of the class you want to share. To ensure that your flyweight objects are shared, you can provide a factory where clients can find flyweights, and you have to enforce the use of this factory. Access modifiers give you some control over how other developers access your code, but nested classes take this control further, letting you guarantee that a class is accessible by only its containing class. By ensuring that clients use your flyweight factory properly, you can provide safe, shared access to what would otherwise be a multitude of fine-grained objects.

PART 3

CONSTRUCTION PATTERNS

CHAPTER 14

INTRODUCING CONSTRUCTION

When you create a C# class, you normally provide for the creation of objects of your class by supplying class constructors. Constructors are useful, though, only if clients know which class to construct and have values for the parameters that a constructor requires. Several design patterns address cases where these conditions or other circumstances of ordinary construction do not hold. Before examining designs for cases where ordinary construction is insufficient, it is useful to review ordinary construction in C#.

A Few Construction Challenges

C# constructors are special methods. In many respects, including access modifiers, overloading, and the syntax of parameter lists, constructors are like ordinary methods. On the other hand, there are a significant number of syntactic and semantic rules that govern the use and behavior of constructors.

Challenge 14.1

List four rules that govern the use and behavior of constructors in C#.

A solution appears on page 381.

C# supplies default constructors and default constructor behavior in some cases. First, if a class has no declared constructor, C# will supply a default. This default constructor is equivalent to a constructor with no arguments and with no statements in its body.

A second default in C# constructors is that if a constructor declaration does not use a variation of :this() or :base() to explicitly invoke another constructor, C# effectively inserts :base() with no arguments. This may cause surprising results, as in the results of compiling following code:

```
using System;
public class Fuse
{
//      private string _name;
//      public Fuse(string name) { this._name = name; }
}
public class QuickFuse : Fuse
{
}
```

This code compiles with no problem until you remove the // comment marks.

Challenge 14.2

Explain the error that will occur if you uncomment the lines that allow the Fuse superclass to accept a fuse name in its constructor.

A solution appears on page 382.

Another subtlety that arises in C# construction comes from the differences between classes and structs. A struct is a value type so, for example, when you create an array of Point structs, you automatically allocate all the space you need to hold the points' data. If Point were a class instead of a struct, you would have to fill each slot in such an array with a new Point object. Using structs can improve efficiency, so certain common elements such as Point and DateTime are structs in C# and .NET. However, you cannot tell just by looking at code whether a type such as Point is a struct or a class. Note in the following code that there is no immediate way to tell which types are structs and which are classes:

```
using System;
using System.Drawing;

public class ShowStructs
{
    static void Main(string[] args)
    {
        Point[] points = new Point[1];
        DateTime[] times = new DateTime[1];
        String[] strings = new String[1];

        Console.WriteLine (points[0].ToString());
        Console.WriteLine (times[0].ToString());
        Console.WriteLine (strings[0].Length);
    }
}
```

This program compiles without problem, but a problem occurs when you execute it.

Challenge 14.3

Knowing that `Point` and `DateTime` are structs and that `String` is a class, explain what happens when you run the `ShowStructs` program.

A solution appears on page 382.

The most common way to instantiate structs and objects is by invoking the `new` operator, but you can also use *reflection*. Reflection provides the ability to work with types and type members as objects. Even if you do not use reflection frequently, you may be able to follow the logic of a working program that relies on reflection, such as the following:

```
using System;
using System.Reflection;
using Fireworks;
public class ShowReflection
{
    public static void Main()
    {
        Type t = typeof(Firework);
        ConstructorInfo c = t.GetConstructor(
            new Type[]{
                typeof(String),
                typeof(Double),
                typeof(Decimal)});
        Console.WriteLine(
            c.Invoke(new Object[]{"Titan", 6500, 31.95M}));
    }
}
```

Challenge 14.4

What does the `ShowReflection` program print out?

A solution appears on page 383.

Reflection lets you achieve results that are otherwise difficult or impossible. For example, the Oozinoz `DataServices` class uses reflection to match a class's properties with a database table's columns. To learn more about using reflection, I recommend reading *C# and the .NET Platform* [Troelson 2001].

Summary

Ordinarily, you will furnish classes and structs that you develop with constructors to provide a means for instantiation. These constructors may form a collaborating suite, and every constructor in classes that you write must ultimately also invoke a superclass constructor. The ordinary way to invoke a constructor is with the new operator, but you can also use reflection to instantiate and use objects.

Beyond Ordinary Construction

C#'s constructor features provide many alternatives when you design a new class. However, constructors are only effective if the user of your class knows which class to instantiate, and knows the required fields for instantiating an object. For example, the choice of which user interface component to compose may depend on whether the program is running on a handheld device or on a larger display. It can also happen that a developer knows which class to instantiate, but does not have all the necessary initial values, or has them in the wrong format. For example, the developer may need to create an object from a dormant or textual version of an object. In such circumstances, you need to go beyond the use of ordinary C# constructors and apply a design pattern.

The following principles describe the intent of patterns that facilitate construction:

If you intend to:	Then apply the pattern:
• Gather the information for an object gradually before requesting its construction,	BUILDER
• Defer the decision of which class to instantiate,	FACTORY METHOD
• Construct a family of objects that share some trait,	ABSTRACT FACTORY
• Specify an object to create by giving an example,	PROTOTYPE
• Reconstruct an object from a dormant version that contains just the object's internal state,	MEMENTO

The intent of each design pattern is to solve a problem in a context. Construction-oriented patterns are designs that let a client construct a new object through a means other than calling a class constructor. For example, when you find the initial values for an object gradually, you may want to follow the BUILDER pattern.

CHAPTER 15

BUILDER

The BUILDER pattern moves the construction logic for an object outside the class to instantiate. There are several reasons why you might make this move. You might simply want to reduce the size of a class that has many methods. You might also want to allow step-by-step construction of a target object. This occurs when you acquire the parameters for a constructor gradually, as happens with parsers and may happen with a user interface.

An Ordinary Builder

A common situation where you can benefit from BUILDER occurs when data that defines a desired object is embedded in a text string. As your code looks through (that is, *parses*) the data, you need to store the data as you find it. Whether your parser is XML-based or hand-crafted, you may not initially have enough data to construct a legitimate target object. The solution that BUILDER provides is to store the data in an intermediate object until the program is ready to ask the storage object to construct (that is, *build*) the target object from the data extracted from text.

Suppose that in addition to manufacturing fireworks, Oozinoz occasionally puts on fireworks displays. Travel agencies email Oozinoz reservation requests that look like:

```
Date, November 5, Headcount, 250, City, Springfield,
DollarsPerHead, 9.95, HasSite, False
```

As you might guess, this protocol originated in the days before XML, but it has thus far proved sufficient. The request tells when a potential customer wants to put on a display, and in what city. The request also specifies the minimum headcount that the customer will guarantee, and the amount of money per guest that the customer will pay. The customer in this example wants to put on a show for 250 guests, and is willing to pay $9.95 per guest, or a total of $2487.50 for Oozinoz's services. The travel agent has also indicated that the customer does not have a site in mind for the display.

The task at hand is to parse the textual request and create a `Reservation` object that represents it. We might approach this task by creating an empty `Reservation` object and setting its parameters as our parser encounters them. This causes the problem that a given `Reservation` object may or may not represent a valid request. For example, we might finish reading the text of a request and then realize that it is missing a date.

To ensure that `Reservation` objects are always valid requests, we can use a `ReservationBuilder` class. The `ReservationBuilder` object can store a reservation request's attributes as a parser finds them, and then build a `Reservation` object, verifying its validity. Figure 15.1 shows the classes we need for this design.

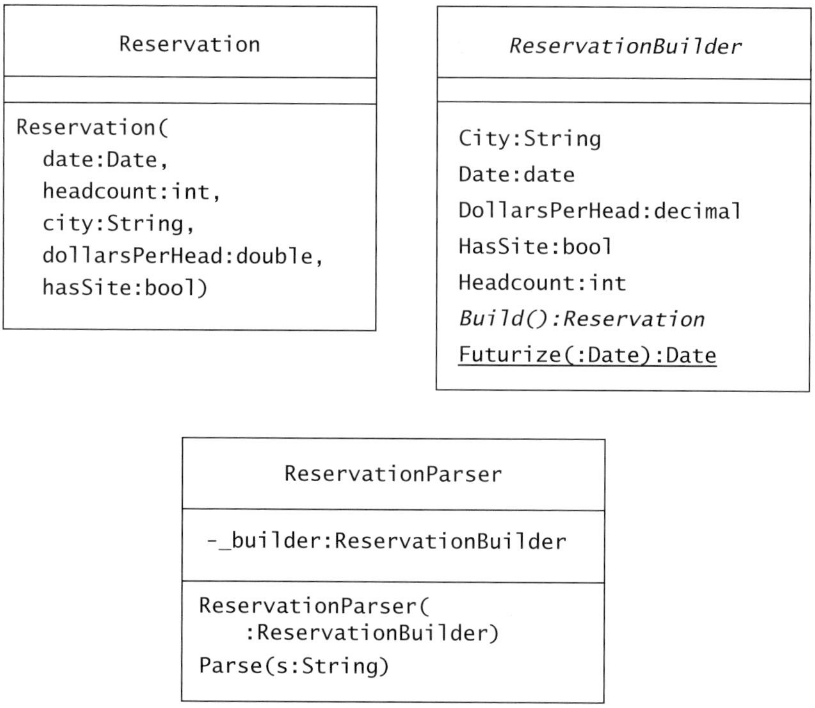

Figure 15.1   A builder class offloads construction logic from a domain class and can accept initialization parameters gradually, as a parser discovers them.

The `ReservationBuilder` class is abstract, as is its `Build()` method. We will create concrete subclasses of `ReservationBuilder` that vary in how aggressively they try to create a `Reservation` object given incomplete data. The `ReservationParser` class constructor accepts a builder to pass information to. The `Parse()` method pulls information out of a reservation string and passes it to a builder as follows:

```
public void Parse(String s)
{
    string[] tokens = new Regex(", ").Split(s);
    for (int i = 0; i < tokens.Length; i += 2 )
    {
        String type = tokens[i];
        String val = tokens[i + 1];

        if (String.Compare("date", type, true) == 0)
        {
            DateTime d = DateTime.Parse(val);
            _builder.Date = ReservationBuilder.Futurize(d);
        }
        else if
            (String.Compare("headcount", type, true) == 0)
        {
            _builder.Headcount = Int32.Parse(val);
        }
        else if (String.Compare("City", type, true) == 0)
        //...
    }
}
```

The `Parse()` code uses a `Regex` object to split up, or *tokenize*, the input string. The code expects a reservation to be a comma-separated list of information types and values. The `String.Compare()` method accepts a Boolean that indicates the comparison should disregard case. When the parser finds the word "date," it parses the following value and moves the date into the future. The `Futurize()` method moves a date's year forward until the date lies in the future. This ensures, for example, that a date of "November 5" will parse to the next November 5th. As you review the code, you may begin to notice several areas where the parser can go astray, beginning with the initial tokenization of the reservation string.

Challenge 15.1

The `Regex` object created by `new Regex(", ")` accepts a `Split(s)` call and divides a comma-separated list into individual strings. Suggest an improvement to this regular expression (or to the entire approach) that will make the parser better at recognizing a reservation's information.

A solution appears on page 383.

Building under Constraints

You want to ensure that invalid `Reservation` objects are never instantiated. Specifically, suppose that every reservation must have a non-null date and city. Suppose too that there is a business rule that says Oozinoz will not perform for less than 25 people, or for less than $495.95. We might want to record these limits in a database, but for now, we will record them as constants in the C# code as follows:

```
public abstract class ReservationBuilder
{
    public static readonly int MINHEAD = 25;
    public static readonly decimal MINTOTAL = 495.95M;
    //...
}
```

To avoid creating an instance of `Reservation` when a request is invalid, you might place business logic checks and exception throwing in the constructor for `Reservation`. But this logic is fairly independent of the normal function of a `Reservation` object once it is created. Introducing a builder will make the `Reservation` class simpler, leaving it with methods that concentrate on behavior other than construction. Using a builder also creates an opportunity to validate the parameters of a `Reservation` object with different reactions to invalid parameters. Finally, moving the construction job to a `ReservationBuilder` subclass lets construction occur gradually as the parser finds a reservation's attributes. Figure 15.2 shows concrete subclasses of `ReservationBuilder` that differ in how forgiving they are regarding invalid parameters.

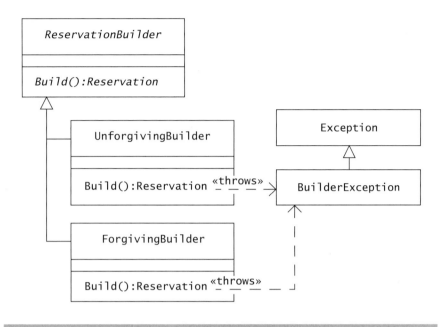

Figure 15.2   Builders may differ in how likely they are to throw an exception given an incomplete reservation string.

The diagram in Figure 15.2 brings out an advantage of applying the BUILDER pattern: By separating the construction logic from the Reservation class itself, we can treat construction as an entirely separate task and can even create a separate hierarchy of approaches for building. Differences in builder behavior may have little to do with reservation logic. For example, the builders in Figure 15.2 differ in how likely they are to throw a BuilderException. Code that uses a builder will look something like:

```
using System;
using Reservations;
public class ShowUnforgiving
{
    public static void Main()
    {
        String sample =
            "Date, November 5, Headcount, 250, "
            + "City, Springfield, DollarsPerHead, 9.95, "
            + "HasSite, False";
        ReservationBuilder b = new UnforgivingBuilder();
        new ReservationParser(b).Parse(sample);
        try
        {
            Reservation r = b.Build();
```

```
                    Console.WriteLine(r);
                }
                catch (BuilderException e)
                {
                    Console.WriteLine(e.Message);
                }
            }
        }
```

Running this program prints out a `Reservation` object.

```
    Date: Nov 5, 2001, Headcount: 250, City: Springfield,
    Dollars/Head: 9.95, Has Site: false
```

Given a reservation request string, the code instantiates a builder and a parser, and asks the parser to parse the string. As the parser reads the string, it passes the reservation attributes to the builder, using the builder's set methods.

After parsing, the code asks the builder to build a valid reservation. This example just prints out an exception's message text rather than taking a more significant action as you would in a real application.

Challenge 15.2

The `Build()` method of the `UnforgivingBuilder` class throws a `BuilderException` if the date or city is null, if the headcount is too low, or if the total cost of the proposed reservation is too low. Write the code for the `Build()` method according to these specifications.

A solution appears on page 384.

A Forgiving Builder

The `UnforgivingBuilder` class rejects requests that are anything less than fully formed. A better business decision might be to make reasonable changes to requests that are missing certain details about the reservation.

Suppose that an Oozinoz analyst asks you to set the headcount for an event to the minimum if this attribute is missing. Similarly, if the dollars/head value is missing, the builder should set it to be high enough so that the total take is above the minimum. These requirements are simple enough, but the design requires some skill. For example, what should the builder do if a reservation string supplies a dollars/head value but does not supply a headcount value?

Challenge 15.3

Write a design for `ForgivingBuilder.Build()`, focusing on how the builder can handle missing values for headcount or dollars/head.

A solution appears on page 385.

Challenge 15.4

After reviewing your design, write the code for the `ForgivingBuilder` class's `Build()` method.

A solution appears on page 385.

The classes `ForgivingBuilder` and `UnforgivingBuilder` let you guarantee that `Reservation` objects are always valid. Your design also gives you flexibility around what action to take when there is a problem in constructing a reservation.

Summary

The BUILDER pattern separates the construction of a complex object from its representation. This has the immediate effect of making a complex target class simpler. It lets a builder class focus on the proper construction of an object, leaving the target class to focus on the operation of a valid instance. This is especially useful when you want to ensure the validity of an object before instantiating it, and don't want the associated logic to appear in the target class's constructors. A builder also accommodates step-by-step construction, which often occurs when you create an object by parsing text.

CHAPTER 16

FACTORY METHOD

When you develop a class, you usually provide class constructors to let clients of your class instantiate it. There are times, though, when a client that needs an object does not or should not know which of several possible classes to instantiate. The FACTORY METHOD pattern lets a class developer define the interface for creating an object while retaining control of which class to instantiate.

A Classic Example—Enumerators

Enumerators in the .NET FCL provide a good example of FACTORY METHOD. The overall design for supporting enumeration is the subject of the ITERATOR pattern (see Chapter 28, "Iterator"). But, GetEnumerator() methods themselves are good examples of the FACTORY METHOD pattern. These methods isolate the caller from knowing which class to instantiate. Consider the following program that loops over a short list:

```
using System;
using Machines;
using System.Collections;
class ShowEnumeration
{
    static void Main()
    {
        Machine[] machines =
            {new Machine(1), new Machine(2)};
        IEnumerator e = machines.GetEnumerator();
        while (e.MoveNext())
        {
            Machine m = (Machine) e.Current;
            Console.WriteLine(m.ID);
        }
    }
}
```

The logic for iterating over an array is almost the same as for iterating over any other type of collection. In fact, we might want to require all collection classes to supply a `GetEnumerator()` method so that we could standardize this logic. There is no such mandate in .NET, but C# links its `foreach` statement to the `GetEnumerator()` method. You can use any class that implements `GetEnumerator()` in a foreach statement. The foreach statement simply provides syntactic convenience. For example, the following program is shorter in syntax but identical in effect to the previous program:

```
using System;
using Machines;
class ShowEnumeration2
{
    static void Main()
    {
        Machine[] machines =
            {new Machine(1), new Machine(2)};
        foreach (Machine m in machines)
        {
            Console.WriteLine(m.ID);
        }
    }
}
```

The convenience of the `foreach` statement springs partly from the power of the FACTORY METHOD pattern. As a client, the `foreach` statement has no way of knowing which type of enumerator is appropriate for enumerating a collection. Collections, on the other hand, can easily specify (and instantiate) an appropriate enumerator. Each collection class's `GetEnumerator()` method creates an enumerator that is appropriate for the collection, isolating clients from the knowledge of which class to instantiate.

You can use C#'s `foreach` statement with your own collection classes so long as you follow the rules that isolate the statement from knowing which class to instantiate when iterating over an instance of your collection. Suppose that you prototype a Set class as follows:

```
using System;
using System.Collections;
namespace Utilities
{
    public class Set
    {
        private Hashtable h = new Hashtable();
        public void Add(Object o)
        {
            h[o] = null;
        }
    }
}
```

This code uses the keys of a `Hashtable` object to ensure that no object can be added twice to a `Set` instance.

Challenge 16.1

Add a method to the `Set` class that will make its instances usable in `foreach` statements.

A solution appears on page 386.

The FACTORY METHOD pattern relieves a client from the burden of knowing which class to instantiate. C# applies this principle to collection enumerators with the result that you can use a `foreach` statement with any collection, including those you create.

Recognizing FACTORY METHOD

You might think any method that creates and returns a new object is a "factory" method. In OO programming, however, methods that return new objects are common and not every such method is an instance of the FACTORY METHOD pattern.

Challenge 16.2

Name two commonly used methods in C# or in the .NET FCL that return a new object.

A solution appears on page 387.

The fact that a method creates a new object does not in itself mean that it is an example of the FACTORY METHOD pattern. The FACTORY METHOD pattern requires that an operation that creates an object also isolates its client from knowing which class to instantiate. In FACTORY METHOD, you will find several classes that implement the same operation, returning the same abstract type, but internally instantiating different classes that implement the type. When a client requests a new object, the precise class of the object that is created depends on the behavior of the object receiving the creation request.

Taking Control of Which Class to Instantiate

The ordinary way for a client to instantiate a class is to use one of the class's constructors. But sometimes a client that needs an object doesn't know exactly which class to create. This happens with enumerators, where the class of the enumerator that a client needs depends on the type of collection that the client wants to enumerate. It also happens frequently in application code.

Suppose that Oozinoz wants to start letting customers buy fireworks on credit. Early in the design of the credit authorization system, you accept responsibility for developing a CreditCheckOnline class that checks to see if a customer can maintain a certain amount of credit with Oozinoz.

As you begin development, you realize there will be times when the credit agency is offline. The analyst on the project determines that in this situation, the business wants to bring up a dialog for the call center representative and make a credit decision based on a few questions. To handle this, you create a CreditCheckOffline class, and you get this working to specification. Initially, you design the classes as Figure 16.1 shows. The CreditLimit() method accepts a customer's identification number and returns that customer's credit limit.

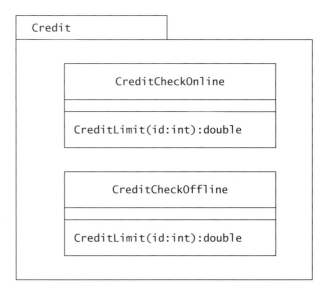

Figure 16.1   You can instantiate one of these classes to check a customer's credit, depending on whether the online credit agency is up.

With the classes in Figure 16.1, you can provide credit limit information whether or not the credit agency is online. The problem now is that the user of your classes needs to know which class to instantiate. But *you* are the one who knows whether or not the agency is up!

In this scenario, you need to commit to the interface for creating an object but keep control of which class to instantiate. One solution is to change both classes to implement a standard interface and create a factory method that returns an object of that type. Specifically, you might:

- Make ICreditCheck a C# interface that includes the CreditLimit() method.

- Change both credit check classes to declare that they implement the ICreditCheck interface.

- Create a CreditCheckFactory class that provides a CreateCreditCheck() method that returns an object whose type is ICreditCheck.

When you implement CreateCreditCheck(), you will use your knowledge of the credit agency's status to decide which class to instantiate.

Challenge 16.3

Draw a class diagram for this new scheme that establishes a way to create a credit-checking object while retaining control of which class to instantiate.

A solution appears on page 387.

By applying FACTORY METHOD, you let the user of your services call the CreateCreditCheck() method to get a credit-checking object that works whether or not the credit agency is online.

Challenge 16.4

Assume that the CreditCheckFactory class has an IsAgencyUp() method that tells whether the credit agency is available and write the code for CreateCreditCheck().

A solution appears on page 388.

FACTORY METHOD in Parallel Hierarchies

The FACTORY METHOD pattern often appears when you use parallel hierarchies to model a problem domain. A *parallel hierarchy* is a pair of class hierarchies in which each class in one hierarchy has a corresponding class in the other hierarchy. Parallel hierarchies usually emerge when you decide to move a subset of behavior out of an existing hierarchy.

Consider the construction of aerial shells, as illustrated in Chapter 5, "Composite." To build these shells, Oozinoz uses the machines that the diagram in Figure 16.2 models.

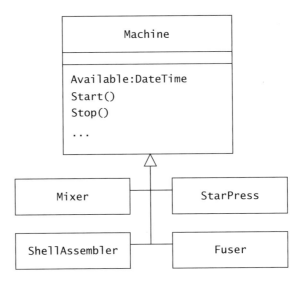

Figure 16.2   The Machine hierarchy contains logic for controlling physical machines and for planning.

To make a shell, we mix chemicals in a mixer and pass them to a star press, which extrudes individual stars. We pack stars into a shell around a core of black powder and place this over a lifting charge, using a shell assembler. We use a fuser to insert the fusing that will ignite both the lifting charge and the shell core.

Suppose that you need the Available property to forecast when a machine will complete its current processing and be available for more work. This method may require several supporting, private methods, adding up to quite a bit of logic to add to each of our machine classes. Rather than adding the planning logic to the Machine hierarchy, you might prefer to have a separate MachinePlanner hierarchy. You need a separate planner class for most machine types, but mixers and fusers are always available for additional work. For these classes, you can use a BasicPlanner class.

Challenge 16.5

Fill in the diagram of the Machine/MachinePlanner parallel hierarchy in Figure 16.3.

A solution appears on page 389.

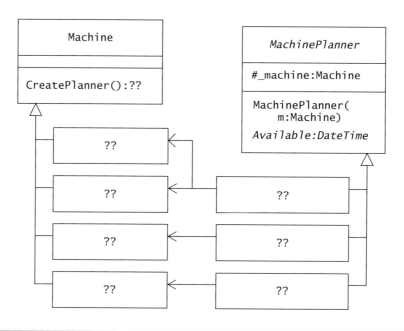

Figure 16.3   Slim down the Machine hierarchy by moving planning logic to a parallel hierarchy.

Challenge 16.6

Write a CreatePlanner() method for the Machine class to return a BasicPlanner object, and write a CreatePlanner() method for the StarPress class.

A solution appears on page 390.

Summary

The intent of the FACTORY METHOD pattern is to let a service provider relieve clients from knowing which class to instantiate. This pattern occurs in the .NET FCL, notably in the `GetEnumerator()` method on which the C# `foreach` statement depends.

FACTORY METHOD often appears in client code, occurring anytime you need to isolate clients from knowing exactly which class to instantiate. This need for isolation occurs when the decision of which class to instantiate depends on a factor that the client is unaware of, such as the status of an online credit bureau. You may also encounter FACTORY METHOD when you introduce a parallel class hierarchy to keep a set of classes from becoming bloated with many different aspects of behavior. FACTORY METHOD lets you connect parallel hierarchies by letting subclasses in one hierarchy determine which class to instantiate in the corresponding hierarchy.

CHAPTER 17

ABSTRACT FACTORY

There will be times when you want to provide for object creation while retaining control of which class to instantiate. In such circumstances, you can apply the FACTORY METHOD pattern with a method that uses an outside factor to determine which class to instantiate. Sometimes the factor that controls which object to instantiate can be thematic, running across several classes. The ABSTRACT FACTORY pattern addresses this situation. Its intent is to provide for the creation of families of related or dependent objects.

A Classic Example—GUI Kits

GUI kits provide a classic example of the ABSTRACT FACTORY pattern. A GUI kit is an object that is an abstract factory, supplying GUI controls to a client that is building a user interface. Each GUI kit object determines how buttons, text areas, and other controls appear. A kit establishes a specific look and feel, including background colors, shapes, and other aspects of GUI design that run across the family of controls the kit provides. You might establish a single look and feel for an entire system. You can also use look and feel changes to reflect changes in versions of the application, changes in company standard graphics, or simply improvements over time. ABSTRACT FACTORY lets you put look and feel to work, making your applications easier to learn and use. The Oozinoz UI class, shown in Figure 17.1, provides an example.

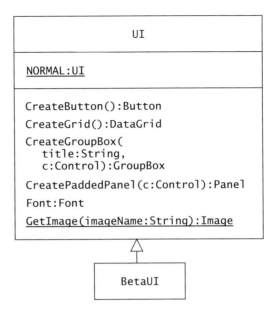

Figure 17.1   Instances of the UI and BetaUI classes are abstract factories that
create families of GUI controls.

The UI class marks all its instance methods and properties as virtual so
subclasses can override any particular element of the user control factory.
An application that builds a GUI from an instance of the UI class can later
produce a different look and feel by building from an instance of a subclass of UI. For example, Oozinoz uses a Visualization class to help engineers lay out new equipment lines. This visualization appears as in
Figure 17.2.

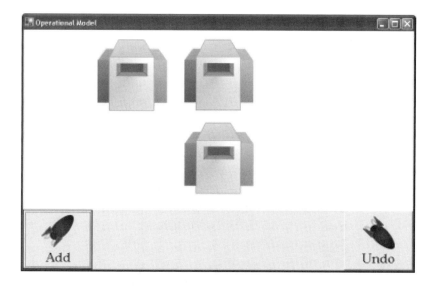

Figure 17.2   This visualization adds machines at the top left location of the panel and lets a user drag machines into place. Users can undo drags or adds.

The visualization in Figure 17.2 lets the user add machines and drag them around the factory floor. (The executable that shows this visualization is the ShowVisualization program in the ShowAbstractFactory directory.) The application gets its buttons from a UI object that the Visualization class accepts in its constructor. Figure 17.3 shows the Visualization class.

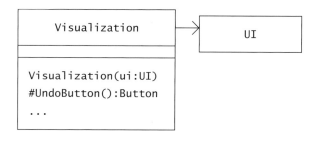

Figure 17.3   The Visualization class builds a GUI using a UI factory object.

The Visualization class builds its GUI using a UI object. For example, the code for the UndoButton() method is as follows:

```
protected Button UndoButton()
{
    if (_undoButton == null)
    {
        _undoButton = _ui.CreateButtonCancel();
        _undoButton.Dock = DockStyle.Right;
        _undoButton.Text = "Undo";
        _undoButton.Click +=
            new System.EventHandler(_mediator.Undo);
        _undoButton.Enabled = false;
    }
    return _undoButton;
}
```

This code creates a "cancel" button and changes its text to "Undo." The UI class determines the size and placement of the image and text on the button. The button-producing code of the UI class is as follows:

```
public virtual Button CreateButtonOk()
{
    Button b = CreateButton();
    b.Image = GetImage("rocket-large.gif");
    b.Text = "Ok!";
    return b;
}
public virtual Button CreateButtonCancel()
{
    Button b = CreateButton();
    b.Image = GetImage("rocket-large-down.gif");
    b.Text = "Cancel!";
    return b;
}
public virtual Button CreateButton()
{
    Button b = new Button();
    b.Size = new Size(128, 128);
    b.ImageAlign = ContentAlignment.TopCenter;
    b.Font = Font;
    b.TextAlign = ContentAlignment.BottomCenter;
    return b;
}
```

To produce a different look and feel for the visualization, we can create a subclass that overrides some of the elements of the UI factory class. We can pass an instance of this GUI factory to the Visualization class's constructor.

Suppose that we release a version of the Visualization class with new features, and while this code is in beta test, we want to change the user interface. Let's say that we want fonts to be italicized, and in place of the rocket images, we want to use cherry-large.gif and cherry-large-down.gif images. The code for a BetaUI class will look something like the following:

```
public class BetaUI : UI
{
    public BetaUI ()
    {
        Font f = Font;
        _font = new Font(f, f.Style ^ FontStyle.Italic);
    }
    public override Button CreateButtonOk()
    {
        // challenge!
    }
    public override Button CreateButtonCancel()
    {
        // challenge!
    }
}
```

Challenge 17.1

Complete the code for the BetaUI class.

A solution appears on page 390.

The following code runs the visualization with the new look and feel:

```
public class ShowBetaVis
{
    static void Main()
    {
        Application.Run(new Visualization(new BetaUI()));
    }
}
```

This program runs the visualization with the look shown in Figure 17.4.

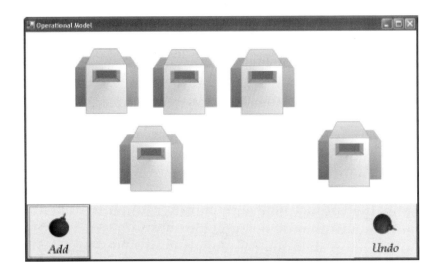

Figure 17.4   With no code changes to the Visualization class, the
                application shows the new look and feel provided by the
                BetaUI class.

Instances of the UI and BetaUI classes supply different families of GUI
controls to provide different looks to a GUI application. Although this is a
useful application of ABSTRACT FACTORY, the design is somewhat fragile.
In particular, the BetaUI class depends on the UI class to mark its creation
methods as virtual, and to give certain instance variables (notably _font)
protected access.

Challenge 17.2

Suggest a design change that would still allow for the development of a
variety of GUI control factories, but that would reduce the reliance of
subclasses on method modifiers in the UI class.

A solution appears on page 391.

ABSTRACT FACTORY frees a client from knowing which classes to instantiate when it needs new objects. In this regard, ABSTRACT FACTORY is similar to FACTORY METHOD. In some cases, a FACTORY METHOD design may
grow into an ABSTRACT FACTORY design.

Abstract Factories and Factory Method

Chapter 16, "Factory Method," introduced a pair of classes that implement the ICreditCheck interface. The CreditCheckFactory class instantiates one of these classes when a client calls its CreateCreditCheck() method. Which class the factory instantiates depends on whether or not the usual credit agency is up and running. This design isolates other developers from the status of the credit agency. Figure 17.5 shows the CreditCheckFactory class and current implementations of the ICreditCheck interface.

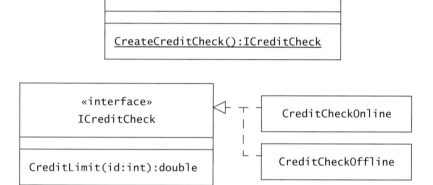

Figure 17.5   A FACTORY METHOD design that isolates clients from knowledge of which class to instantiate for performing credit checks.

The CreditCheckFactory class usually provides credit agency information about a customer's credit. In addition, the Credit package has classes that can look up shipping and billing information for a customer. Figure 17.6 shows the current Credit package.

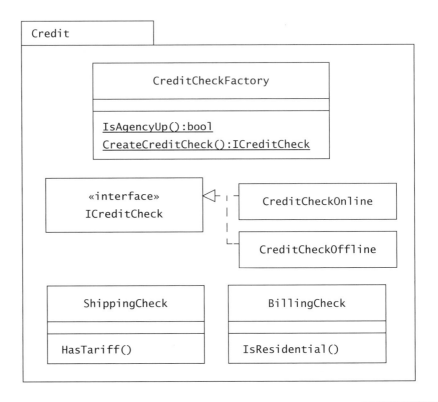

Figure 17.6   Classes in this package check a customer's credit, shipping
                address, and billing address.

Now suppose that a requirements analyst tells you that Oozinoz wants to
start servicing customers in Canada. To do business in Canada, you will
use a different credit agency and different data sources to establish U.S.
shipping and billing information.

When a customer calls, the call center application needs a *family* of objects
to perform a variety of checks. The family to use depends on whether the
call is from Canada or from the U.S. You can apply the ABSTRACT FAC-
TORY pattern to provide for the creation of these object families.

Expanding to Canada will nearly double the number of classes that support credit checks. Suppose that you decide to maintain these classes in
three namespaces. The Credit namespace will now contain three "check"
interfaces and one abstract factory class. This class will have three creation methods that supply appropriate objects for checking credit, billing,
and shipping information. You will also put CreditCheckOffline in this
package, since you can use this class for offline checks regardless of a
call's origin. Figure 17.7 shows the new contents of the Credit namespace.

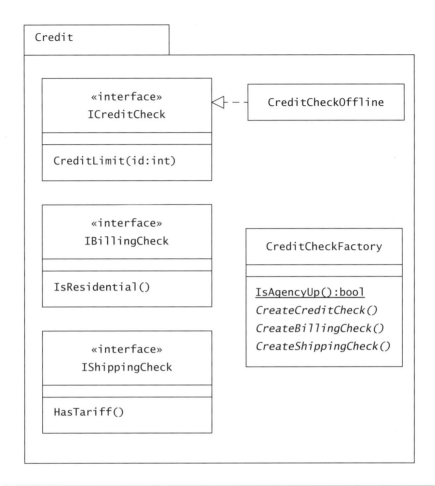

Figure 17.7   The revised package contains primarily interfaces and an abstract factory class.

To implement the interfaces in `Credit` with concrete classes, you can introduce two new namespaces: `Credit.Canada` and `Credit.US`. Each of these namespaces can contain a concrete version of the factory class and classes to implement each of the interfaces in `Credit`.

Challenge 17.3

Complete the diagram in Figure 17.8 that shows the classes in `Credit.Canada` and their relationships to classes and interfaces in `Credit`.

A solution appears on page 391.

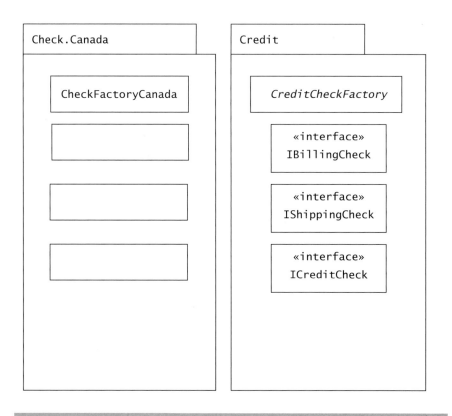

Figure 17.8   Show the classes in the Check.Canada namespace and their
                relationships to classes in Credit.

The concrete factory classes for Canadian and U.S. calls are fairly simple.
They return the Canadian or U.S. versions of the "check" interfaces, with
the exception that both concrete factories return a CreditCheckOffline
object if the local credit agency is offline. As in the previous chapter, the
CreditCheckFactory class has an IsAgencyUp() method that tells whether
or not the credit agency is available.

Challenge 17.4

Complete the code for `CheckFactoryCanada.cs`.

```
using System;
using Credit;
namespace Credit.Canada
{
    public class CheckFactoryCanada : CreditCheckFactory
    {
        // ??
    }
}
```

A solution appears on page 392.

At this point, you have a design that applies the ABSTRACT FACTORY pattern to provide for the creation of families of objects that conduct checks of different kinds of customer information. An instance of the abstract `CreditCheckFactory` class will either be a `CheckFactoryCanada` object or a `CheckFactoryUS` class. These objects are abstract factories, capable of creating billing, shipping, and credit check objects that are appropriate for the country the factory object represents.

Namespaces and Abstract Factories

Speaking loosely, a namespace usually contains a "family" of classes and an abstract factory produces a "family" of objects. In the previous example, we used separate namespaces to support abstract factories for Canada and the U.S., with a third namespace that provided common interfaces for the objects the factories produced.

Challenge 17.5

Write an argument supporting the decision to place each factory and its related classes in a separate namespace. Or, argue that another approach is superior.

A solution appears on page 393.

Summary

The ABSTRACT FACTORY pattern lets you arrange for a client to create objects that are part of a family of related or dependent objects. A classic application of this pattern is for look and feel families, or "kits" of GUI controls. Other themes that run across a family of objects are possible, such as a customer's country of residence. As with FACTORY METHOD, ABSTRACT FACTORY isolates clients from knowing which class to instantiate. ABSTRACT FACTORY lets you provide a client with a factory that produces objects that are related by a common theme.

CHAPTER 18

PROTOTYPE

When you develop a class, you ordinarily furnish it with constructors to let client applications instantiate it. In some circumstances, you may decide to isolate users of your class from directly calling a constructor. The construction-oriented patterns covered so far—BUILDER, FACTORY METHOD, and ABSTRACT FACTORY—all provide this isolation. These patterns establish methods that instantiate an appropriate class on a client's behalf. The PROTOTYPE pattern also conceals object creation from clients, but uses a different approach. Instead of bringing forth new, uninitialized instances of a class, the intent of the PROTOTYPE pattern is to provide new objects by copying an example.

Prototypes as Factories

Suppose that you are using the ABSTRACT FACTORY pattern at Oozinoz to provide user interfaces for several different contexts. Figure 18.1 shows the user interface factories that might evolve.

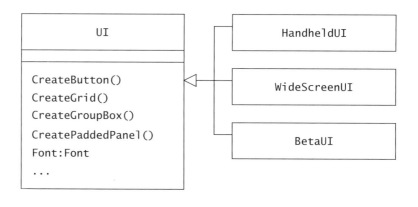

Figure 18.1   Three abstract factories, or "kits," produce different user
               interface looks.

The users at Oozinoz enjoy the productivity that results from applying
the right user interface in the right context. The problem you face is that
they want several more user interface kits, and it's becoming burdensome
to create a new class for each context your users envision. Suppose a
developer at Oozinoz suggests halting the proliferation of user interface
factory classes by applying the PROTOTYPE pattern. Specifically, she suggests:

- Drop the subclasses of UI.

- Let each *instance* of UI become a user interface factory that works
  by handing out copies of prototypical controls.

- Place the code that creates new UI objects in static methods on the
  UI class.

With this design, a UI object will have a complete set of prototypical
instance variables: a Button object, a Grid object, a GroupBox object, a Pad-
dedPanel object, and so on. The code that creates a new UI object will set
the values of these prototypical controls to produce the desired look and
feel. The Create-() methods will return copies of these prototypical controls.

For example, we can create a static CreateHandheldUI() method on the UI
class. This method will instantiate UI, set this object's instance variables to

values that are appropriate for a handheld display, and return the object for use as a GUI kit.

Challenge 18.1

A PROTOTYPE design will cut down on the number of classes that Oozinoz uses to maintain multiple GUI kits. Name two other pros or cons of this design approach.

A solution appears on page 394.

The normal way to create an object is to invoke a class constructor. The PROTOTYPE pattern offers a flexible alternative, letting you determine at runtime which object to use as a model for the new one. However, the PROTOTYPE approach in C# does not allow new objects to have different methods than their parent. You may need to evaluate the advantages and disadvantages of a prototyping scheme, and you may want to experiment with PROTOTYPE to see how if it suits your needs. Whether or not you're just experimenting, to employ PROTOTYPE, you'll need to master the mechanics of copying objects in C#.

Prototyping with Clones

The intent of the PROTOTYPE pattern is to provide new objects by copying an example. When you create an object as a copy, the new object will have the same attributes and behavior as its parent. The new object may also inherit some or all of the parent object's data values. For example, a copy of a padded panel should have the same padding value as the original.

An important question to ask is: When you copy an object, does the copy operation provide copies of the original object's attribute values, or does the copy share these values with the original? As a developer, it is easy to forget to ask this question or to answer it incorrectly. Defects commonly arise when developers make mistaken assumptions about the mechanics of copying. Many classes in the .NET FCL offer support for copying, but as a developer, you must understand how copying works, especially if you want to use PROTOTYPE.

Challenge 18.2

The Object class includes a MemberwiseClone() method that all objects inherit. If you're not familiar with this method, look it up in online help or other documentation. Then write in your own words what this method does.

A solution appears on page 394.

Suppose that Machine class had just two attributes: an integer ID and a Location, where Location is a separate class.

Challenge 18.3

Draw an object diagram that shows a Machine object, its Location object, and any other objects that result from invoking MemberwiseClone() on the Machine object.

A solution appears on page 395.

The MemberwiseClone() method makes it easy to add a Copy() method to a non-sealed class. For example, you might create a class of cloneable group boxes with the following code:

```
using System;
using System.Windows.Forms;
namespace UserInterface
{
    public class OzGroupBox : GroupBox
    {
        // dangerous!
        public OzGroupBox Copy()
        {
            return (OzGroupBox) this.MemberwiseClone();
        }
        // ...
    }
}
```

The Copy() method in this code makes cloning publicly available and casts the copy to the appropriate type. The problem with this code is that the MemberwiseClone() method will create copies of all of a GroupBox object's attributes, whether you understand the function of those attributes or not. Note that the attributes of the GroupBox class include the attributes of all ancestors of GroupBox, as Figure 18.2 highlights.

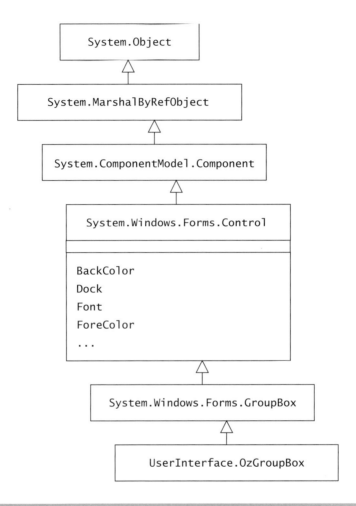

Figure 18.2   The OzGroupBox class inherits numerous methods and variables from its superclasses.

As Figure 18.2 suggests, the GroupBox class inherits numerous properties from the Control class, and these are often the only attributes that you need to copy when working with GUI objects.

Challenge 18.4

Write an OzGroupBox.Copy2() method that copies a group box without relying on MemberwiseClone(). Assume that the only attributes that are important to copy are BackColor, Dock, Font, and ForeColor.

A solution appears on page 395.

Summary

The PROTOTYPE pattern lets a client create new objects by copying an example. A major difference between calling a constructor and copying an object is that a copy typically includes some of the state of the original object. You can use this to your advantage, particularly when different "classes" of objects differ only in their attributes and not in their behaviors. In such a case, you can create new classes at runtime by crafting prototypical objects for a client to copy.

When you need to create a copy, the Object.MemberwiseClone() method can help, but you must remember that this method creates a new object with the same fields. This object may not be a suitable copy and any difficulties related to deeper copying are your responsibility. If a prototypical object has too many fields, you can create a copy by instantiating a new object and setting its fields to match just the aspects of the original object you need to copy.

CHAPTER 19

MEMENTO

Sometimes the object you want to create is one that existed previously. This occurs when you want to let a user undo operations, revert to an earlier version of work, or resume work that he or she previously suspended. The intent of the MEMENTO pattern is to provide storage and restoration of an object's state.

A Classic Example—Using Memento for Undo

Chapter 17, "Abstract Factory," introduced a visualization application that let users perform operational modeling experiments with material flow through a factory. Suppose that the functionality for the Undo button has not yet implemented. We can apply the MEMENTO pattern to make the Undo button work.

A memento is an object that holds state information. In the visualization application, the state we need to preserve is the state of the application. Whenever a user adds or moves a machine, he or she should be able to undo that change by clicking Undo. To add the undo function to the visualization, we will need to decide how to capture the state of the application in a memento. We will also have to decide *when* to capture this state and how to restore the application to a previously captured state. When the application starts up, it appears as in Figure 19.1.

Figure 19.1   When the visualization application starts up, the work panel is
               blank and the Undo button is disabled.

The visualization starts up in an empty state, which is a state nonetheless. Anytime the visualization is in this empty state, the Undo button should be disabled. After a few adds and drags, the visualization might appear as in Figure 19.2.

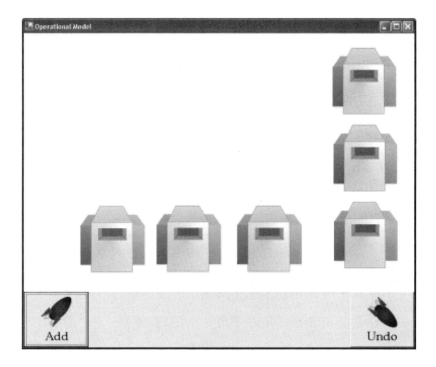

Figure 19.2   Users can add and rearrange machines in the visualization.

The state we need to capture in a memento consists of a list of machine locations that the user has placed. We can keep a stack of these mementos, popping one each time the user clicks Undo.

To summarize:

- Each time the user adds or moves a machine in the visualization, your code will create a memento of the simulated factory and add it to a stack.

- Each time the user clicks the Undo button, your code will pop the most recent memento, and then restore the simulation to the state stored at the top of the stack.

When your visualization starts up, you will stack an initial, empty memento and never pop it to ensure that the top of the stack is always a valid memento. Anytime the stack contains just one memento, you will disable the Undo button.

We might write the code for this program in a single class, but we expect to add features that support operational modeling and other features that your users may request. Eventually, the application may grow large, so it is wise to use an MVC design that you can build on. Figure 19.3 shows a design that moves the work of modeling the factory into a separate class.

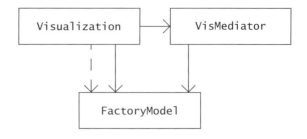

Figure 19.3   This design divides the application's work into separate classes
              for modeling the factory, providing GUI elements, and
              handling a user's clicks.

This design lets you first focus on developing a FactoryModel class that
has no GUI controls and no dependency on the GUI.

The FactoryModel class is at the center of our design. It is responsible for
maintaining the current configuration of machines, and for maintaining
mementos of previous configurations.

Each time a client asks the factory to add or move a machine, the factory
will create a copy—a memento—of its current locations and push this
onto its stack of mementos. In this example, we do not need a special
Memento class. Each memento is merely a list of points, the list of machine
locations at a particular time.

The factory model must provide events that let clients register interest in
changes to the factory state. This lets the visualization GUI inform the
model of changes that the user makes. Suppose that you decide the factory should let clients register for events of adding a machine, dragging a
machine, and for rebuilding the entire factory configuration. Figure 19.4
shows a design for such a FactoryModel class.

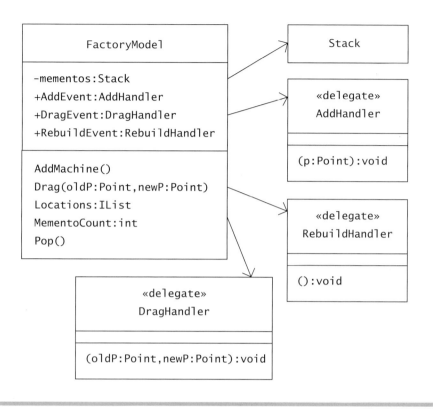

Figure 19.4 The `FactoryModel` class maintains a stack of factory configurations and lets clients register for notification of changes in the factory.

The design in Figure 19.4 calls for the `FactoryModel` class to provide clients with the ability to register for the notification of several events. For example, consider the event of adding a machine. The `AddHandler` delegate type defines a method signature that takes a `Point` argument and returns nothing. The code for this type is:

```
public delegate void AddHandler(Point p);
```

The `AddHandler` and `RebuildHandler` delegate type declarations are in a `FactoryDelegates.cs` file in the `lib/Visualizations` directory of the code available from www.oozinoz.com.

The `AddEvent` instance variable in the `FactoryModel` class is a variable whose type is `AddHandler`. As the following code shows, the `AddEvent` field declaration marks the `AddEvent` variable with the event keyword to limit the access that clients have to this public field:

```
public class FactoryModel
{
    private Stack _mementos;
    public event AddHandler AddEvent;
    public event DragHandler DragEvent;
    public event RebuildHandler RebuildEvent;
    public static readonly Point DEFAULT_LOCATION =
        new Point(10, 10);

    public FactoryModel()
    {
        _mementos = new Stack();
        _mementos.Push(new ArrayList());
    }
    //...
}
```

The declarations in the FactoryModel class make the model's events accessible to clients. The constructor starts off the factory's initial configuration
as an empty list. The remaining methods in the class maintain the stack of
machine configuration mementos and fire events that correspond to any
changes. For example, to add a machine to the current configuration, a
client can call the following method:

```
public void AddMachine()
{
    IList newLocs = new ArrayList();
    Point newP = DEFAULT_LOCATION;
    newLocs.Add(newP);
    foreach (Point p in (IList)_mementos.Peek())
    {
        newLocs.Add(new Point(p.X, p.Y));
    }
    _mementos.Push(newLocs);
    if (AddEvent != null) AddEvent(newP);
}
```

This code creates a new list of machine locations and pushes the list on
the stack of mementos that the factory model maintains. A subtlety here is
that the code ensures that the new machine is first in this list. This is a
clue to the visualization that a picture of this machine should appear in
front of any other machines that the picture may overlap.

A client that registers for the AddEvent event might update its view of the
factory model by using the new Point value the event provides. Alternatively, a client might rebuild itself entirely when receiving any event from
the factory model. The factory model's latest configuration is always
available in the Locations property, whose code is as follows:

```
public IList Locations
{
    get
    {
        return (IList)_mementos.Peek();
    }
}
```

The Pop() method of the FactoryModel class lets a client change the model of machine locations to be a previous version. When this code executes, it raises the RebuildEvent event.

Challenge 19.1

Write the code for the FactoryModel class's Pop() method.

A solution appears on page 396.

An interested client can provide undo support by registering for notification of the RebuildEvent event, supplying a method that rebuilds the client's view of the factory. The Visualization class is one such client.

The MVC design in Figure 19.3 separates the tasks of translating user actions from the tasks of maintaining the GUI. The Visualization class creates its GUI controls but passes off the handling of GUI events to a mediator. The VisMediator class translates GUI events into appropriate changes in the factory model. When the model changes, the GUI may need to update. The Visualization class registers for the events that the FactoryModel class provides. Note the division of responsibility:

- The visualization changes factory events into GUI changes.

- The mediator translates GUI events into factory changes.

Figure 19.5 shows the three collaborating classes in more detail.

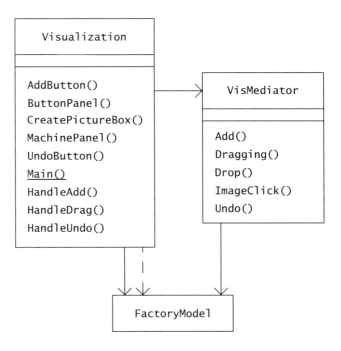

Figure 19.5   The mediator translates GUI events into factory model changes, and the visualization reacts to factory events to update the GUI.

Suppose that while dragging a machine image, a user accidentally drops it in the wrong spot and clicks "Undo." To be able to handle this click, the visualization registers the mediator for notification of button events. The code for the Undo button in the `Visualization` class is:

```
protected Button UndoButton()
{
    if (_undoButton == null)
    {
        _undoButton = new Button();
        _undoButton.Dock = DockStyle.Right;
        _undoButton.Font = UI.NORMAL.Font;
        _undoButton.Width = UI.NORMAL.Font.Height * 4;
        _undoButton.Text = "Undo";
        _undoButton.Click +=
            new System.EventHandler(_mediator.Undo);
        _undoButton.Enabled = false;
    }
    return _undoButton;
}
```

This code passes responsibility for handling a click to the mediator. The mediator informs the factory model of any requested changes. The mediator translates an undo request to a factory change with the following code:

```
internal void Undo(object sender, System.EventArgs e)
{
    _factoryModel.Pop();
}
```

The _factoryModel variable in this method is an instance of FactoryModel, which the Visualization class creates and passes the mediator in the Vis-Mediator class's constructor.

We have already examined the FactoryModel class's Pop() command. The flow of messages that occurs when the user clicks "Undo" appears in Figure 19.6.

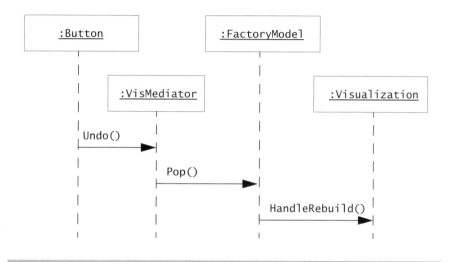

Figure 19.6   The message flow that occurs when the user clicks "Undo."

When the FactoryModel class pops its current configuration, exposing the previous configuration it stored as a memento, the Pop() method fires the RebuildEvent event. The Visualization class registers for this event in its constructor.

```
public Visualization()
{
    _factoryModel.AddEvent += new AddHandler(HandleAdd);
    _factoryModel.DragEvent += new DragHandler(HandleDrag);
    _factoryModel.RebuildEvent +=
        new RebuildHandler(HandleUndo);
    _mediator = new VisMediator(_factoryModel);
    Controls.Add(MachinePanel());
    Controls.Add(ButtonPanel());
    Text = "Operational Model";
}
```

For each machine location in the factory model, the visualization maintains a PictureBox object that it creates with its CreatePictureBox() method. The HandleUndo() method must clear all the picture box controls from the machine panel and re-add new picture boxes from the now-current set of locations in the factory model. The HandleUndo() method must also disable the Undo button if the factory has only a single memento left on its stack.

Challenge 19.2

Write the HandleUndo() method for the Visualization class.

A solution appears on page 397.

The MEMENTO pattern lets you save and restore an object's state. A common use of MEMENTO is related to providing undo support in applications. In some applications, as in the factory visualization example, the repository for the information you need to store can be another object. In other cases, you may need to store mementos in a form more durable than an object.

Memento Durability

A *memento* is a tiny repository that saves an object's state. You can create a memento using another object, a string, or a file. The anticipated duration between the storage and reconstruction of an object has an effect on the strategy that you can use in designing a memento. The time that elapses can be moments, hours, days, or years.

Challenge 19.3

List two reasons that might drive you to save a memento in a file rather than as an object.

A solution appears on page 397.

Persisting Mementos across Sessions

A *session* occurs when a user runs a program, conducts transactions in the program, and exits. Suppose your users want to be able to save a simulation in one session and restore it in another session. This ability is a matter normally referred to as *persistent storage*. Persistent storage fulfills the intent of the MEMENTO pattern and is a natural extension to the undo functionality we have already implemented.

Suppose that you subclass the Visualization class with a Visualization2 class that has a menu bar with a File menu with "Save As..." and "Restore From..." items.

```
using System;
using System.Collections;
using System.Windows.Forms;
public class Visualization2 : Visualization
{
    public Visualization2()
    {
        Menu = ApplicationMenu();
    }
    protected MainMenu ApplicationMenu()
    {
        MenuItem fileMenu =
            new MenuItem("File", new MenuItem[]
            {
                new MenuItem(
                    "Save As...",
                    new EventHandler(_mediator.Save)),
                new MenuItem(
                    "Restore From...",
                    new EventHandler(_mediator.Restore))
            });
        return new MainMenu(new MenuItem[]{fileMenu});
    }
    static void Main()
    {
        Application.Run(new Visualization2());
    }
}
```

This code requires the addition of Save() and Restore() methods to the VisMediator class. The MenuItem constructors associate these methods with menu item Click events. When the Visualization2 class runs, the GUI appears as in Figure 19.7.

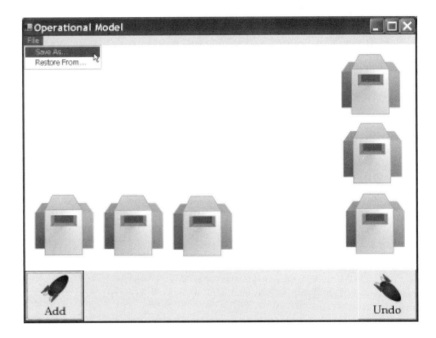

Figure 19.7   The addition of a File menu lets a user save a memento from
               which the application can later restore.

An easy way to serialize an object such as the factory model's top-most
configuration is to write it out in SOAP format. The code for the `Save()`
method in the `VisMediator` class might appear as follows:

```
internal void Save(object sender, System.EventArgs e)
{
    SaveFileDialog d = new SaveFileDialog();
    if (d.ShowDialog() == DialogResult.OK)
    {
        using (FileStream fs = File.Create(d.FileName))
        {
            new SoapFormatter().Serialize(
                fs, _factoryModel.Locations);
        }
    }
}
```

Challenge 19.4

Write the code for the `Restore()` method of the `VisMediator` class.

A solution appears on page 397.

Design Patterns states the intent of the MEMENTO pattern as: "Without violating encapsulation, capture and externalize an object's internal state so that the object can be restored to this state later."

Challenge 19.5

Write a short statement of whether, in your opinion, saving a memento in textual form violates encapsulation.

A solution appears on page 398.

Depending on your answer to Challenge 19.5, you might or might not agree that a SOAP-formatted serialization is a kind of memento. Regardless, if a developer says he or she creates mementos by storing an object's data in a SOAP message, you should understand what he or she means. And that's the point of design patterns: By using a common vocabulary, we can readily discuss design concepts and their application.

Summary

The MEMENTO pattern lets you capture an object's state so you can restore the object later. The means of storage may depend on whether you need to be able to restore an object after a few clicks and keystrokes, or after days or years. The most common reason for saving and restoring objects during an application session is to support undo operations. In such cases, you can store an object's state in another object. To let an object persist across sessions, you can save a memento through object serialization.

PART 4

OPERATION PATTERNS

CHAPTER 20

INTRODUCING OPERATIONS

When you write a C# method, you produce a fundamental unit of work that is a level up from writing a statement. Your methods have to participate in an overall design, architecture, and test plan, but no activity is more central to programming than writing methods. Ironically, despite the central role of methods, it is easy to get confused about what methods are and how methods function. This confusion may stem from the tendency of many developers (and authors) to mix the meaning of the words *method* and *operation*. In addition, delegates in C# introduce new concepts for many developers. The concepts of "algorithm" and "polymorphism" are more abstract than methods, and yet they are ultimately realized by methods.

Having a clear understanding of the terms *algorithm*, *polymorphism*, *method*, and *operation* will help you understand several design patterns. In particular, STATE, STRATEGY, and INTERPRETER all work by implementing an operation in methods across several classes—but such observations are only useful if we agree on the meaning of *method* and *operation*.

Operations and Methods

Of the many terms that relate to the work a class may be called on to perform, it is especially useful to distinguish "operation" from "method." The UML defines the difference between an operation and a method as follows:

- An *operation* is a specification of a service that can be requested from an instance of a class.

- A *method* is an implementation of an operation.

An operation specifies something that a class does, and specifies the interface for calling this service. Multiple classes may implement the same operation in different ways. For example, many classes implement the ToString() operation. Every class that implements an operation implements it with a method. That method contains (or *is*) the code that makes the operation work for that class.

The definitions of *method* and *operation* help to clarify the structure of many design patterns. The meaning of *operation* is a level of abstraction up from the idea of *method*. Since design patterns are also a level up from classes and methods, it is no surprise that operations feature prominently in many patterns. For example, COMPOSITE arranges for operations to apply to both items and groups. PROXY lets an intermediary that has the same operations as a target object interpose itself to manage access to the target.

Challenge 20.1

Use the words *operation* and *method* to explain how CHAIN OF RESPONSIBILITY implements an operation.

A solution appears on page 398.

In C#, a method declaration includes a *header* and a *body*. A method's *body* is the series of instructions that can be called into action by invoking the method's signature. A method's *header* includes the method's return type and signature, and may include modifiers and a `throws` clause. Section 10.5 of the *C# Language Specification* [Wiltamuth] gives the form of a method header as:

attributes modifiers return-type signature

Attributes in C# let you mark classes and methods with information. For example, the section "Remote Proxies" in Chapter 11 shows the use of a `WebMethod` attribute to mark a method as a Web service. The list of modifiers that can apply to a method is extensive, including access modifiers such as `protected` and polymorphism-related modifiers such as `virtual`.

Challenge 20.2

List as many of the 11 C# method modifiers as you can think of.

An answer appears on page 398.

After attributes and modifiers, a C# method header declares a method's return type and signature.

Signatures

On the surface the meaning of *operation* is similar to the meaning of *signature*. Both words refer to the interface into a method. When you write a method, it becomes available for invocation according to its signature. Section 3.6 of the *C# Language Specification* [Wiltamuth] says:

> The *signature* of a method consists of the name of the method and the type and kind (value, reference, or output) of each of its formal parameters. The signature of a method specifically does not include the return type, nor does it include the `params` modifier that may be specified for the right-most parameter.

Note that although a method's signature does not include return type, if a method declaration overrides the declaration of another method, then a compile-time error occurs if they have different return types.

Challenge 20.3

The method `Bitmap.MemberwiseClone()` returns `object`, even though the method always returns an instance of the `Bitmap` class. Wouldn't this method be more effective if its return type were `Bitmap`?

An answer appears on page 398.

A *signature* specifies which method is invoked when a client makes a call. An *operation* is a specification of a service that can be requested from an instance of a class. The meanings of the terms "signature" and "operation" are similar, and yet the words are not synonyms. The difference between the meaning of these terms is mainly in the context in which they apply. The term *operation* applies when discussing the idea that methods in different classes may have the same interface. The term *signature* applies when discussing the rules that govern how C# matches a method call to a method in the receiving object.

A signature depends on a method's name and parameters, but not on the method's return type. In some situations, what is important or known about a method is its return type and parameters, but not its name. That is, you may know what type of information will be passed to a method and what type of information the method will return, without knowing which specific method should execute. Delegates fit precisely this case.

Delegates

A delegate declaration defines the type of information that flows in and out of a method without specifying a specific method to provide this flow. The decision of which method or methods a delegate should represent is deferred to runtime when the delegate is instantiated.

Several previous examples have drawn on the usefulness of the delegate construct. Chapter 2, "Introducing Interfaces," explored the similarity between delegates and interfaces. Chapter 4, "Facade," used a Function delegate to allow a plotting control to accept a function to plot. Chapter 9, "Observer" explained how delegates support the OBSERVER pattern, and Chapter 19, "Memento," used delegates in a complete MVC application.

The syntax for using delegates is fairly simple, but the concepts behind delegates can be confusing. In addition, some texts use the word "delegate" to refer to the idea of delegates, or to a delegate declaration, or to the result of a delegate declaration, or to a variable whose type is a delegate, or to a delegate instance.

Suppose that you want your LoadImage() method to execute when a user clicks a button. You can pass off this responsibility by wrapping a reference to the method in a delegate and passing it to the button with code something like:

```
_button.Click += new System.EventHandler(LoadImage);
```

Which part of this statement is a delegate: Click, System.EventHandler, or the entire expression on the right side of the equation? Strictly speaking, the delegate in this code is System.EventHandler. There are many other facts that you might observe about this single C# statement.

Challenge 20.4

Line up the following numbers and letters so that each number/letter pair creates a true statement about delegates in C#.

1. A delegate declaration	a. is an instance variable whose type is `System.EventHandler`.
2. A delegate instance	b. defines a class that derives from the class `System.Dele-gate`.
3. The expression on the right side of the += operator	c. creates a delegate instance.
4. `Click`	d. must have the same parameters and return type as `System.EventHandler`.
5. The `System.EventHandler` delegate	e. specifies the parameters and return type, but no name for the method.
6. The `LoadImage()` method	f. encapsulates one or more methods.

A solution appears on page 399.

Like any other method, a method contained by a delegate normally completes by executing the code of its body and returning. But another, less healthy way for control to return from an executing method is through an exception.

Exceptions

In *Illness as Metaphor,* Susan Sontag observes that "Everyone who is born holds dual citizenship, in the kingdom of the well and in the kingdom of the sick." This metaphor applies to methods as well as people: Instead of returning normally, methods may throw an exception or may call another method that causes an exception to be thrown. When a method returns normally, program control returns to the point just after the method call. A different set of rules applies to the kingdom of exceptions.

When an exception is thrown, the C# execution environment must find a containing `try`/`catch` statement that matches the exception. The `try`/`catch` statement may exist in the method that threw the exception, or in the method that called the current method, or in the method that called the previous method, and so on back through the current tree of method calls. If no matching `try`/`catch` statement is found, the programs stops—it crashes.

Any method can throw an exception with a `throw` statement. For example:

```
throw new Exception("Good Luck!");
```

If your application uses a method that throws an exception you haven't planned for, your application can unceremoniously crash. To prevent this sort of behavior, you need to have an architectural plan that specifies the points in your application that catch and react appropriately to exceptions. You might also think that it would be useful for C# to force a method that throws an exception to declare this possibility. Java, for example, requires methods that throw certain types of exceptions to declare this possibility in the method header.

Challenge 20.5

C# differs from Java in that it does not require methods to declare any exceptions they might throw. Give your opinion of whether or not this is a beneficial feature of C#.

A solution appears on page 399.

Algorithms and Polymorphism

Algorithms and polymorphism are important ideas in programming, but it can be difficult to explain what we mean by these terms. If you want to show someone a method, you can edit the source code for a class and point to lines of code. Occasionally, an algorithm may exist entirely within one method, but often, an algorithm's work relies on the interplay of several methods. *Introduction to Algorithms* [Cormen] says:

- An *algorithm* is any well-defined computational procedure that takes some value, or set of values, as input and produces some value, or set of values, as output.

An *algorithm* is a procedure—a sequence of instructions—that accepts inputs and produces outputs. In this regard, an algorithm is similar to a method. A *method* accepts inputs (its parameter list) and produces an output (its return value). However, many algorithms require more than one method to execute in an OO program. For example, the `IsTree()` algorithm in Chapter 3, "COMPOSITE," requires four methods, as shown in Figure 20.1.

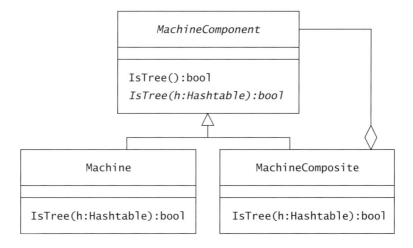

Figure 20.1   Four `IsTree()` methods collaborate to effect the algorithm for determining whether an instance of `MachineComponent` is a tree.

Challenge 20.6

How many algorithms, operations, and methods does Figure 20.1 depict?

An answer appears on page 400.

Algorithms get something done. They may appear as part of a method, or they may involve many methods. In OO computing, algorithms that require more than one method often rely on polymorphism to allow multiple implementations of a single operation.

- *Polymorphism* is the principle that method invocation depends on both the operation invoked and the class of the invocation receiver.

For example, you might ask which method executes when C# encounters the expression `m.IsTree()`. The answer is, *it depends*. If m is an instance of `Machine`, then C# will invoke `Machine.IsTree()`. If m is an instance of `MachineComposite`, then C# will invoke `MachineComposite.IsTree()`. Informally, polymorphism means that the right method gets invoked for the right type of object. Many patterns employ polymorphism, and in some cases, this ties directly to the intent of the pattern.

Summary

Although it is common to intermingle the meanings of *operation*, *method*, *signature*, and *algorithm*, preserving distinctions between these terms helps to describe important concepts. An operation is, like a signature, a specification of a service. The word *operation* applies when talking about the idea that many methods may have the same interface. The word *signature* applies when discussing method lookup rules. A method definition includes its signature (its name and parameter list), along with attributes, modifiers, return type, and the method's body. A method *has* a signature and *implements* an operation.

The normal way to invoke a method is to call it. C# also provides, through delegates, the powerful ability to manage when and by whom a method is invoked. The normal way for a method to conclude is for it to return, but any method will stop executing when it encounters an unhandled exception.

An *algorithm* is a procedure that accepts inputs and produces outputs. Methods accept inputs, produce outputs, and contain a procedural method body; some authors may refer to a method body as an "algorithm." However, an algorithm's procedure may involve many operations and methods, or it may exist as part of another method. The word *algorithm* best applies when you are discussing a procedure that produces a result.

Many design patterns involve distributing an operation across several classes. You can also say that these patterns rely on *polymorphism*, the principle that method selection depends on the class of the object receiving a method call.

Beyond Ordinary Operations

Different classes can implement an operation in different ways. In other words, C# supports polymorphism. The power of this seemingly simple idea appears in several design patterns.

If you intend to:	Then apply the pattern:
• Implement an algorithm in a method, deferring the definition of some steps of the algorithm so that subclasses can redefine them,	TEMPLATE METHOD
• Distribute an operation so that each class represents a different state,	STATE
• Encapsulate an operation, making implementations interchangeable,	STRATEGY
• Encapsulate a method call in an object,	COMMAND
• Distribute an operation so that each implementation applies to a different type of composition,	INTERPRETER

Operation-oriented patterns address contexts where you need more than one method, usually with the same signature, to participate in a design. For example, the TEMPLATE METHOD pattern allows subclasses to implement methods that adjust the effect of a procedure defined in a superclass.

CHAPTER 21

TEMPLATE METHOD

Ordinary methods have bodies that define a sequence of instructions. It is also quite ordinary for a method to invoke methods on the current object and on other objects. Ordinary methods are, in this sense, "templates" that outline a series of instructions for the computer to follow. The TEMPLATE METHOD pattern, however, involves a more specific type of template.

When you write a method, you may want to define the outline of an algorithm while allowing for the fact that there may be differences in how you want to implement certain steps. In this case, you can define the method but leave some steps as abstract methods, as stubbed-out methods, or as methods defined in a separate interface. This produces a more rigid "template" that specifically defines which steps of an algorithm other classes can or must supply. The intent of TEMPLATE METHOD is to implement an algorithm in a method, deferring the definition of some steps of the algorithm so that other classes can redefine them.

A Classic Example—Sorting

Sorting algorithms are ancient and highly reusable. Suppose that a prehistoric woman devised a method for sorting arrows by the sharpness of their heads. Perhaps she lined up the arrows and made a series of left-to-right sweeps, switching each arrow with one on its left if the left arrowhead was sharper. Having worked out this algorithm, she may then have realized that she could reapply the method to sort the arrows by their flight distance or by any other attribute.

Sorting algorithms vary in approach and speed, but every sorting algorithm relies on the primitive step of comparing two items or attributes. If you have a sorting algorithm and you can compare an attribute of any two items, then your sorting algorithm will let you sort a collection of items by that attribute.

Sorting is an ancient example of Template Method. It is a procedure that lets us change one critical step—the comparison of two objects—to reuse the algorithm for various attributes of various collections of objects.

In recent times, sorting probably reigns as the most frequently reimplemented algorithm, with implementations likely outnumbering the number of existing programmers. But unless you are sorting a huge collection, there is no reason to write your own sorting algorithm.

The `Array` class and `ArrayList` class both provide `Sort()` methods. The `Array` class's `Sort()` method is static and takes an array to sort as an argument. The `ArrayList` class's `Sort()` method is an instance method that sorts the recipient of the `Sort()` message. In other regards, these methods share a common strategy that depends on the `IComparable` and `IComparer` interfaces shown in Figure 21.1.

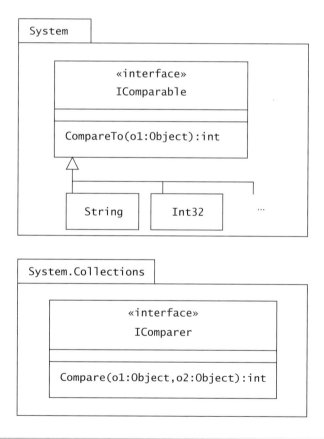

Figure 21.1   The `Sort()` methods in the `Array` class and the `ArrayList` class depend on the two interfaces shown here.

The `Sort()` methods in the `Array` class and `ArrayList` class are overloaded, allowing you to provide an instance of the `IComparer` interface if you choose. If you use a Sort() method without providing an instance of IComparer, the method will rely on the CompareTo() method of the ICompa-rable interface. An exception will occur if you attempt to sort items without providing an IComparer instance and the items do not implement the IComparable interface. But note that most basic types, such as String and Int32, do implement IComparable.

The Sort() methods provide an example of TEMPLATE METHOD; they provide an algorithm that lets you supply one critical step—the step of comparing two items. The CompareTo() methods return a number less than, equal to, or greater than 0. These values correspond to the idea that, in a sense that you define, object o1 is less than, equal to, or greater than object o2. For example, the following code sorts a collection of rockets by their apogees. (The rocket constructor accepts the name, mass, price, apogee, and thrust of the rocket.)

```
using System;
using System.Collections;
using Fireworks;
public class ShowComparator
{
    public static void Main()
    {
        Rocket r1 = new Rocket(
            "Mach-it",  1.1, 22.95m, 1000, 70);
        Rocket r2 = new Rocket(
            "Pocket",   0.3,  4.95m,  150, 20);
        Rocket r3 = new Rocket(
            "Sock-it",  0.8, 11.95m,  320, 25);
        Rocket r4 = new Rocket(
            "Sprocket", 1.5, 22.95m,  270, 40);
        Rocket[] rockets = new Rocket[] { r1, r2, r3, r4 };
        Array.Sort(rockets, new ApogeeCompare());
        foreach (Rocket r in rockets)
        {
            Console.WriteLine(r);
        }
    }
    private class ApogeeCompare : IComparer
    {
        // challenge!
    }
}
```

The program printout depends on how Rocket implements ToString(), but shows the rockets sorted by apogee.

```
Pocket
Sprocket
Sock-it
Mach-it
```

Challenge 21.1

Fill in the missing code in the ApogeeCompare class so that the program will sort a collection of rockets by apogee.

A solution appears on page 400.

Sorting is a general algorithm that, except for one step, has nothing to do with the specifics of your domain or application. The critical step is the comparison of items. No sorting algorithm includes, for example, a step that compares the apogees of two rockets—an application needs to supply that step. The Sort() methods and IComparer interface let you supply a specific step to a general sorting algorithm. It is not always the case that TEMPLATE METHOD applies where only the missing step is domain-specific. Sometimes the entire algorithm applies to a specific application domain.

Completing an Algorithm

The TEMPLATE METHOD pattern is similar to the ADAPTER pattern in that both patterns allow one developer to simplify and specify the way in which another developer's code completes a design. In ADAPTER, one developer may specify the interface for an object a design requires. A second developer creates an object that provides the interface the design expects, but using the services of an existing class with a different interface. In TEMPLATE METHOD, one developer may provide a general algorithm while a second developer supplies a key step of the algorithm. Consider the Aster star press that Figure 21.2 shows.

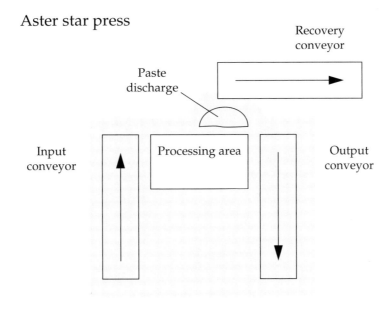

Figure 21.2   An Aster star press comes with input and output conveyors that move star press molds. Oozinoz adds a recovery conveyor that saves discarded star press paste.

A star press from Aster Corporation accepts empty metal molds and presses fireworks stars into them. The machine has hoppers that dispense the chemicals that the machine mixes into a paste and presses into the molds. When the machine shuts down, it stops working on the mold in the processing area and *ushers* any molds on its input conveyor through the processing area to the output, without actually processing the molds. Then the machine discharges its current batch of paste and flushes its processing area with water. The machine orchestrates all this activity using an onboard computer and the `AsterStarPress` class shown in Figure 21.3.

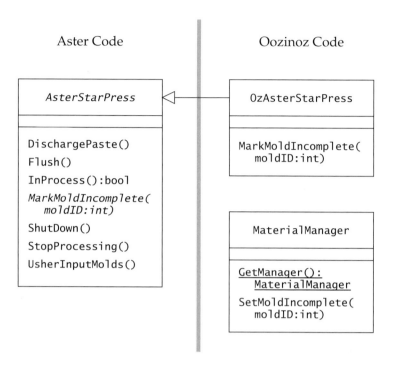

Figure 21.3   Star presses from Aster Corporation come with an abstract class
               that you must subclass to work at Oozinoz.

The Aster star press is smart and independent, and it is also aware that it
may be running in a smart factory with which it must communicate. For
example, the ShutDown() method informs the factory if the mold it was
processing was left incomplete.

```
public virtual void ShutDown()
{
    if (InProcess())
    {
        StopProcessing();
        MarkMoldIncomplete(_currentMoldID);
    }
    UsherInputMolds();
    DischargePaste();
    Flush();
}
```

The MarkMoldIncomplete() method and AsterStarPress class are abstract.
At Oozinoz, you create a subclass that implements the required method
and download this code to the star press computer. You can implement
MarkMoldIncomplete() by passing the information about the incomplete
mold to the MaterialManager singleton that tracks material status.

Challenge 21.2

Write the code for the `MarkMoldIncomplete()` method of the `OzAsterStarPress` class.

```
using System;
using Aster;
using BusinessCore;
public class OzAsterStarPress : AsterStarPress
{
    // challenge!
}
```

A solution appears on page 400.

The Aster star press developers are well aware of how fireworks factories work and have done a good job of communicating with the factory at the right processing points. Nonetheless, it may happen that you need to establish communication at a point that the Aster developers have not foreseen.

TEMPLATE METHOD Hooks

A *hook* is a method call that a developer places in his or her code to give other developers a chance to insert code at a specific spot in a procedure. When you are adapting another developer's code and you need control at a point where you don't currently have it, you can request a hook. An obliging developer can add a method call at the point that you need it. The developer will also usually supply a stubbed-out version of the hook method so that other clients need not necessarily override the hook method.

Consider the Aster star press that discharges its chemical paste and flushes itself with water when shutting down. The press has to discharge this paste to keep it from drying and clogging the machine. At Oozinoz you recover this paste so that you can dice it for use as tiny stars in Roman candles. (A *Roman candle* is a stationary tube that contains a mixture of explosive charges, sparks, and stars.) After the star press discharges the paste, you arrange for a robot to move the paste to a separate conveyor, as Figure 21.2 shows. It is important to remove the paste before the machine flushes its processing area with water. The problem is that you want to gain control between the following two statements in the `ShutDown()` method:

```
DischargePaste();
Flush();
```

You might override `DischargePaste()` with a method that adds a call to collect the paste.

```
public override void DischargePaste()
{
    base.DischargePaste();
    GetFactory().CollectPaste();
}
```

This method effectively inserts a step after discharging paste. The added step uses a `Factory` singleton to collect discarded paste. When the `Shut-Down()` method executes, the factory robot will now collect discarded paste before the `ShutDown()` method flushes the press. Unfortunately, the `DischargePaste()` code is now dangerous because paste collection is a surprising side effect. Developers at Aster will certainly be unaware that you're defining `DischargePaste()` in this way. If they modify their code to discharge paste at a time when you don't want to collect it, an error will occur.

Developers usually strive to solve problems by writing code. But here, the challenge is to solve a problem by communicating with other developers.

Challenge 21.3

Write a note to the developers at Aster, asking for a change that will let you safely collect discarded star paste before the machine flushes its processing area.

A solution appears on page 401.

The step that a subclass supplies in TEMPLATE METHOD may be required to complete the algorithm, or it may be an optional step that hooks in a subclass's code, often at another developer's request. Although the intent of the pattern is to let a separate class define part of an algorithm, you can also apply TEMPLATE METHOD when you refactor an algorithm that appears in multiple methods.

Refactoring to TEMPLATE METHOD

When TEMPLATE METHOD is at work, you will find classes in a hierarchy where a superclass provides the outline of an algorithm and subclasses provide certain steps of the algorithm. You may introduce this arrangement, refactoring to TEMPLATE METHOD, when you find similar algorithms in different methods. Consider the `Machine` and `MachinePlanner` parallel hierarchy that you worked with in Chapter 16, "Factory Method." As Figure 21.4 shows, the `Machine` class provides a CreatePlanner() method as a FACTORY METHOD that returns an appropriate subclass of MachinePlanner.

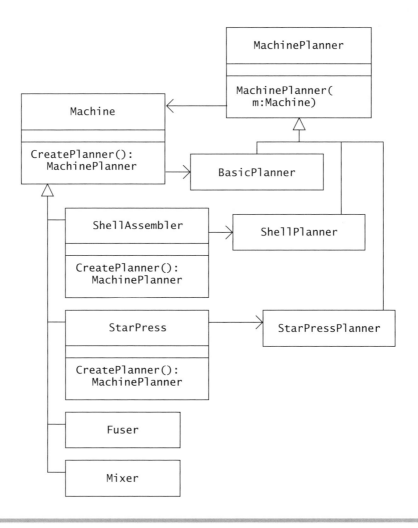

Figure 21.4   A Machine object can create an appropriate MachinePlanner instance for itself.

Two of the subclasses of Machine instantiate specific subclasses from the MachinePlanner hierarchy when asked to create a planner. These classes—ShellAssembler and StarPress—have a common problem in that they want to create a MachinePlanner only on demand.

Looking at the code for these classes, you might notice that the subclasses use similar techniques for lazy-initializing a planner. For example, the ShellAssembler class has a GetPlanner() method that lazy-initializes a _planner attribute.

```
public ShellPlanner GetPlanner()
{
    if (_planner == null)
    {
        _planner = new ShellPlanner(this);
    }
    return _planner;
}
```

In the ShellPlanner class, the _planner attribute is of type ShellPlanner. The StarPress class also has a _planner attribute, but declares it to be of type StarPressPlanner. The GetPlanner() method of the StarPress class also lazy-initializes the planner attribute.

```
public StarPressPlanner GetPlanner()
{
    if (_planner == null)
    {
        _planner = new StarPressPlanner(this);
    }
    return _planner;
}
```

The other subclasses of Machine have similar approaches to creating a planner only when it is first needed. This presents a refactoring opportunity, letting you clean up and reduce the amount of code that you maintain. Suppose that you decide to provide the Machine class with a _planner attribute of type MachinePlanner, removing this attribute from subclasses and eliminating the existing GetPlanner() methods.

Challenge 21.4

Write the code for the GetPlanner() method in the Machine class.

A solution appears on page 401.

You can often refactor your code into an instance of TEMPLATE METHOD by abstracting the outline of the similar methods, moving the outline method up to a superclass, and letting subclasses supply just the step where they differ in their implementation of the algorithm.

Summary

The intent of TEMPLATE METHOD is to define an algorithm in a method, leaving some steps abstract, stubbed-out, or defined in an interface so that other classes can fill them in.

TEMPLATE METHOD may function as a contract between developers. One developer supplies the outline of an algorithm and another developer supplies a certain step of the algorithm. This may be a step that lets the algorithm complete, or it may be a step that the algorithm developer includes to hook in code at specific points in the procedure.

The intent of TEMPLATE METHOD does not imply that you will always write the template method in advance of defining subclasses. You may discover similar methods in an existing hierarchy. In this case, you may be able to distill the outline of an algorithm and move it up to a super-class, applying TEMPLATE METHOD to simplify and organize your code.

CHAPTER 22

STATE

The *state* of an object is a combination of the current values of its attributes. When you call an object's `Set-` method or assign a value to one of the object's variables or properties, you are changing the object's state. Objects also commonly change their own state as their methods execute.

We sometimes use the word *state* to refer to a single, changing attribute of an object. For example, we may say that the state of a machine is up or down. In such a case, the changeable part of an object's state may be the most prominent aspect of its behavior. As a result, logic that depends on the object's state may spread through many of the class's methods. Similar or identical logic may appear many times, creating a maintenance burden.

One way to counter the spread of state-specific logic is to introduce a new group of classes where each class represents a different state. Then you can place state-specific behavior into each of these classes. This is the intent of the STATE pattern: to distribute state-specific logic across classes that represent an object's state.

Modeling States

When you model an object whose state is important, you may find that you have a particular variable that tracks how the object should behave, depending on its state. This variable may appear in complex, cascading `if` statements that focus on how to react to the events that an object can experience. The problem with this approach to modeling state is not just that `if` statements can become complex, but also that when you adjust how you model the state, you often have to adjust `if` statements in several methods. The STATE pattern offers a cleaner, simpler approach using a distributed operation. STATE lets you model states as objects, encapsulating state-specific logic in separate classes. To see STATE at work, it will help to first look at a system that models states without using the STATE pattern. In the next section, we will refactor this code to investigate whether the STATE pattern can improve the design.

Consider the software at Oozinoz that models the state of a carousel door. A *carousel* is a large, smart rack that accepts material through a doorway and stores it according to a barcode ID on the material. The door operates with a single button. If the door is closed, touching the button makes the door start opening. If you touch the button again before the door opens fully, the door will begin closing. If you let the door open all the way, it will automatically begin closing after a two-second timeout. You can prevent this by touching the button again when the door is open. Figure 22.1 shows the states and transitions of the carousel's door.

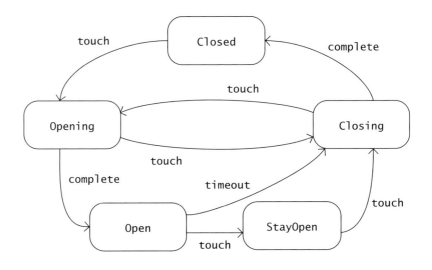

Figure 22.1   A carousel door provides "one-touch" control with a single button that changes the door's state.

The diagram in Figure 22.1 is a UML *state machine*. Such diagrams can be much more informative than a corresponding textual description.

Challenge 22.1

Suppose you open the door and place a material bin in the doorway. Is there a way to make the door begin closing without waiting for it to time out?

A solution appears on page 402.

You can supply the carousel software with a `Door` object that the carousel software will update with state changes in the carousel. Figure 22.2 shows the `Door` class.

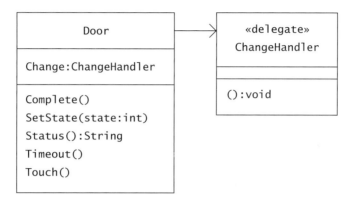

Figure 22.2   The Door class models a carousel door, relying on state change events sent by the carousel machine.

The `Door` class maintains a `ChangeHandler` variable so that clients such as a GUI can observe a door. The class definition establishes the states that a door can enter.

```
using System;
namespace Carousel
{
    public class Door
    {
        public const int CLOSED   = -1;
        public const int OPENING  = -2;
        public const int OPEN     = -3;
        public const int CLOSING  = -4;
        public const int STAYOPEN = -5;
        //
        public ChangeHandler Change;
        private int _state = CLOSED;

    }
    // ...
}
```

Not surprisingly, a textual description of the state of a door depends on the door's state.

```
public String Status()
{
    switch (_state)
    {
        case OPENING :
            return "Opening";
        case OPEN :
            return "Open";
        case CLOSING :
            return "Closing";
        case STAYOPEN :
            return "StayOpen";
        default :
            return "Closed";
    }
}
```

When a user touches the carousel's "one-touch" button, the carousel generates a call to a Door object's Touch() method. The Door code for a state transition mimics the information in Figure 22.1.

```
public void Touch()
{
    if (_state == CLOSED)
    {
        SetState(OPENING);
    }
    else if (_state == OPENING || _state == STAYOPEN)
    {
        SetState(CLOSING);
    }
    else if (_state == OPEN)
    {
        SetState(STAYOPEN);
    }
    else if (_state == CLOSING)
    {
        SetState(OPENING);
    }
}
```

The SetState() method of the Door class notifies observers of the door's change.

```
private void SetState(int state)
{
    this._state = state;
    if (Change != null) Change();
}
```

Challenge 22.2

Write the code for the `Complete()` and `Timeout()` methods of the `Door` class.

A solution appears on page 402.

Refactoring to STATE

The code for `Door` is somewhat complex because the use of the `_state` variable is spread throughout the class. In addition, you might find it difficult to compare the state transition methods, particularly `Touch()`, with the state machine in Figure 22.1. The STATE pattern can help you simplify this code. To apply STATE in this example, make each state of the door a separate class, as shown in Figure 22.3.

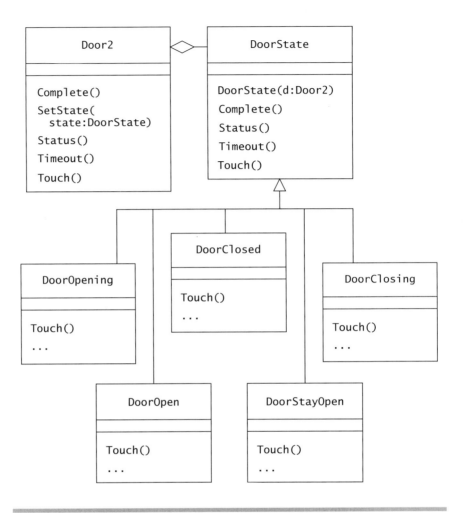

Figure 22.3   This diagram shows a door's states as classes in an
                arrangement that mirrors the door's state machine.

The refactoring shown in Figure 22.3 creates a special class for each state
that the door might be in. Each of these classes contains the logic for
responding to a touch of the "one-touch" button while the door is in a
specific state. For example, the DoorClosed.cs file contains the following
code:

```
namespace Carousel
{
    public class DoorClosed : DoorState
    {

        public DoorClosed(Door2 door) : base (door)
        {
        }

        public override void Touch()
        {
            _door.SetState(_door.OPENING);
        }
    }
}
```

The Touch() method in the DoorClosed class informs a Door2 object of the door's new state. The Door2 object is the object received by the DoorClosed constructor. The design at play here requires each state object to hold a reference to a Door2 object so that the state object can inform the door of state transitions. This design approach requires a state object to refer to a particular door, so a state object can apply only to a single door. The next section addresses how to modify this design so that a single set of states would suffice for any number of doors. The current design requires the generation of a Door2 object to be accompanied by the creation of a suite of states that belong to the door.

```
using System;
namespace Carousel
{
    public class Door2
    {
        public readonly DoorState CLOSED;
        public readonly DoorState CLOSING;
        public readonly DoorState OPEN;
        public readonly DoorState OPENING;
        public readonly DoorState STAYOPEN;

        public ChangeHandler Change;
        private DoorState _state;

        public Door2()
        {
            CLOSED    = new DoorClosed(this);
            CLOSING   = new DoorClosing(this);
            OPEN      = new DoorOpen(this);
            OPENING   = new DoorOpening(this);
            STAYOPEN  = new DoorStayOpen(this);
            _state = CLOSED;
        }
        // ...
    }
}
```

The abstract `DoorState` class requires subclasses to implement `Touch()`.
This is consistent with the state machine, in which every state has a
`Touch()` transition. The `DoorState` class stubs out other transitions so that
subclasses can override or ignore irrelevant messages.

```csharp
using System;
namespace Carousel
{
    public abstract class DoorState
    {
        protected Door2 _door;

        public DoorState(Door2 door)
        {
            _door = door;
        }

        public abstract void Touch();
        public virtual void Complete() {}
        public virtual void Timeout() {}

        public String Status()
        {
            return this.GetType().Name;
        }

    }
}
```

Note that the `Status()` method works for all the states and is much simpler than its predecessor before refactoring.

The new design doesn't change the role of a `Door2` object in receiving state
changes from the carousel, but now the `Door2` object simply passes these
changes to its current _state object.

```csharp
using System;
namespace Carousel
{
    public class Door2
    {
        // variables and constructor ...

        public void Touch()
        {
            _state.Touch();
        }

        public void Complete()
        {
            _state.Complete();
        }

        public void Timeout()
        {
            _state.Timeout();
        }
```

```
            public String Status()
            {
                return _state.Status();
            }

            internal void SetState(DoorState state)
            {
                this._state = state;
                if (Change != null) Change();
            }
        }
    }
```

The Touch(), Complete(), Timeout(), and Status() methods show the role
of polymorphism in this design. Each of these methods is still a kind of
switch. In each case, the operation is fixed, but the class of the receiver—
the class of state—varies. The rule of polymorphism is that the method
that actually executes depends on the operation signature and the class of
the receiver. What happens when you call Touch()? The answer depends
on the door's state. The code still effectively performs a switch, but by
relying on polymorphism, the code is simpler than before.

The SetState() method in the Door2 class is now used by subclasses of
DoorState. These subclasses closely resemble their counterparts in the
state machine in Figure 22.1. For example, the code for DoorOpen handles
calls to Touch() and Timeout(), the two transitions from the Open state in
the state machine.

```
        namespace Carousel
        {
            public class DoorOpen : DoorState
            {
                public DoorOpen(Door2 door) : base (door)
                {
                }

                public override void Touch()
                {
                    _door.SetState(_door.STAYOPEN);
                }

                public override void Timeout()
                {
                    _door.SetState(_door.CLOSING);
                }
            }
        }
```

Challenge 22.3

Write the code for `DoorClosing.cs`.

A solution appears on page 402.

The new design leads to much simpler code, but you might feel a bit dissatisfied that the "constants" the `Door` class uses are actually local variables.

Making States Constant

The STATE pattern moves state-specific logic across classes that represent an object's state. However, STATE does not specify how to manage communication and dependencies between state objects and a central object to which they apply. In the previous design, each state class accepted a `Door` object in its constructor. The state objects retain this object and use it to update the door's state. This is not necessarily a bad design, but it does create the effect that instantiating a `Door` object causes the instantiation of a complete set of `DoorState` objects. You might prefer a design that created a single, static set of `DoorState` objects and required the `Door` state to manage all updates resulting from state changes.

To make the state objects constant, one approach is to have the state classes simply identify the next state, leaving it to the `Door` class to actually update its state variable. In this design, the `Door` class's `Touch()` method, for example, updates the _state variable as follows:

```
public void Touch()
{
    _state = _state.Touch();
}
```

Note that the `Door` class's `Touch()` method's return value is `void`. Subclasses of `DoorState` will also implement `Touch()`, but these implementations will provide a `DoorState` value in their returns. For example, the `DoorOpen` class's `Touch()` method now reads as follows:

```
public override DoorState Touch()
{
    return DoorState.STAYOPEN;
}
```

In this design, the `DoorState` objects do not retain a reference to a `Door` object, so the application needs only a single instance of each `DoorState` object.

Another approach to making the DoorState objects constants is to pass around the central Door object during state transitions. You can add a Door parameter to the Complete(), Timeout(), and Touch() state change methods. These methods receive the central Door object as a parameter and update its state without retaining a reference to it.

Challenge 22.4

Complete the class diagram in Figure 22.4 to show a design that lets DoorState objects be constants and that passes around a Door object during state transitions.

A solution appears on page 403.

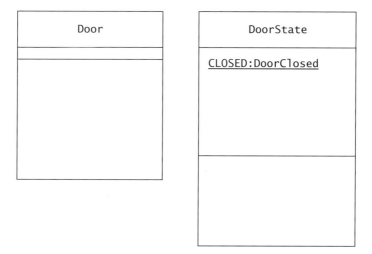

Figure 22.4   Complete this diagram to show a design that makes door states constants.

When you apply the STATE pattern, you have complete freedom in how your design arranges for the communication of state changes. State classes can retain a reference to the central object whose state is being modeled. Alternatively, you can pass this object around during transitions. You can also make state subclasses mere information providers that determine the next state but that do not update the central object. Which approach you use may depend on the context of your application or on esthetics. Regardless of how your design manages state transitions, the power of the STATE pattern is that the logic for any given state is central-ized in a single class.

Summary

Generally speaking, the state of an object depends on the collective value of the object's instance variables. In some cases, most of an object's attributes are fairly static once set, and one attribute is dynamic and plays a prominent role in the class's logic. This attribute may represent the state of the entire object and may even be named "state."

A dominant state variable may occur when an object is modeling a real-world entity whose state is important, such as a transaction or machine. In such a case, logic that depends on the object's state may appear in many methods. You may be able to simplify such code by moving state-specific behavior to a hierarchy of state objects. This lets each state class contain the behavior for one state in the domain. It also allows the state classes to correspond directly to states in a state machine.

To handle transitions between states, you can let the central object retain references to a set of states. Alternatively, you can pass around—in state transition calls—the central object whose state is changing. You can also make state classes information providers that only indicate a following state without actually updating the central object. Regardless of how you manage state transitions, the STATE pattern simplifies your code by dis-tributing an operation across a collection of classes that represents an object's different states.

CHAPTER 23

STRATEGY

A *strategy* is a plan or approach for achieving an aim given certain input conditions. A strategy is thus similar to an algorithm, a procedure that produces outputs from a set of inputs. Usually there is more latitude in how a "strategy" pursues its goal than in an "algorithm." This latitude also means that strategies often appear in groups or families of alternatives.

When multiple strategies appear in a computer program, the code may become complex. The logic that surrounds the strategies must select a strategy, and this selection code may itself become complex. The execution of various strategies may also lie along different code paths, but in code that all resides in a single method. If the choice and execution of various strategies leads to complex code, you can apply the STRATEGY pattern to clean it up.

The intent of STRATEGY is to encapsulate alternative approaches (that is, strategies) in separate classes that each implement a common operation. The strategic operation defines the inputs and output of a strategy, but leaves implementation up to the individual classes. Classes that implement the various approaches implement the same operation and are thus interchangeable, presenting different strategies but the same interface to clients. The STRATEGY pattern allows a family of strategies to coexist without their code intermingling. STRATEGY also separates the logic for selecting a strategy from the strategies themselves.

Modeling Strategies

The STRATEGY pattern helps organize and simplify code by encapsulating different approaches to a problem in different classes. To see STRATEGY at work, it is useful to first look at a program that models strategies without applying STRATEGY. In the next section, we will refactor this code, applying STRATEGY to improve the quality of the code.

Consider the advertising policy at Oozinoz that suggests a fireworks item to purchase when the customer visits the Oozinoz Web site or calls the call center. Oozinoz uses two commercial, off-the-shelf recommendation engines to help choose the right item to offer to a customer. The Customer class chooses and applies one of these engines to decide on which item to recommend to a customer.

One of the recommendation engines, the Re18 engine, suggests a purchase based on the customer's similarity to other customers. For this to work, the customer must have "registered" and given information about likes and dislikes regarding fireworks and other entertainments.

If the customer has not registered, Oozinoz uses a LikeMyStuff engine from another vendor that suggests a purchase based on the customer's recent purchases. If there is not enough data for either engine to function, the advertising software picks an item at random. However, a special promotion can override all these considerations to promote a specific item that Oozinoz wants to sell. Figure 23.1 shows the classes that collaborate to suggest an item to a customer.

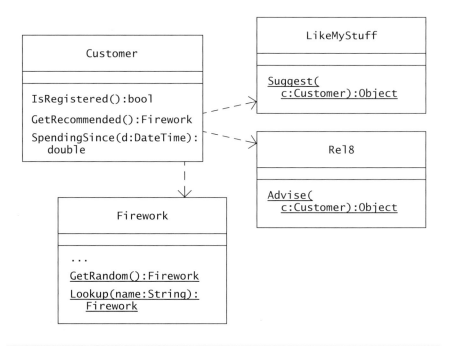

Figure 23.1   The Customer class relies on other classes for recommendations, including two off-the-shelf recommendation engines.

The LikeMyStuff and Re18 engines both accept a Customer object and both suggest something to advertise to the customer. Both engines are configured at Oozinoz to work for fireworks, although LikeMyStuff requires a database and Re18 works entirely from an object model. The code for GetRecommended() in class Customer mirrors Oozinoz's advertising policies.

```
public Firework GetRecommended()
{
    // if we're promoting a particular firework, return it
    try
    {
        String s = FileFinder.GetFileName(
            "config", "strategy.xml");
        StreamReader r = new StreamReader(s);
        XmlSerializer xs =
            new XmlSerializer(typeof(String));
        String promotedName = (String) xs.Deserialize(r);
        r.Close();

        Firework f = Firework.Lookup(promotedName);
        if (f != null)
        {
            return f;
        }
    }
    catch {}

    // if registered, compare to other customers
    if (IsRegistered())
    {
        return (Firework) Re18.Advise(this);
    }
    // check spending over the last year
    if (SpendingSince(DateTime.Now.AddYears(-1)) > 1000)
    {
        return (Firework) LikeMyStuff.Suggest(this);
    }
    // oh well!
    return Firework.GetRandom();
}
```

This code is in the lib/Recommendations directory of the Oozinoz codebase available from www.oozinoz.com. The GetRecommended() method expects that if a promotion is on, it will be named in a strategy.xml file in a config directory. Such a file would look as follows:

```
<?xml version="1.0" encoding="utf-8"?>
<string>Byebaby</string>
```

It there is no such file, the GetRecommended() code will use the Re18 engine if the customer is registered. If there is no promotion strategy file and the customer is not registered, the code will use the LikeMyStuff engine if the customer has spent a certain amount of money in the past year. If no better recommendation is possible, the code selects and recommends an item at random. The method works, and you might feel like this is not the worst code you've ever seen. But we can make it better.

Refactoring to STRATEGY

The GetRecommended() method presents several problems. First, it's long—so long that comments have to explain its various parts. Short methods are easy to understand, seldom need explanation, and are usually preferable to long methods. In addition, the GetRecommended() method chooses a strategy and then executes it; these are two different and separable functions. We can clean up this code by applying STRATEGY. To do so:

- Create an interface that defines the strategic operation.

- Implement the interface with classes that represent each strategy.

- Refactor the code to select and use an instance of the right strategic class.

Suppose that you create an Advisor interface as shown in Figure 23.2.

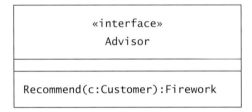

«interface»
Advisor

| |

| Recommend(c:Customer):Firework |

Figure 23.2   The Advisor interface defines an operation that various classes can implement with different strategies.

The Advisor interface declares, essentially, that a class that implements the interface can accept a customer and recommend a fireworks item. The next step in refactoring the Customer class's GetRecommended() code is to create classes that each represent one of the recommendation strategies. Each class will provide a different implementation of the Recommend() method that the Advisor interface specifies.

Challenge 23.1

Fill in the class diagram in Figure 23.3 that shows the recommendation logic refactored into a collection of strategy classes.

A solution appears on page 403.

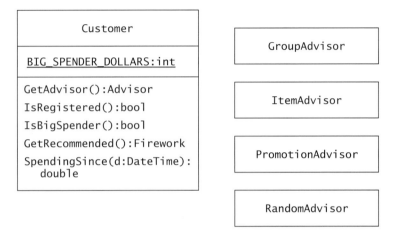

Figure 23.3   Complete this diagram to show a refactoring of the
recommendation software, with strategies appearing as
implementations of a common interface.

With the strategy classes in place, the next step is to move code from the existing `GetRecommended()` method of the `Customer` class into the new classes. The two simplest classes will be `GroupAdvisor` and `ItemAdvisor`. They must simply wrap calls into the off-the-shelf recommendation engines. Interfaces can define only instance methods, so `GroupAdvisor` and `ItemAdvisor` must be instantiated to support the `Advisor` interface. However, only one such object is ever necessary, and so these classes define publicly-accessible singletons. Figure 23.4 shows the design of these classes.

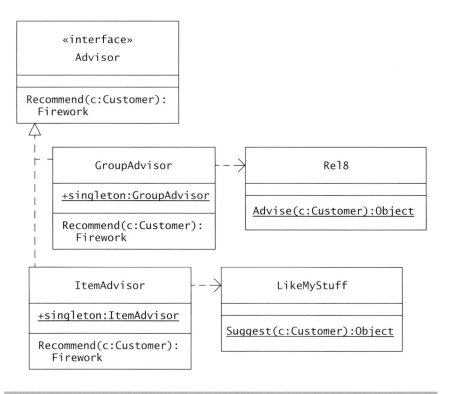

Figure 23.4   Implementations of the Advisor interface provide the strategic
               Recommend() operation, relying on off-the-shelf engines.

The advisor classes translate calls to Recommend() into the interfaces that
the underlying engines require. For example, the GroupAdvisor class
translates calls to Recommend() into the Advise() interface that the Rel8
engine requires.

```
public Firework Recommend(Customer c)
{
    return (Firework) Rel8.Advise(c);
}
```

Challenge 23.2

In addition to SINGLETON and STRATEGY, what pattern appears in the
GroupAdvisor and ItemAdvisor classes?

A solution appears on page 404.

The GroupAdvisor and ItemAdvisor classes work by translating a call to
the Recommend() method into a call to a recommendation engine. We also
need to create a PromotionAdvisor class and a RandomAdvisor class by

refactoring code from the current `GetRecommended()` method of the Customer class. As with the `GroupAdvisor` and `ItemAdvisor` classes, the remaining classes will each supply a singleton that offers the `Recommend()` operation. We might correspondingly give each class a single, private constructor to prevent other classes from instantiating it.

The constructor for `PromotionAdvisor` should investigate whether a promotion is on. You might then supply this class with a `HasItem()` method that indicates whether there is a promoted item.

```
public class PromotionAdvisor : Advisor
{
    public static readonly PromotionAdvisor singleton =
        new PromotionAdvisor();
    private Firework _promoted;

    private PromotionAdvisor()
    {
        try
        {
            String s = FileFinder.GetFileName(
                "config", "strategy.xml");
            StreamReader r = new StreamReader(s);
            XmlSerializer xs =
                new XmlSerializer(typeof(String));
            String name = (String) xs.Deserialize(r);
            r.Close();
            _promoted = Firework.Lookup(name);
        }
        catch {}
    }

    public bool HasItem()
    {
        return _promoted != null;
    }

    public Firework Recommend(Customer c)
    {
        return _promoted;
    }
}
```

The `RandomAdvisor` class is simple:

```
public class RandomAdvisor : Advisor
{
    public static readonly RandomAdvisor singleton =
        new RandomAdvisor();

    private RandomAdvisor()
    {
    }

    public Firework Recommend(Customer c)
    {
        return Firework.GetRandom();
    }
}
```

The refactoring of Customer separates the *selection* of a strategy (or "advisor") from the *use* of the strategy. An _advisor attribute of a Customer object holds the current choice of the strategy to apply. The refactored Customer class lazy-initializes this attribute with logic that reflects Oozinoz's advertising policies.

```
private Advisor GetAdvisor()
{
    if (_advisor == null)
    {
        if (PromotionAdvisor.singleton.HasItem())
        {
            _advisor = PromotionAdvisor.singleton;
        }
        else if (IsRegistered())
        {
            _advisor = GroupAdvisor.singleton;
        }
        else if (IsBigSpender())
        {
            _advisor = ItemAdvisor.singleton;
        }
        else
        {
            _advisor = RandomAdvisor.singleton;
        }
    }
    return _advisor;
}
```

```
private bool IsBigSpender()
{
    return SpendingSince(DateTime.Now.AddYears(-1)) >
        BIG_SPENDER_DOLLARS;
}
```

Challenge 23.3

Write the new code for `Customer.GetRecommended()`.

A solution appears on page 404.

Challenge 23.4

In the new design, four singletons implement the `Advisor` interface in four ways, encapsulating four strategies. Is the presence of multiple, similar singletons reminiscent of a design pattern?

A solution appears on page 404.

Comparing STRATEGY and STATE

The refactored code consists almost entirely of simple methods in simple classes. This is an advantage in its own right and makes adding new strategies easy. The refactoring relies primarily on the idea of distributing an operation across a related group of classes. In this regard, STRATEGY is identical to STATE. In fact, many developers wonder whether these are really different patterns.

On one hand, in the real world, strategies (like recommending a fireworks item) and states (like a carousel door with a one-touch control button) are clearly different ideas. This real difference leads to different problems in modeling states and strategies. For example, transitions are important when modeling states, but usually irrelevant when choosing a strategy. Another difference is that STRATEGY might allow a client to select or provide a strategy, an idea that rarely applies to STATE.

On the other hand, the differences in modeling states and strategies may seem subtle. Certainly, the reliance on polymorphism makes STATE and STRATEGY appear almost identical structurally.

Either way, if you decide that these are, or are not, two separate patterns, you will be in good company.

Comparing STRATEGY and TEMPLATE METHOD

Chapter 21, "TEMPLATE METHOD," described sorting as an example of the TEMPLATE METHOD pattern. You can use the Sort() algorithm from the Array or ArrayList classes to sort any list of objects, so long as you supply a step to compare two objects. But you might argue that when you supply a comparison step to a sorting algorithm, you are changing the strategy. For instance, if you are selling rockets, presenting them sorted by price is a different marketing strategy than presenting them sorted by thrust.

Challenge 23.5

Provide an argument that the Array.Sort() method provides an example of TEMPLATE METHOD, or that it is an example of STRATEGY.

A solution appears on page 405.

Summary

Logic that models alternative strategies may appear in a single class, often in a single method. Such methods may be too complicated and may mix strategy selection logic with the execution of a strategy.

To simplify such code, create a group of classes, one for each strategy. Define an operation and distribute it across these classes. This lets each class encapsulate one strategy, creating simpler code. You also need to arrange for the client that uses a strategy to be able to select one. This selection code may be complex even after refactoring, but you should be able to reduce this code so that it is nearly equivalent to pseudocode that describes strategy selection in the problem domain.

Typically, a client will hold a selected strategy in a context variable. This makes the execution of a strategy a simple matter of forwarding the strategic operation call to the context, using polymorphism to execute the right strategy. By encapsulating alternative strategies in separate classes that each implement a common operation, the STRATEGY pattern lets you create clean, simple code that models a family of approaches to solving a problem.

CHAPTER 24

COMMAND

The ordinary way to cause a method to execute is to call it. There may be times, though, when you cannot control the timing of or the context in which a method should execute. In these situations, you can encapsulate a method inside an object. By storing the information necessary for invoking a method in an object, you can pass the method as a parameter, allowing a client or service to determine when to invoke the method.

Fortunately, delegates in C# expressly support the ability to encapsulate a method in an object. However, this is a good example of how language support does not eliminate the role of patterns. Although C# provides direct support for the COMMAND pattern, developers must still understand how to employ the purpose of the pattern, which is to encapsulate a request in an object.

A Classic Example—Menu Commands

Architectures that include support for menus usually apply the COMMAND pattern. Each menu item is outfitted with an object that knows how to behave when the user clicks the item. This design keeps GUI logic and application logic separate. The .NET framework applies this approach, associating a delegate type variable with each menu item.

A delegate type variable in C# retains a list of one or more delegate instances that contain references to methods. For example, the `MenuItem` class in the .NET FCL has a `Click` variable whose type is the `EventHandler` delegate type. When a user clicks a mouse on a menu item, the appropriate `MenuItem` object interprets this hardware event by invoking its `Click` delegate. This, in turn, invokes any methods that have been stored in the `Click` delegate. The following code shows the construction of a menu that includes an "Exit" menu item within a "File" menu:

```
using System;
using System.Windows.Forms;
public class ShowCommand : Form
{
    public ShowCommand()
    {
        MenuItem exitItem = new MenuItem();
        exitItem.Text = "Exit";
        exitItem.Click += // challenge!

        MenuItem fileItem = new MenuItem();
        fileItem.Text = "File";
        fileItem.MenuItems.Add(exitItem);

        Menu = new MainMenu();
        Menu.MenuItems.Add(fileItem);
        Text = "Show Command";
    }

    static void Main()
    {
        Application.Run(new ShowCommand());
    }

    // challenge: anything else?
}
```

Suppose you want to execute `Application.Exit()` to close the application when a user clicks the "Exit" menu item. Essentially, you want the menu item to invoke `Application.Exit()`. You can arrange this by adding a delegate instance to the menu item's `Click` delegate. However, you must respect that the `Click` delegate's type is `EventHandler`. The `EventHandler` delegate type declares a `void` return value and two arguments whose types are `object` and `EventArgs`.

Challenge 24.1

Fill in the code in the `ShowCommand` program to assign a delegate instance to the menu item's Click variable.

A solution appears on page 405.

The architecture of .NET menus applies COMMAND, encapsulating requests for action in instances of the `EventHandler` delegate type. This approach provides an OO version of what is sometimes called a *callback* scheme. Menu items call back your code when a user clicks. In menus, the need for this callback is timing. The menu item knows when it is clicked, and application code knows how to respond. There are also times when you need your code to be called under certain circumstances, such as when a service needs to execute code before and after your code executes. In such cases, you can apply the COMMAND pattern to allow code to run within a service.

Using COMMAND to Supply a Service

A common programming problem arises when using resources that must be released when they are no longer needed. For example, code that uses a database resource often reads as follows:

```
OleDbConnection conn = CreateConnection();
try
{
    conn.Open();
    // use connection...
}
finally
{
    if (conn != null)
    {
        conn.Dispose();
    }
}
```

When the logic that uses the database connection terminates—either normally or through an exception—this code releases the resourced used by the connection. The situation of needing to release a resource is so common that C# builds in special syntax to support it. The following code is precisely equivalent to, although more compact than, the try/finally code:

```
using (OleDbConnection conn = CreateConnection())
{
    conn.Open();
    // use connection...
}
```

The using statement helps compact the code, but a problem remains that the logic of creating and releasing a resource is quite different from the logic of using a resource in an application. You may have seen codebases that have try/finally or using statements everywhere a system resource is used. The COMMAND pattern will let you replace such code with a single resource lending service.

Chapter 2, "Introducing Interfaces," compares delegates and interfaces and uses an example of "lending" a database reader. The DataServices class in the DataLayer namespace provides a LendReader() method whose code is as follows:

```
public static object LendReader(
    string sel, BorrowReader borrower)
{
    using (OleDbConnection conn = CreateConnection())
    {
        conn.Open();
        OleDbCommand c = new OleDbCommand(sel, conn);
        OleDbDataReader r = c.ExecuteReader();
        return borrower(r);
    }
}
```

This code acquires a database connection, creates a reader from it, lets client code use the reader, and releases the reader. In other words, this method executes before *and* after client code—by applying the COMMAND pattern. The parameters for LendReader() are a SQL select statement (in a string) and an instance of the BorrowReader delegate type. That delegate type's declaration is:

```
public delegate object BorrowReader(IDataReader reader);
```

To use the LendReader() method, a developer can instantiate the Borrow-Reader delegate type with a method that accepts a database reader. For example, the following code (from the DataServices class) converts a select statement into a DataTable object:

```
public static DataTable CreateTable(string select)
{
    return (DataTable) LendReader(
        select, new BorrowReader(CreateTable));
}
internal static object CreateTable(IDataReader reader)
{
    DataTable table = new DataTable();
    for (int i = 0; i < reader.FieldCount; i++)
    {
        table.Columns.Add(
        reader.GetName(i), reader.GetFieldType(i));
    }
    while (reader.Read())
    {
        DataRow dr = table.NewRow();
        for (int i = 0; i < reader.FieldCount; i++)
        {
            dr[i] = reader.GetValue(i);
        }
        table.Rows.Add(dr);
    }
    return table;
}
```

The public CreateTable() method creates a COMMAND object from the internal CreateTable() method when the first method instantiates the BorrowReader delegate type. This design lets LendReader() do work before and after executing the command.

Now suppose that you want to add a new service that returns the time it takes for a method to execute. A class that supplies this service, along with a test, might look as follows:

```
using System;
delegate void Command();
class ShowTimerCommand
{
    static void Main()
    {
        Console.WriteLine(TimeThis(new Command(Snooze)));
    }
    static void Snooze()
    {
        System.Threading.Thread.Sleep(2000);
    }
    static TimeSpan TimeThis(Command c)
    {
        // challenge!
        return DateTime.Now.Subtract(t1);
    }
}
```

Challenge 24.2

Complete the TimeThis() method so that it will measure the execution time of a supplied command.

A solution appears on page 406.

The mechanics of delegates are always the same, but when you use delegates to apply the COMMAND pattern, the intent you have in mind may vary. Menu items use the COMMAND pattern to let client code respond to an event. Services use COMMAND to let client code execute within context-setting code provided by the service. Another use of COMMAND is as a hook, allowing clients to provide a step within an algorithm. In this scenario, the COMMAND pattern can function as an alternative to the TEMPLATE METHOD pattern.

COMMAND Hooks

Chapter 21, "Template Method," introduced the Aster star press, a smart machine that includes code that relies on TEMPLATE METHOD. The star press's code lets you override a method that marks a mold as incomplete if the mold is in process when the press shuts down.

The AsterStarPress class is abstract, requiring you to subclass it with a class that has a MarkMoldIncomplete() method. The ShutDown() method of

AsterStarPress relies on this method to ensure that your domain object knows the mold is incomplete.

```
public virtual void ShutDown()
{
    if (InProcess())
    {
        StopProcessing();
        MarkMoldIncomplete(_currentMoldID);
    }
    UsherInputMolds();
    DischargePaste();
    Flush();
}
```

You might find it inconvenient to subclass AsterStarPress with a class that you have to move to the star press's onboard computer. Suppose that you ask the developers at Aster to provide the hook in a different way, using the COMMAND pattern. Figure 24.1 shows a Hook delegate that the AsterStarPress class can use, letting you parameterize the star press code at runtime.

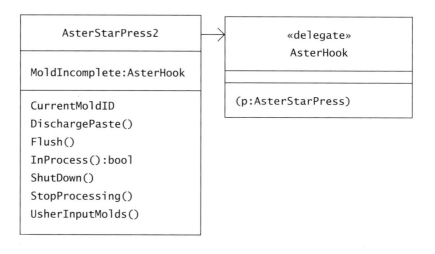

Figure 24.1   A class can provide a hook—a way to insert custom code—by
                invoking a supplied delegate at a specific point in a procedure.

In the original AsterStarPress class, the ShutDown() method relied on a step that subclasses would provide. In the new design, the ShutDown() method now uses a hook to execute client code after processing stops but before completing the shutdown process.

```
public virtual void ShutDown()
{
    if (InProcess())
    {
        StopProcessing();
        // challenge!
    }
    UsherInputMolds();
    DischargePaste();
    Flush();
}
```

Challenge 24.3

Complete the code for the new ShutDown() method.

A solution appears on page 406.

The COMMAND pattern affords an alternative design to a TEMPLATE METHOD for hooks, and is similar in intent or structure to several other patterns.

COMMAND in Relation to Other Patterns

COMMAND is similar to INTERPRETER. The section titled "An Interpreter Example" in Chapter 25 compares them. COMMAND is also similar to a pattern in which a client knows when an action is required, but doesn't know exactly which operation to call.

Challenge 24.4

Which pattern addresses the situation where a client knows *when* to create an object, but doesn't know which class to instantiate?

A solution appears on page 407.

In addition to bearing similarities to other patterns, COMMAND often collaborates with other patterns. For example, you might combine COMMAND and MEDIATOR in an MVC design. Chapter 19, "Memento," shows an example of this. The Visualization class handles GUI control logic, but passes off any model-related logic to a mediator. For example, the Visualization class uses the following code to lazy-initialize its "Undo" button:

```
        protected Button UndoButton()
        {
            if (_undoButton == null)
            {
                _undoButton = new Button();
                // ...
                _undoButton.Text = "Undo";
                _undoButton.Click +=
                    new System.EventHandler(_mediator.Undo);
                _undoButton.Enabled = false;
            }
            return _undoButton;
        }
```

This code applies COMMAND, packaging an Undo() method in an instance of the EventHandler delegate type. This code also applies MEDIATOR, letting a central object mediate events that pertain to an underlying object model. For the Undo() method to work, the mediator code has to restore a previous version of the simulated factory, bringing up the opportunity to apply one more pattern that often accompanies COMMAND.

Challenge 24.5

Which pattern provides for the storage and restoration of an object's state?

A solution appears on page 407.

Summary

The COMMAND pattern lets you encapsulate a request in an object, allowing you to manage method calls as objects, passing them and invoking them when the timing or conditions are right. Delegates in C# provide the mechanics to support COMMAND, but you may use delegates for a variety of intents. A classic example of the usefulness of COMMAND comes with menus. Menu items know *when* to execute an action, but don't know which method to call. COMMAND lets you parameterize a menu with method calls that correspond to menu labels.

Another use for COMMAND is to allow the execution of client code in the context of a service. A service often runs code both before and after invoking client code. Finally, in addition to controlling the timing or context in which a method executes, the COMMAND pattern can provide a clean mechanism for providing hooks, allowing optional client code to execute as part of an algorithm.

COMMAND encapsulates a request in an object, so that anything that you can do with an object, you can do with a method encapsulated in a delegate instance. Perhaps because this idea is so fundamental, COMMAND has interesting relationships to several other patterns. COMMAND can provide an alternative to TEMPLATE METHOD, and COMMAND often collaborates with MEDIATOR and MEMENTO.

CHAPTER 25

INTERPRETER

As with the COMMAND pattern, the INTERPRETER pattern produces an executable object. The patterns differ in that INTERPRETER involves the creation of a class hierarchy in which each class implements (or *interprets*) a common operation in a way that matches the class's name. In this regard, INTERPRETER is similar to the STATE and STRATEGY patterns. In INTERPRETER, STATE, and STRATEGY, a common operation appears throughout a collection of classes, with each class implementing the operation in a different way.

The INTERPRETER pattern is also similar to the COMPOSITE pattern that defines a common interface for individual items and groups of items. COMPOSITE does not require different, interesting ways of forming groups, although it allows this. For example, the ProcessComponent hierarchy in Chapter 5, "Composite," allows sequences and alternations of process flows. In INTERPRETER, the idea that there are different types of composition is essential. The way that a class composes other components defines how an INTERPRETER class will implement (that is, interpret) a distributed operation. The intent of the INTERPRETER pattern is to let you compose executable objects according to a set of composition rules that you define.

An INTERPRETER Example

The robots that Oozinoz uses to move material along a processing line come with an interpreter that controls the robot and that has limited control of machines on the line. You might think of interpreters as programming languages, but the INTERPRETER pattern has at its heart a collection of classes that allow for the composition of instructions. The Oozinoz robot interpreter comes as a hierarchy of classes that encapsulate robot commands. At the head of the hierarchy is an abstract Command class. Distributed across the hierarchy is an Execute() operation. Figure 25.1 shows the Robot class and two of the commands the robot interpreter supports.

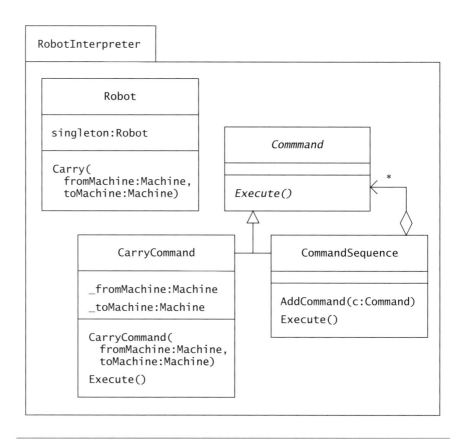

Figure 25.1   An interpreter hierarchy provides for runtime programming of
a factory robot.

A glance at Figure 25.1 might suggest that the COMMAND pattern is at
work in this design, with a Command class at the top of the hierarchy. However, the COMMAND pattern has the intent of encapsulating a method in
an object. The Command hierarchy in Figure 25.1 doesn't do that. Rather,
this hierarchy's design requires Command subclasses to reinterpret the
meaning of the Execute() operation. This is the intent of INTERPRETER: to
allow you to compose executable objects.

A typical INTERPRETER hierarchy will include more than two subclasses,
and we will extend the Command hierarchy shortly. The two classes shown
in Figure 25.1 are sufficient for an initial example as follows:

```
using System;
using Machines;
using RobotInterpreter;
public class ShowInterpreter
{
    public static void Main()
    {
        MachineComposite dublin = ExampleMachine.Dublin();
```

```
            ShellAssembler sa = (ShellAssembler)
                dublin.Find("ShellAssembler:3302");
            StarPress sp = (StarPress)
                dublin.Find("StarPress:3404");
            UnloadBuffer ub = (UnloadBuffer)
                dublin.Find("UnloadBuffer:3501");

            sa.Load(new Bin(11011));
            sp.Load(new Bin(11015));

            CarryCommand c1 = new CarryCommand(sa, ub);
            CarryCommand c2 = new CarryCommand(sp, ub);

            CommandSequence seq = new CommandSequence();
            seq.AddCommand(c1);
            seq.AddCommand(c2);

            seq.Execute();
        }
    }
```

This demonstration code causes a factory robot to move two bins of material from operational machines to an unload buffer. The code works with a machine composite returned by the Dublin() method of the ExampleMachine class. This data model represents a factory planned for a new Oozinoz facility in Dublin, Ireland. The code locates three machines within this factory, loads material bins onto two of them, and then builds up commands from the Command hierarchy. The last statement of the program calls the Execute() method of a CommandSequence object. This causes the robot to take the actions contained in the seq command.

A CommandSequence object interprets the Execute() operation by forwarding the call to each subcommand.

```
using System;
using System.Collections;
namespace RobotInterpreter
{
    public class CommandSequence : Command
    {
        protected IList _commands = new ArrayList();

        public void AddCommand(Command c)
        {
            _commands.Add(c);
        }
        public override void Execute()
        {
            foreach (Command c in _commands)
            {
                c.Execute();
            }
        }
    }
}
```

The CarryCommand class interprets the Execute() operation by interacting with the factory's robot to move a bin from one machine to another.

```
using System;
using Machines;
namespace RobotInterpreter
{
    public class CarryCommand : Command
    {
        protected Machine _fromMachine;
        protected Machine _toMachine;

        public CarryCommand(
            Machine fromMachine, Machine toMachine)
        {
            _fromMachine = fromMachine;
            _toMachine = toMachine;
        }

        public override void Execute()
        {
            Robot.singleton.Carry(_fromMachine, _toMachine);
        }
    }
}
```

The CarryCommand class is designed to work specifically within the domain of a robot-controlled factory line. We can easily imagine other domain-specific classes, such as a StartUpCommand class or a ShutdownCommand class, for controlling machines. It will also be useful to have a command for a ForCommand class that executes a command across a given collection of machines. Figure 25.2 shows these extensions to the Command hierarchy.

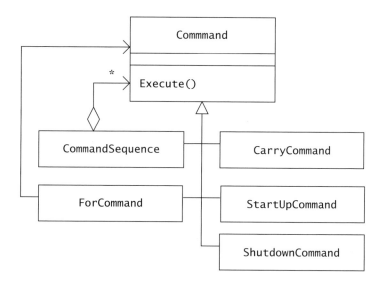

Figure 25.2   The INTERPRETER pattern allows for many subclasses to reinterpret the meaning of a common operation.

Part of the design for a `ForCommand` class is immediately clear: The constructor for this class would presumably accept a collection of machines and a COMMAND object to execute as the body of a `for` loop. The more difficult part of this design comes in the connection of the loop and the body. The `for` and `foreach` statements in C# establish a variable that receives a new value each time the body executes. Consider the following statement:

```
foreach (Command c in _commands)
{
    c.Execute();
}
```

C# links the `c` identifier that the `foreach` statement declares with the `c` variable in the loop's body. To create an INTERPRETER class that emulates a `for` loop, we need an approach for handling variables. Figure 25.3 shows a `Term` hierarchy that provides for handling and evaluating variables.

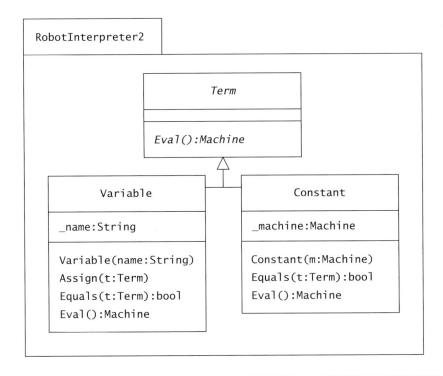

Figure 25.3   The Term hierarchy allows for variables that can evaluate to machines.

The Term hierarchy is similar to the Command hierarchy in that a common operation (Eval()) appears throughout the hierarchy. You might argue that this hierarchy is itself an example of INTERPRETER, although it does not show composition classes (such as CommandSequence), which usually accompany INTERPRETER.

The Term hierarchy lets us wrap individual machines as constants and lets us assign variables to these constants or to other variables. It also lets us make domain-specific INTERPRETER classes more flexible. For example, the StartUpCommand code can arrange to work with a Term object rather than a specific machine as follows:

```
using System;
using Machines;
namespace RobotInterpreter2
{
    public class StartUpCommand : Command
    {
        protected Term _term;
        public StartUpCommand(Term term)
        {
            _term = term;
```

```
        }
        public override void Execute()
        {
            Machine m = _term.Eval();
            m.StartUp();
        }
    }
}
```

Similarly, to add flexibility to the `CarryCommand` class, we can modify it to work with `Term` objects as follows:

```
using System;
using Machines;
namespace RobotInterpreter2
{
    public class CarryCommand : Command
    {
        protected Term _from;
        protected Term _to;

        public CarryCommand(Term fromTerm, Term toTerm)
        {
            _from = fromTerm;
            _to = toTerm;
        }

        public override void Execute()
        {
            Robot.singleton.Carry(_from.Eval(), _to.Eval());
        }
    }
}
```

Once we design the `Command` hierarchy to work with terms, we can write the `ForCommand` class so that it sets the value of a variable and executes a body command in a loop.

```
using System;
using System.Collections;
using Machines;
namespace RobotInterpreter2
{
    public class ForCommand : Command
    {
        protected MachineComponent _root;
        protected Variable _variable;
        protected Command _body;
        public ForCommand(
            MachineComponent mc, Variable v, Command body)
        {
            _root = mc;
            _variable = v;
            _body = body;
        }
        public override void Execute()
        {
            Execute(_root);
```

```
        }
        private void Execute(MachineComponent mc)
        {
            Machine m = mc as Machine;
            if (m != null)
            {
                // challenge!
                // challenge!
                return;
            }
            MachineComposite comp = mc as MachineComposite;
            foreach (
                MachineComponent child in comp.Children)
            {
                Execute(child);
            }
        }
    }
}
```

The Execute() code in the ForCommand class uses casting to walk through a machine component tree. Chapter 28, "Iterator," will review faster and more elegant techniques for iterating over a composite. For the INTER-PRETER pattern, the important point is to properly interpret the Execute() request for each node in the tree.

Challenge 25.1

Complete the code in the Execute() method of the ForCommand class.

A solution appears on page 407.

The ForCommand class lets us begin to compose "programs" or "scripts" of commands for the factory. For example, here is a C# program that composes an interpreter object that shuts down all the machines in a factory:

```
using System;
using Machines;
using RobotInterpreter2;
class ShowDown
{
    static void Main()
    {
        MachineComposite dublin = ExampleMachine.Dublin();
        Variable v = new Variable("machine");
        Command c = new ForCommand(
            dublin, v, new ShutDownCommand(v));
        c.Execute();
    }
}
```

When this program calls the Execute() method, the ForCommand object c interprets Execute() by traversing the provided machine component, and for each machine:

- Sets the value of the variable v

- Calls the Execute() operation of the provided ShutDownCommand object

We can build richer interpreters if we add classes that control the flow of logic, such as an IfCommand class and a WhileCommand class to the interpreter hierarchy. These classes will require a way to model a Boolean condition. For example, we might need a way to model whether a machine variable is equal to a particular machine. We might introduce a new hierarchy of terms, but it may be simpler to borrow an idea from the C language: let null represent falsity and anything else represent truth. With this idea in mind, we can extend the Term hierarchy as Figure 25.4 shows.

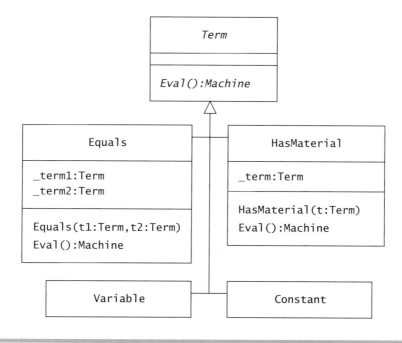

Figure 25.4   The Term hierarchy includes classes that model Boolean conditions.

The Equals class compares two terms and returns null to indicate false. A reasonable design is to have the Eval() method of the Equals class return one of its terms if the terms are equal.

```
using System;
using Machines;
namespace RobotInterpreter2
{
    public class Equals : Term
    {
        protected Term _term1;
        protected Term _term2;
        public Equals(Term term1, Term term2)
        {
            this._term1 = term1;
            this._term2 = term2;
        }
        public override Machine Eval()
        {
            Machine m1 = _term1.Eval();
            Machine m2 = _term2.Eval();
            bool b = m1.Equals(m2);
            return b ? m1 : null;
        }
    }
}
```

The HasMaterial class extends the idea of the value of a Boolean class to a domain-specific example with code as follows:

```
using System;
using Machines;
namespace RobotInterpreter2
{
    public class HasMaterial : Term
    {
        protected Term _term;
        public HasMaterial(Term term)
        {
            _term = term;
        }
        public override Machine Eval()
        {
            Machine m = _term.Eval();
            return m.HasMaterial() ? m : null;
        }
    }
}
```

Now that we have added the idea of Boolean terms to our interpreter package, we can add flow control interpreter classes as Figure 25.5 shows.

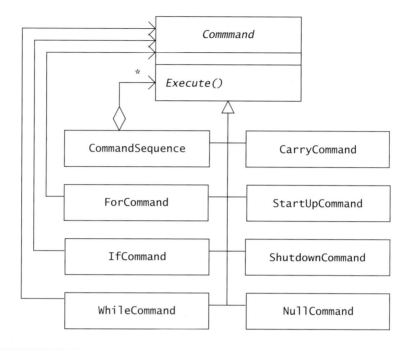

Figure 25.5   We can provide for richer composition interpreters by adding
logical flow control classes to the interpreter hierarchy.

The NullCommand class is useful for when we need a command that does
nothing, as when the else branch of an "If" command is empty.

```
using System;
namespace RobotInterpreter2
{
    public class NullCommand : Command
    {
        public override void Execute()
        {
        }
    }
}
```

The NullCommand class lets us code the IfCommand class as follows:

```
using System;
namespace RobotInterpreter2
{
    public class IfCommand : Command
    {
        protected Term _term;
        protected Command _body;
        protected Command _elseBody;
        public IfCommand(
            Term term, Command body, Command elseBody)
        {
            _term = term;
```

```
                    _body = body;
                    _elseBody = elseBody;
                }
                public override void Execute()
                {
                    // challenge!
                }
            }
        }
```

Challenge 25.2

Complete the code in the Execute() method of the IfCommand class.

A solution appears on page 408.

Challenge 25.3

Write the code for WhileCommand.cs.

A solution appears on page 408.

You might put your WhileCommand class into use with an interpreter that unloads a star press.

```
using System;
using Machines;
using RobotInterpreter2;
public class ShowWhile
{
    public static void Main()
    {
        MachineComposite dublin = ExampleMachine.Dublin();
        Term sp = new Constant(
            (Machine) dublin.Find("StarPress:1401"));
        Term ub = new Constant(
            (Machine) dublin.Find("UnloadBuffer:1501"));
        WhileCommand wc = new WhileCommand(
            new HasMaterial(sp),
            new CarryCommand(sp, ub));
        wc.Execute();
    }
}
```

The wc object is an interpreter that interprets `Execute()` to mean unload all bins from star press "1401."

Challenge 25.4

Close this book and write a short explanation of the difference between COMMAND and INTERPRETER.

A solution appears on page 409.

We can add more classes to the interpreter hierarchy for more types of control or for other domain-specific tasks. We can also extend the `Term` hierarchy. For example, it might be useful to have a `Term` subclass that finds an unload buffer that is near another machine.

Users of the `Command` and `Term` hierarchies can compose arbitrarily rich, complex "programs" of execution. For example, it is not too difficult to create an object that, when it executes, unloads all material from all machines (except unload buffers) in a factory. We might sketch this program in pseudocode as follows:

```
for (m in factory) // (this is not c#!)
{
    if (not (m is unloadBuffer))
    {
        ub = findUnload for m;
        while (m hasMaterial)
        {
            carry (m, ub);
        }
    }
}
```

If we write C# code to perform these tasks, the C# code will be more voluminous and less straightforward than the pseudocode. So why not change the "pseudocode" into real code by creating a parser that reads a domain-specific language for manipulating material in our factory and creates interpreter objects for us?

Interpreters, Languages, and Parsers

The INTERPRETER pattern addresses how interpreters work, but does not specify how you should instantiate or compose interpreters. In this chapter, you have built new interpreters "manually" by writing lines of C# code. But a more common way to create a new interpreter is with a parser. A *parser* is an object that can recognize text and decompose its structure, according to a set of rules, into a form suitable for further processing. For example, you can write a parser that will create a machine command interpreter object that corresponds to a textual program in the pseudocode above.

At this writing, there are not many tools for parser writing in C#, nor are there any books on the topic. By the time you read this, there may be more support available; try searching the Web for "C# parser tools."

Most parser toolkits include a parser generator. To use a generator, you use a special syntax to describe the pattern (the grammar) of your language and the tool generates a parser from your description. The generated parser will recognize instances of your language. Rather than using a parser generator tool, it turns out that you can write a general-purpose parser by applying the INTERPRETER pattern. *Building Parsers in Java* [Metsker] explains this technique, although its examples are in Java rather than C#.

Summary

The INTERPRETER pattern lets you compose executable objects from a class hierarchy that you create. Each class in the hierarchy implements a common operation that usually has necessarily vague names such as `Execute()`. Each class's name usually implies how the class implements (or interprets) the common operation. Each class either defines a way of composing commands or is a terminal command that causes some action.

Interpreters are often accompanied by a design for introducing variables and for Boolean or arithmetic expressions. Interpreters also often partner with a parser for a little language that simplifies the creation of new interpreter objects.

PART 5

EXTENSION PATTERNS

CHAPTER 26

INTRODUCING EXTENSIONS

When you program in C#, you do not begin from scratch—you "inherit" all the power of the .NET FCL. You also usually inherit the code of your predecessors and coworkers. When you're not reorganizing or improving this legacy code, you're extending it. You might say that programming in C# *is* extension.

If you've ever inherited a codebase, you may have grumbled about its quality. But is the new code you're adding really better? The answer is sometimes subjective, but this chapter reviews a few principles of OO software development that you can use to assess your work.

In addition to normal techniques for extending a codebase, you may be able to apply design patterns to add new behavior. This chapter reviews earlier patterns that contain an element of extension and introduces the remaining extension-oriented patterns in this section, after a look at principles of OO design in ordinary development.

Principles of OO Design

Stone bridges have been around for thousands of years and we have lots of time-tested, well-agreed-upon principles for designing them. Object-oriented programming has been around for less than a century, so it's not surprising that we do not have time-tested, well-agreed-upon principles for OO design. We do, however, have excellent forums for discussing prospective principles. One of the best is the "Portland Pattern Repository" at www.c2.com [Cunningham]. If you browse this Web site, you will find a few principles that have shown value in assessing OO designs. One principle in particular that you should consider in your designs is the Liskov Substitution Principle.

The Liskov Substitution Principle

New classes should be logical, consistent extensions of their super-classes—but what does it mean to be logical and consistent? A C# compiler will ensure a certain level of consistency, but there are many principles of consistency that will elude a compiler. One rule that may help improve your designs is the Liskov Substitution Principle [Liskov], or LSP, which can be paraphrased as:

> *An instance of a class should function as an instance of its superclass.*

Basic LSP compliance is built into OO languages like C#. For example, it is legal to refer to an `UnloadBuffer` object as a `Machine`, since `UnloadBuffer` is a subclass of `Machine`.

```
Machine m = new UnloadBuffer(3501);
```

Some aspects of LSP compliance require human-level intelligence, or at least more intelligence than today's compilers possess. Consider the class hierarchies shown in Figure 26.1.

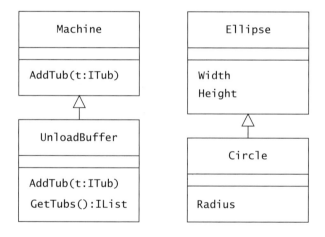

Figure 26.1   This diagram applies to the following questions: Is an unload buffer a machine? Is a circle an ellipse?

An unload buffer is certainly a machine, but modeling this fact in a class hierarchy can lead to problems. In the case of machines at Oozinoz, every machine except an unload buffer can receive a tub of chemicals. Since nearly every machine can accept chemical tubs and can report on the collection of tubs that it has nearby, it is useful to move this behavior up to the `Machine` class. But it's a mistake to invoke `AddTub()` or `GetTubs()` on an `UnloadBuffer` object. If it's a mistake, should we throw exceptions if these methods are called?

Suppose that another developer writes a method that interrogates all the machines in a bay to create a complete list of all the chemical tubs in that bay. When this code encounters an unload buffer, it will encounter an exception if the GetTubs() method in the UnloadBuffer class throws one. This is a strong violation of LSP: Use an UnloadBuffer object as a Machine object and your program may crash! Suppose that instead of throwing an exception, we decide to simply ignore calls to GetTubs() and AddTub() in the UnloadBuffer class. This still violates LSP: If you add a tub to a machine, the tub may disappear!

Violating LSP is not always a design flaw. In the case of Oozinoz machines, you have to weigh the value of letting the Machine class have behaviors that apply to most machines against the disadvantages of violating LSP. The important point is to be aware of LSP and to be able to articulate why other design considerations may warrant a breach of LSP.

Challenge 26.1

A circle is certainly a special case of an ellipse, or is it? Say whether the relationship of the Ellipse and Circle classes in Figure 26.1 is a violation of LSP.

A solution appears on page 409.

The Law of Demeter

In the late 1980s, members of the "Demeter Project" at Northeastern University attempted to codify rules that would ensure the good health of OO programs. The project team referred to these rules as "The Law of Demeter," or the LoD. Karl Lieberherr and Ian Holland provided a thorough summary of the rules in "Assuring Good Style for Object-Oriented Programs" [Lieberherr]. This paper states that

> *Informally, the law [of Demeter] says that each method can send messages to only a limited set of objects: to argument objects, to the [this] pseudovariable, and to the immediate subparts of [this].*

The paper goes on to give formal definitions of the law. It is easier to point out violations of the LoD than to fully grasp the law's intent.

Suppose you have a MaterialManager object with a method that receives a Tub object as a parameter. Tub objects have a Location property that returns the Machine object that represents where the tub is placed. Suppose that in the MaterialManager method you need to know if this

machine is up and available. You might find yourself writing the following code in your method:

```
if (tub.Location.IsUp())
{
    //...
}
```

This code violates the LoD because it invokes a method ("sends a message") to tub.Location. The tub.Location object is neither a parameter,
nor this (the MaterialManager object whose method is executing), nor an
attribute of this.

Challenge 26.2

Explain why the expression tub.Location.IsUp() might be viewed as
unhealthy.

A solution appears on page 409.

This challenge may trivialize the value of the LoD if the challenge suggests that the LoD means only that expressions of the form a.b.c are bad.
In fact, Lieberherr and Holland hope that the LoD will go beyond this and
answer the following question affirmatively: Is there some formula or
rule that you can follow to write good OO programs? It is well worth
reading the original papers that explain the LoD.

Like the LSP, the LoD will help you write better code if you know the
rules, generally follow them, and know when your designs merit a violation of the rules.

You may find that by following a set of guidelines, your extensions will
automatically generate good code. But to many practitioners, OO development is still an art. The artful extension of a codebase appears to result
from a set of practices acquired by artisans who are still only beginning to
articulate and codify their art. *Refactoring* refers to a collection of tools for
code modification that can improve a codebase's quality without altering
its functionality.

Removing Code Smells

You may believe that the LSP and LoD may prevent you from ever writing bad code, but more likely you will use these principles to find bad
code and fix it. This is normal practice: Write code that runs, then
improve its quality by finding and fixing quality problems. But how
exactly do you find problems? The answer, according to some, is *smell*.

In *Refactoring: Improving the Design of Existing Code*, Kent Beck and Martin Fowler describe 22 "smells," or indications that code quality can be improved through one or more corresponding refactorings.

This book has used refactoring many times to reorganize and improve existing code by applying a pattern. But you need not always apply a design pattern when refactoring. Anytime a method's code smells, the code may merit refactoring.

Challenge 26.3

Provide an example of a method that smells—that cries out for improvement—without violating either the LSP or LoD.

A solution appears on page 410.

Beyond Ordinary Extensions

Many design patterns, including many that this book has already covered, have a purpose that relates to extending behavior. Extension-oriented patterns often clarify the roles of two developers. For example, in the ADAPTER pattern, a developer may provide a useful service along with an interface for objects that want to use the service.

Challenge 26.4

Fill in the blanks in Table 26.1 to give examples of using design patterns to extend a class's or an object's behavior.

Table 26.1: Extending Behavior with Design Patterns

Example	Pattern at Play
A fireworks simulation designer establishes an interface that defines the behaviors your object must possess to participate in the simulation	ADAPTER
A toolkit that lets you compose executable objects at runtime	?
?	TEMPLATE METHOD
?	COMMAND
A code generator inserts behavior that provides the illusion that an object executing on another machine is local	?
?	OBSERVER
A design lets you define abstract operations that depend on a well-defined interface and lets you add new drivers that fulfill the interface	?

A solution appears on page 410.

In addition to the patterns already covered, three patterns remain whose intent applies primarily to extension.

If you intend to:	Then apply the pattern:
• Let developers compose an object's behavior dynamically	DECORATOR
• Provide a way to access the elements of collection sequentially	ITERATOR
• Let developers define a new operation for a hierarchy without changing the hierarchy classes	VISITOR

Summary

Writing code is primarily a matter of extension to provide new features, followed by reorganization that improves the quality of the code. A complete, objective technique for assessing code quality does not yet exist, but some principles of good OO code have been proposed.

The LSP suggests that an instance of a class should function as an instance of its superclass. You should be aware of and able to justify any violations of LSP in your code. The LoD is a collection of rules that help to reduce the dependencies among classes and that help lead to cleaner code.

Kent Beck and Martin Fowler have organized a large collection of rules, or "smells," that suggest that code is of imperfect quality. Each smell is subject to one or more refactorings, some of which include refactoring to a design pattern. Many design patterns serve as techniques for clarifying, simplifying, or facilitating extension.

Chapter 27

Decorator

To extend a codebase, you ordinarily add new classes or methods to it. Sometimes, though, you want to compose an object with new behavior at runtime. The Interpreter pattern, for example, lets you compose an executable object whose behavior changes radically depending on how you compose it. In some cases, you may need small variations in behavior and want to be able to mix them together. The Decorator pattern addresses this need. Decorator lets you compose new variations of an operation at runtime.

A Classic Example—Streams

The .NET FCL provide a classic example of the Decorator pattern in the overall design of input and output streams. A *stream* is a serial collection of bytes or characters, such as those that appear in a document. In C#, some stream classes have constructors that accept another stream, so that you create a stream from a stream. This sort of slim composition is the typical structure of Decorator. The Decorator pattern is at work in .NET streams, to a degree. But, as we shall see, with a small amount of code, we can leverage Decorator to greatly expand our ability to mix in variations of the read and write operations of streams.

For an example of Decorator in .NET, consider the following code that creates a small text file:

```
using System;
using System.IO;
public class ShowDecorator
{
    public static void Main()
    {
        FileStream fs =
            new FileStream("sample.txt", FileMode.Create);
        StreamWriter sw = new StreamWriter(fs);
        sw.WriteLine("a small amount of sample text");
        sw.Close();
    }
}
```

Running this program will produce a `sample.txt` file that contains a small amount of sample text. The program uses a `FileStream` object to create a new file. The `FileStream` object will only accept `byte` data, so the program wraps this stream inside a `StreamWriter` object. The `StreamWriter` class handles the conversion from characters into bytes.

The main point to note in the program is that we can compose one stream from another—the code composes a `StreamWriter` object from a `FileStream` object. We can expand on this idea by building a framework of stream decorators. These decorator classes will let us compose a large variety of output stream filters.

To develop a collection of filter classes, it is useful to first create an interface that defines the operations you want your filters to support. By selecting operations that already exist in the `StreamWriter` class, you can create, almost effortlessly, a class that inherits all its behavior from `StreamWriter` and that also serves as an implementation of your interface. Figure 27.1 shows this design.

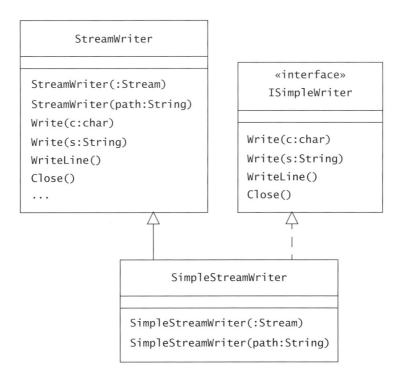

Figure 27.1   The ISimpleWriter interface narrows the functionality that the
StreamWriter class provides.

The ISimpleWriter interface simply defines which operations your filters
will have.

```
namespace Filters
{
    public interface ISimpleWriter
    {
        void Write(char c);
        void Write(string s);
        void WriteLine();
        void Close();
    }
}
```

The main point of creating the ISimpleWriter interface is to establish the
behavior that we expect from streams. This will let us define a filter class
that accepts a stream in its constructor and that mixes in new behaviors in
its Write() methods. Before looking at that filter, note that the operations
in the ISimpleWriter interface match operations in the StreamWriter class.
This lets us create the SimpleStreamWriter with no behavior of its own as
follows:

```
using System.IO;
namespace Filters
{
    public class SimpleStreamWriter :
        StreamWriter, ISimpleWriter
    {
        public SimpleStreamWriter(Stream s) : base (s)
        {
        }
        public SimpleStreamWriter(string path) : base (path)
        {
        }
    }
}
```

The value of the SimpleStreamWriter class is that it inherits all the stream-writing behavior of the StreamWriter class and we can use SimpleStream-Writer objects as instances of the ISimpleWriter type.

To create a toolkit of composable output streams, the next step is to introduce a filter superclass that has several critical attributes. The filter class will:

- Implement the ISimpleWriter interface

- Accept in its constructor another ISimpleWriter object

- Act as the superclass of a filter hierarchy

- Provide default implementations of all ISimpleWriter methods except Write(:char)

Figure 27.2 shows this design.

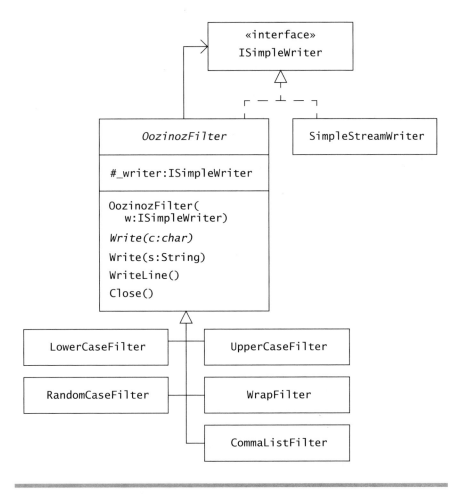

Figure 27.2   The OozinozFilter class constructor will accept an instance of
any subclass of OozinozFilter, or an instance of
SimpleStreamWriter.

The OozinozFilter class meets its design goals with a small amount of
code:

```
using System;
namespace Filters
{
    public abstract class OozinozFilter : ISimpleWriter
    {
        protected ISimpleWriter _writer;

        public OozinozFilter(ISimpleWriter writer)
        {
                _writer = writer;
        }
        public abstract void Write(char c);
        public virtual void Write(String s)
```

```
            {
                foreach(char c in s.ToCharArray())
                {
                    Write(c);
                }
            }
            public virtual void WriteLine()
            {
                _writer.WriteLine();
            }
            public virtual void Close()
            {
                _writer.Close();
            }
        }
    }
```

This code is all we need to start putting DECORATOR to work. Subclasses of OozinozFilter can supply new implementations of Write(:char) that modify a character before passing it on to the underlying stream's Write(:char) method. The other methods in the OozinozFilter class supply the behavior that subclasses will usually want. The class simply passes WriteLine() and Close() calls to the underlying stream (the stream supplied in the constructor). The OozinozFilter class also interprets Write(:String) in terms of the Write(:char) method that it leaves abstract.

Now it is easy to create and use new stream filters. For example, the following code forces text to be lowercase:

```
using System;
namespace Filters
{
    public class LowerCaseFilter : OozinozFilter
    {
        public LowerCaseFilter(ISimpleWriter writer) :
            base (writer)
        {
        }
        public override void Write(char c)
        {
            _writer.Write(Char.ToLower(c));
        }
    }
}
```

An example of a program that uses a lowercase filter is:

```
using System;
using Filters;
public class ShowLowerCase
{
    static void Main(string[] args)
    {
        ISimpleWriter w =
            new SimpleStreamWriter("sample.txt");
        ISimpleWriter x = new LowerCaseFilter(w);
        x.Write("This Text, notably ALL in LoWeR casE!");
        x.Close();
    }
}
```

This program produces a sample.txt file that contains "this text, notably all in lower case!"

The code for the UpperCaseFilter class is identical to the code for LowerCaseFilter, except for the Write() method, which is:

```
public override void Write(char c)
{
    _writer.Write(Char.ToUpper(c));
}
```

The code for the TitleCaseFilter class is slightly more complex, as it has to keep track of whitespace:

```
using System;
namespace Filters
{
    public class TitleCaseFilter : OozinozFilter
    {
        protected bool inWhite = true;
        public TitleCaseFilter(ISimpleWriter writer) :
            base (writer)
        {
        }
        public override void Write(char c)
        {
            _writer.Write(inWhite
                ? Char.ToUpper(c)
                : Char.ToLower(c));
            inWhite = Char.IsWhiteSpace(c) || c == '\"';
        }
        public override void WriteLine()
        {
            base.WriteLine();
            inWhite = true;
        }
    }
}
```

The CommaListFilter class puts a comma between elements as follows:

```
using System;
namespace Filters
{
    public class CommaListFilter : OozinozFilter
    {
        protected bool needComma = false;
        public CommaListFilter(ISimpleWriter writer) :
            base (writer)
        {
        }
        public override void Write(char c)
        {
            if (needComma)
            {
                _writer.Write(',');
                _writer.Write(' ');
            }
            _writer.Write(c);
            needComma = true;
        }
        public override void Write(string s)
        {
            if (needComma)
            {
                _writer.Write(", ");
            }
            _writer.Write(s);
            needComma = true;
        }
    }
}
```

The theme of these filters is the same: The development task consists of overriding the appropriate Write() methods. The Write() methods decorate the received stream of text and pass the modified text on to a subordinate stream.

Challenge 27.1

Write the code for RandomCaseFilter.cs.

A solution appears on page 411.

The code for the WrapFilter class is considerably more complex than the other filters. It offers to center its output and thus must buffer and count characters before passing them to its subordinate stream. You can inspect the code for WrapFilter.cs by downloading it from www.oozinoz.com (see Appendix C, "Oozinoz Source," for details on downloading).

The constructor for the WrapFilter class accepts an ISimpleWriter object as well as a width parameter that tells where to wrap lines. You can mix this filter and other filters together to create a variety of effects. For exam-

ple, the following program wraps, centers, and title-cases the text of an
input file:

```
using System;
using System.IO;
using Filters;
public class ShowFilters
{
    static void Main(string[] args)
    {
        StreamReader   r = new StreamReader(args[0]);
        ISimpleWriter w1 = new SimpleStreamWriter(args[1]);
        ISimpleWriter w2 = new TitleCaseFilter(w1);
        WrapFilter    w3 = new WrapFilter(w2, 40);
        w3.Center = true;
        String line;
        while ((line = r.ReadLine()) != null)
        {
            w3.Write(line);
        }
        r.Close();
        w3.Close();
    }
}
```

To see this program in action, suppose that an adcopy.txt file contains the
following text:

```
The "SPACESHOT" shell        hovers
         at 100 meters for 2 to 3
minutes,         erupting star bursts  every 10 seconds that
generate              ABUNDANT reading-level light for a
typical    stadium.
```

You can execute the ShowFilters program with the command line:

```
>ShowFilters adcopy.txt adout.txt
```

The contents of the adout.txt file will be something like:

```
   The "Spaceshot" Shell Hovers At 100
  Meters For 2 To 3 Minutes, Erupting Star
   Bursts Every 10 Seconds That Generate
    Abundant Reading-level Light For A
              Typical Stadium.
```

Rather than writing to a file, it can be useful to direct output characters to
the console. Figure 27.3 shows the design of a class that implements ISimpleWriter and that will direct its characters to the console.

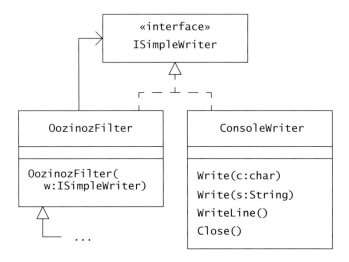

Figure 27.3   A `ConsoleWriter` object can serve as an argument to the constructor of any of the `OozinozFilter` subclasses.

Challenge 27.2

Write the code for `ConsoleWriter.cs`.

A solution appears on page 411.

I/O streams provide a classic example of how the DECORATOR pattern lets you assemble the behavior of an object at runtime. Another important application of DECORATOR occurs when you need to create mathematical functions at runtime.

Function Wrappers

The idea of composing new behaviors at runtime using the DECORATOR pattern applies as nicely to mathematical functions as it does to I/O streams. The ability to create new functions at runtime is something you can pass along to your users, letting them specify new functions through a GUI or through a little language. You may also simply want to reduce the number of methods in your code by creating mathematical functions as objects instead of new methods.

To create a library of function decorators (or function "wrappers") we can apply the same ideas we used for I/O streams. For the function wrapper superclass name, we can use "Frapper" as an abbreviation of "function wrapper." For an initial design of the Frapper class, we can mimic the design for the OozinozFilter class, as Figure 27.4 shows.

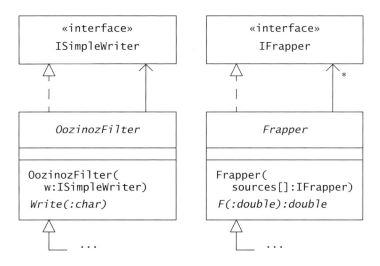

Figure 27.4   This initial design of the function wrapper hierarchy closely models the design of I/O filters.

The OozinozFilter class implements the ISimpleWriter interface, and its constructor expects to receive another ISimpleWriter object. The design for the Frapper class is similar, but instead of accepting a single IFrapper object, it accepts an array. Some functions, such as arithmetic functions, will require more than one subordinate function to work from.

In the case of function wrappers, there is no existing class like Stream-Writer that already implements the operation we need. As a result, there is no need for an IFrapper interface. We can more simply define the Frapper hierarchy without this interface, as Figure 27.5 shows.

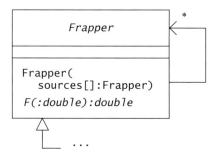

Figure 27.5   A simplified design for the Frapper class works without
              defining a separate interface.

As with the OozinozFilter class, the Frapper class defines a common operation that its subclasses must implement. A natural choice for the name of this operation is F. We can plan to implement parametric functions, basing all functions on a normalized "time" parameter that varies 0 to 1. See the sidebar, "Parametric Equations," in Chapter 4, for background on the power of using parametric equations.

We will create a subclass of Frapper for every function we want to wrap around another function. Figure 27.6 shows an initial Frapper hierarchy.

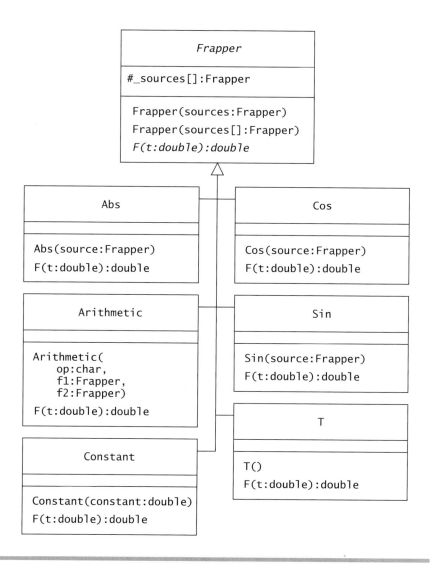

Figure 27.6   Each subclass of Frapper implements F(t) in a way that corresponds to the class's name.

The code for the Frapper superclass serves mainly to declare the _sources array.

```
using System;
namespace Functions
{
    public abstract class Frapper
    {
        protected Frapper[] _sources;
        public Frapper(Frapper[] sources)
        {
            _sources = sources;
```

```
        }
        public Frapper(Frapper f) :
            this(new Frapper[] { f })
        {
        }
        public abstract double F(double t);
    }
}
```

The Frapper subclasses are also generally simple. For example, here is code for the Cos class:

```
using System;
namespace Functions
{
    public class Cos : Frapper
    {
        public Cos(Frapper f) : base (f)
        {
        }
        public override double F(double t)
        {
            return Math.Cos(_sources[0].F(t));
        }
    }
}
```

The Cos class constructor expects a Frapper argument and passes this argument up to the superclass constructor where the argument is stored in the _sources array. The Cos.F() method evaluates the source function at time t, passes this value to Math.Cos(), and returns the result.

The Abs and Sin classes are nearly identical to the Cos class. The Constant class lets you create a Frapper object that holds a constant value to return in response to calls to the F() method. The Arithmetic class accepts an operator indicator that it applies in its F() method. The code for the Arithmetic class is:

```
using System;
namespace Functions
{
    public class Arithmetic : Frapper
    {
        protected char _op;
        public Arithmetic(Char op, Frapper f1, Frapper f2) :
            base (new Frapper[]{f1, f2})
        {
            _op = op;
        }
        public override double F(double t)
        {
            switch (_op)
            {
                case '+' : return
                    _sources[0].F(t) + _sources[1].F(t);
                case '-' : return
                    _sources[0].F(t) - _sources[1].F(t);
```

```
                case '*' : return
                    _sources[0].F(t) * _sources[1].F(t);
                case '/' : return
                    _sources[0].F(t) / _sources[1].F(t);
                default :
                    return 0;
        }
    }
  }
}
```

The T class returns the passed-in value of t. This behavior is useful if you want a variable to vary linearly with time. For example, the following expression creates a Frapper object whose F() value will vary from 0 to 2π as time varies from 0 to 1:

```
new Arithmetic('*', new T(), new Constant(2 * Math.PI))
```

You can use the Frapper classes to compose new mathematical functions without writing new methods. The PlotPanel2 class in the UserInterface namespace accepts Frapper arguments for its x and y functions. This class also makes the functions fit within the plotting canvas. You can put this panel to work with a program such as the following:

```
using System;
using System.Windows.Forms;
using Functions;
using UserInterface;
public class ShowFun
{
    public static void Main()
    {
        Frapper theta  = new Arithmetic(
            '*', new T(), new Constant(2 * Math.PI));
        Frapper theta2 = new Arithmetic(
            '*', new T(), new Constant(2 * Math.PI * 5));
        Frapper x = new Arithmetic(
            '+', new Cos(theta), new Cos(theta2));
        Frapper y = new Arithmetic(
            '+', new Sin(theta), new Sin(theta2));

        PlotPanel2 p = new PlotPanel2(300, x, y);
        Form f = new Form();
        f.DockPadding.All = 10;
        f.Text = "Chrysanthemum";
        f.Controls.Add(p);
        Application.Run(f);
    }
}
```

This program draws a function that lets one circle revolve around another multiple times. Running this program creates the display shown in Figure 27.7.

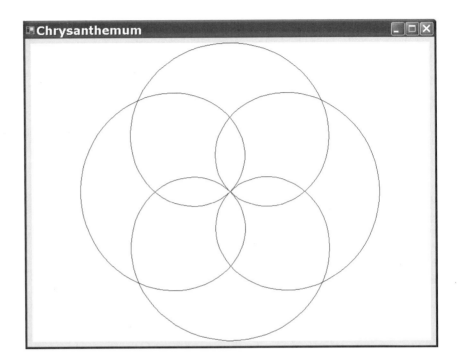

Figure 27.7   A complex mathematical function created without introducing any new methods.

To extend your toolkit of function wrappers, it is easy to add new mathematical functions into the Frapper hierarchy.

Challenge 27.3

Write the code for an Exp function wrapper class (and try closing the book while you do this!).

A solution appears on page 412.

Suppose that the brightness of a star is a sine wave that decreases exponentially.

$$brightness = e^{-4t} \cdot \sin(\pi t)$$

As before, we can compose a function without writing new classes or methods for it.

```
using System;
using System.Windows.Forms;
using Functions;
using UserInterface;
public class ShowBrightness
{
    public static void Main()
    {
        Frapper brightness = // ??

        PlotPanel2 p =
            new PlotPanel2(100, /* ?? */, brightness);

        Panel p2 = UI.NORMAL.CreatePaddedPanel(p);
        GroupBox gb = UI.NORMAL.CreateGroupBox(
            "Brightness vs. Total Burn Time", p2);
        gb.Font = UI.NORMAL.Font;
        Form f = new Form();
        f.DockPadding.All = 10;
        f.Text = "Brightness";
        f.Controls.Add(gb);
        Application.Run(f);
    }
}
```

This code produces the plot in Figure 27.8.

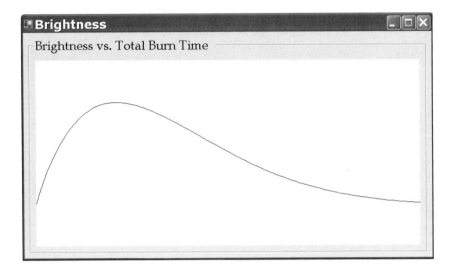

Figure 27.8   A star's brightness peaks quickly and then tails off.

Challenge 27.4

Write the code to define a brightness object that represents the brightness function.

A solution appears on page 412.

You can add other functions to the Function hierarchy as needed. For example, you might add Random, Sqrt, and Tan classes. You can also create new hierarchies that work on different types—such as strings—or that have a different notion of how to define the F() operation. For example, you might define F() as a two- or three-dimensional function of time. Regardless of the hierarchy you create, you can apply DECORATOR to develop a rich set of functions you can compose at runtime.

Decorator in GUIs

One of the original applications of DECORATOR (and presumably the application from which DECORATOR derives its name) lies in the construction of GUI components. Many GUI controls in .NET can contain other controls. Consider the following lines from the ShowBrightness program:

```
PlotPanel2 p = new PlotPanel2(100, /* ?? */, brightness);
Panel p2 = UI.NORMAL.CreatePaddedPanel(p);
GroupBox gb = UI.NORMAL.CreateGroupBox(
    "Brightness vs. Total Burn Time", p2);
```

These statements "decorate" a `PlotPanel2` object with a `Panel` object, and decorate the `Panel` object with a `GroupBox` object.

Decorator in Relation to Other Patterns

The mechanics of DECORATOR include a common operation implemented across a hierarchy. In this regard, DECORATOR is similar to STATE, STRATEGY, and INTERPRETER. In DECORATOR, classes usually have a constructor that requires another, subordinate decorator object. DECORATOR resembles COMPOSITE in this regard. DECORATOR also resembles PROXY in that decorator classes typically implement the common operation by forwarding the call to the subordinate decorator object.

Summary

The DECORATOR pattern lets you mix together variations of an operation at runtime. A classic example of this appears in input and output streams, where you can compose one stream from another. The .NET FCL support DECORATOR in the implementation of I/O streams. You can extend this idea to create your own set of I/O filters. You can also apply DECORATOR to set up function wrappers that let you create a large family of function objects from a fixed set of function classes. The DECORATOR pattern offers a flexible design for cases where a common operation has implementation variations that you want to combine into new composite variations at runtime.

CHAPTER 28

ITERATOR

The intent of the ITERATOR pattern is to provide a way to access the elements of a collection sequentially. You might think that in C# there is little to explore in this topic, because the C# language and the .NET FCL build in support for iteration. However, if you extend a codebase by adding a new type of collection, you may find that you need to extend your extension by adding an iterator. This chapter examines the particular case of iterating over a composite. In addition to iterating over new types of collections, the topic of iterating in a multi-threaded environment brings up a number of interesting problems that warrant review. Iteration is not a completely solved problem, even though iteration in C# ordinarily works just as you might expect.

Ordinary Iteration

In C#, iteration normally just works. The collection classes in the FCL provide iteration by implementing the GetEnumerator() method, which allows iteration over the collection in a foreach statement. Chapter 16, "Factory Method," explained how to implement your own collection classes so that you could iterate over them with foreach.

Thread-Safe Iteration

Rich applications often use threads to undertake tasks with the appearance of simultaneity. In particular, it is common to let time-consuming tasks happen in the background, without slowing down GUI responsiveness. Threading is useful, but it is also perilous. Many applications have crashed because of threaded tasks that did not cooperate effectively. Methods that iterate over collections can certainly be at fault when multi-threaded applications fail.

311

312   Chapter 28 • Iterator

The collection classes in the System.Collections library offer a measure of
thread safety in their respective Synchronized() methods. These methods
return, essentially, a version of the underlying collection that will detect
the problem that occurs if the collection changes in one thread while
another thread is iterating over it. To see this behavior in action, suppose
that the Oozinoz Factory singleton can tell us which machines are up at a
given moment, and we want to display a list of "up" machines. The sample code in the BusinessCore namespace actually hard-codes this list as
follows:

```
public class Factory
{
    //...
    public static ArrayList UpMachineNames()
    {
        return new ArrayList(
            new String[] {
                "Mixer:1201",
                "ShellAssembler:1301",
                "StarPress:1401",
                "UnloadBuffer:1501" } );
    }
}
```

The following program displays a list of the machines that are currently
"up," but simulates the condition that a new machines comes up while
the program is displaying the list:

```
using System;
using System.Collections;
using System.Threading;
using BusinessCore;
public class ShowConcurrentWhile
{
    private ArrayList _list;
    protected void DisplayUpMachines()
    {
        _list = ArrayList.Synchronized(
            Factory.UpMachineNames());
        IEnumerator i = _list.GetEnumerator();
        int counter = 0;
        while (i.MoveNext())
        {
            if (++counter == 2)
            { // simulate wake-up
                new Thread(
                    new ThreadStart(
                        NewMachineComesUp)).Start();
            }
            Thread.Sleep(100); // give other threads a chance
            Console.WriteLine(i.Current);
        }
    }
    public void NewMachineComesUp()
```

```
    {
        _list.Insert(0, "Fuser:1101");
    }
    public static void Main()
    {
        new ShowConcurrentWhile().DisplayUpMachines();
    }
}
```

The `Main()` method in this code constructs an instance of the class and calls the `DisplayUpMachines()` method. The `DisplayUpMachines()` method iterates over the list of "up" machines, taking care to construct a "synchronized" version of the list. This code simulates the condition that another machine comes up while this method iterates over the list. The `NewMachineComesUp()` method modifies the list, running in a separate thread.

The `ShowConcurrentWhile` program prints a machine or two and then crashes.

```
> ShowConcurrentWhile
Mixer:1201
ShellAssembler:1301
Unhandled Exception: System.InvalidOperationException:
Collection was modified;
...
```

The program crashes because the iterator object detects that the list has changed during the iteration. You don't actually need to create a new thread to show this behavior; you can create a program that crashes just by altering a "synchronized" collection from within an iteration loop. In practice, a multi-threaded application is much more likely to accidentally modify a list while an iterator is traversing it.

We can devise a thread-safe approach for iterating over a list, but first it is important to note that the `ShowConcurrentWhile` program only crashes because it uses the iterator that the `GetEnumerator()` method provides. Iterating over a "synchronized" list with a for loop will *not* trigger the exception encountered by the previous program. Consider the following variation of the program:

```
using System;
using System.Collections;
using System.Threading;
using BusinessCore;
public class ShowConcurrentFor
{
    private ArrayList _list;
    protected void DisplayUpMachines()
    {
        _list = ArrayList.Synchronized(
            Factory.UpMachineNames());
        for (int i = 0; i < _list.Count; i++)
        {
            if (i == 2)
            { // simulate wake-up
```

```
                  new Thread(
                      new ThreadStart(
                          NewMachineComesUp)).Start();
                }
                Thread.Sleep(100); // give other threads a chance
                Console.WriteLine(_list[i]);
            }
        }
        public void NewMachineComesUp()
        {
            _list.Insert(0, "Fuser:1101");
        }
        public static void Main()
        {
            new ShowConcurrentFor().DisplayUpMachines();
        }
    }
```

Running this program prints the following:

```
Mixer:1201
ShellAssembler:1301
ShellAssembler:1301
StarPress:1401
UnloadBuffer:1501
```

Challenge 28.1

Explain the output of the ShowConcurrentFor program.

A solution appears on page 413.

We have looked at two versions of the program: One that crashes and one that produces incorrect output. Neither of these results is acceptable, so we need some other way to protect a list while iterating over it.

There are two common approaches to providing safe iteration over a collection in a multi-threaded application. Both approaches involve the use of an object (sometimes called a *mutex*) that is shared by threads that vie for control of the object's lock. In one approach, your design can require that all threads gain control of the mutex lock before accessing the collection. The following program shows this approach:

```
using System;
using System.Collections;
using System.Threading;
using BusinessCore;
public class ShowConcurrentMutex
{
    private ArrayList _list;
    private Object _mutex = new Object();

    protected void DisplayUpMachines()
    {
```

```
        _list = Factory.UpMachineNames();
        lock (_mutex)
        {
            IEnumerator i = _list.GetEnumerator();
            int counter = 0;
            while (i.MoveNext())
            {
                if (++counter == 2)
                { // simulate wake-up
                    new Thread(
                        new ThreadStart(
                            NewMachineComesUp)).Start();
                }
                Thread.Sleep(100);
                Console.WriteLine(i.Current);
            }
        }
    }
    public void NewMachineComesUp()
    {
        lock (_mutex)
        {
            _list.Insert(0, "Fuser:1101");
        }
    }
    public static void Main()
    {
        new ShowConcurrentMutex().DisplayUpMachines();
    }
}
```

This program will print the original list as follows:

```
Mixer:1201
ShellAssembler:1301
StarPress:1401
UnloadBuffer:1501
```

The output shows the list as it exists before the NewMachineComesUp()
method inserts a new object. The program outputs a consistent result (with
no duplicates) because the program logic requires the NewMachineComesUp()
method to wait for the iteration in the DisplayUpMachines() method to
complete. Although the output is correct, the design may be impractical:
You may not be able to afford to have other threads block while one thread
iterates over a collection.

An alternative approach is to clone a collection in a mutex operation and
then work on the clone. The advantage of cloning a list before traversing
it is speed. Cloning a collection is often much faster than waiting for
another method to finish operating on the collection's contents. However,
cloning a collection and iterating over the clone may cause problems.

The Clone() method for ArrayList produces a *shallow* copy: It merely creates a new collection that refers to the same objects as the original. Relying on a clone will fail if other threads can change the underlying objects
in a way that interferes with your method. But in some cases, this risk is

small. For example, if you just want to display a list of machine names, it may be unlikely or inconsequential if the names change while your method iterates over a clone of the list.

To summarize, we have discussed four approaches for iterating over a list in a multi-threaded environment. Two of these approaches use a `Synchronized()` method and fail, either crashing or producing an incorrect result. The latter two approaches (using locking and possibly using cloning) may produce correct results, but do not use a `Synchronized()` method.

Challenge 28.2

Provide an argument against using the `Synchronized()` methods, or argue that a locking-based approach isn't always the answer either.

A solution appears on page 413.

C# and the .NET FCL libraries provide substantial support for iteration in a multi-threaded environment, but this support does not free you from the complexities of concurrent design. The FCL libraries also build in good support for iterating over the many collections that the libararies provides, but if you introduce your own collection type, you may need to also introduce an accompanying iterator.

Iterating over a Composite

It is usually easy to design algorithms that *traverse* a composite structure, visiting every node and performing some function. You may recall that Challenge 3.3 (from Chapter 3, "Composite") asked you to design several algorithms that execute by recursively traversing a composite structure. Creating an iterator may be much more difficult than creating a recursive algorithm. The difficulty lies in returning control to another part of the program and saving some kind of bookmark that lets the iterator pick up where it left off. Composites provide a good example of an iterator that is challenging to develop.

You might think that you will need a new iterator class for each domain-specific composite that you create. In fact, you can design a fairly reusable composite iterator, although you will have to modify your composite classes to return the right sort of iterator.

The design for a composite iterator is as naturally recursive as composites themselves. To iterate over a composite, we iterate over its children, although this is a bit more complex than it may initially sound. First, we have a choice as to whether we return a node before or after its descendants (called *preorder* and *postorder* traversal). If we choose a preorder traversal, then after returning the head, we must iterate over the children, noting that each child may be a composite. A subtlety here is that we must maintain two iterators. One iterator (labeled "1" in Figure 28.1) keeps track of which is the current child. This iterator is a simple list iterator that iterates over the list of children. A second iterator (labeled "2") iterates over the current child as a composite. Figure 28.1 shows the three aspects of determining the current node in a composite iteration.

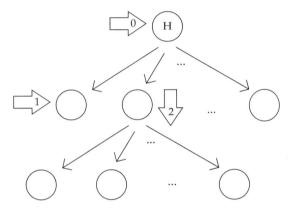

Figure 28.1   Iteration over a composite requires: 0) noting a head node, 1) iterating sequentially across its children, and 2) iterating over each child as a composite.

To work out the design for a composite iterator, we might expect that iterating over a leaf will be trivial, while iterating over a node with children will be more difficult. We can anticipate a design for these iterators something like the one shown in Figure 28.2.

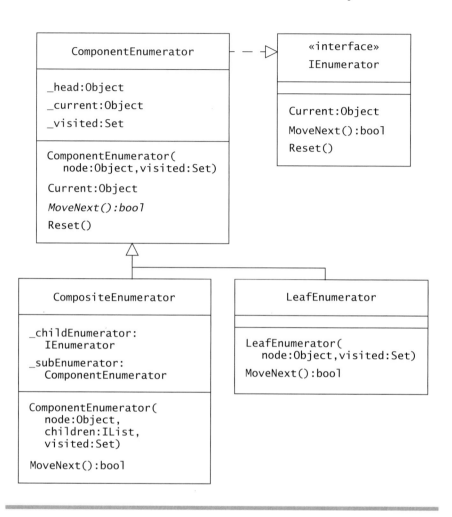

Figure 28.2   An initial design for a family of composite enumerators.

The class names in Figure 28.2 use the word "enumerator" rather than the word "iterator," to be more consistent with iteration classes in the .NET FCL. The classes also use the method names MoveNext() and Reset(), and the property name Current, so that the ComponentEnumerator class implements the IEnumerator interface from the System.Collections library.

The design shows that the enumerator class constructors will accept an object to enumerate. In practice, this object will be a composite such as a machine composite or a process composite. The design also anticipates that we will need a _visited variable to keep track of nodes that we have already enumerated. This will keep us from stepping into an infinite loop when a composite has cycles. The code for ComponentEnumerator at the top of the hierarchy will initially look like the following:

```
using System;
using System.Collections;
using Utilities;
namespace Enumerators
{
    public abstract class ComponentEnumerator : IEnumerator
    {
        protected Object _head;
        protected Set _visited;
        protected Object _current;
        public ComponentEnumerator(Object head, Set visited)
        {
            _head = head;
            _visited = visited;
        }
        public Object Current
        {
            get
            {
                return _current;
            }
        }
        public abstract bool MoveNext();
        public void Reset()
        {
            throw new InvalidOperationException(
                "Reset is not yet supported");
        }
    }
}
```

This class leaves most of the difficult design to its subclasses.

In the CompositeEnumerator subclass, we can anticipate the need for a list enumerator to enumerate a composite node's children. This is the enumeration marked "1" in Figure 28.1, represented by the _childEnumerator variable in Figure 28.2. Composites also need an enumerator for the enumeration marked "2" in Figure 28.1. The _subEnumerator variable in Figure 28.2 can fill this need. The CompositeEnumerator class constructor can initialize the child enumerator as follows:

```
public CompositeEnumerator(
    Object node, IList children, Set visited) :
    base (node, visited)
{
    _childEnumerator = children.GetEnumerator();
}
```

When we begin an enumeration of a composite, we know that the first node to return is the head node (marked "H" in Figure 28.1). Thus, the code for the MoveNext() method of a CompositeEnumerator class must look like:

```
public override bool MoveNext()
{
    if (!_visited.Contains(_head))
    {
        _visited.Add(_head);
        _current = _head;
        return true;
    }
    return SubenumeratorNext();
}
```

The MoveNext() method uses the _visited set to record whether the enumerator has already returned the head node. If the enumerator has
already returned the head of a composite node, the SubenumeratorNext()
method must find the next node.

At any given time, the _subEnumerator variable may be partway through
an enumeration of a child that is itself a composite node. If this enumerator is active, the MoveNext() method of the CompositeEnumerator class can
"move" the sub-enumerator and set the value of _current to be the value
of the _subEnumerator variable's Current property. If the sub-enumerator
cannot move, the code must increment _childEnumerator, get a new sub-
enumerator for it, and move that enumerator. The following code for the
SubenumeratorNext() method shows this logic:

```
protected bool SubenumeratorNext()
{
    while (true)
    {
        if (_subEnumerator != null)
        {
            if (_subEnumerator.MoveNext())
            {
                _current = _subEnumerator.Current;
                return true;
            }
        }
        if (!_childEnumerator.MoveNext())
        {
            _current = null;
            return false;
        }
        ICompositeEnumerable c =
            (ICompositeEnumerable) _childEnumerator.Current;
        if (!_visited.Contains(c))
        {
            _subEnumerator = c.GetEnumerator(_visited);
        }
    }
}
```

This method introduces the first constraint we have encountered regarding the kind of objects that we can enumerate: The code requires that children in a composite implement a GetEnumerator(:Set) method that is part
of an ICompositeEnumerable interface. To see where this interface fits in

the overall design, consider an example of a composite structure such as the ProcessComponent hierarchy that Chapter 5, "Composite," introduced. Figure 28.3 shows the process composite hierarchy that Oozinoz uses for modeling the manufacturing work flows that produce different types of fireworks.

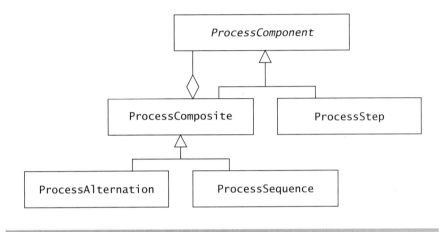

Figure 28.3   Manufacturing process flows at Oozinoz are composites.

The MoveNext() method of the CompositeEnumerator class needs to enumerate the nodes of each child that belongs to a composite object. We need the child's class to implement a GetEnumerator(:Set) method that the MoveNext() code can use. We can create an interface to encapsulate this requirement as follows:

```
using System;
using System.Collections;
using Utilities;
namespace Enumerators
{
    public interface ICompositeEnumerable : IEnumerable
    {
        ComponentEnumerator GetEnumerator(Set visited);
    }
}
```

This code declares ICompositeEnumerable to be an extension of the IEnumerable interface. The IEnumerable interface declares a GetEnumerator() method with no arguments. We shall see that this simplifies the creation of an enumerator over a domain composite such as a machine or process composite.

We have two types of interfaces: one for domain classes such as Process-Component to implement, and one that defines how an enumerator behaves. Figure 28.4 shows the relationship of these classes and interfaces.

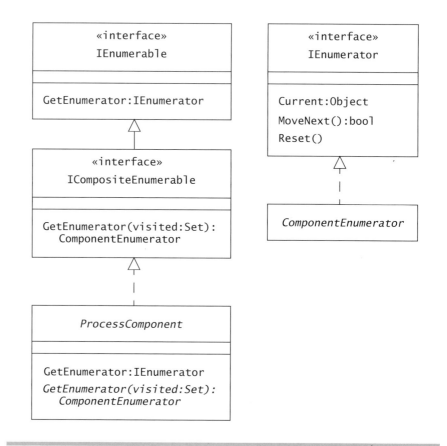

Figure 28.4   Composite structures must be able to provide appropriate
              enumerators.

To update the ProcessComponent hierarchy so that we can enumerate it,
we need to declare that it implements the ICompositeEnumerable interface.

```
using System;
using System.Collections;
using Enumerators;
using Utilities;
namespace Processes
{
    public abstract class ProcessComponent :
        ICompositeEnumerable
    {
        //...
```

```
public IEnumerator GetEnumerator()
    {
        return GetEnumerator(new Set());
    }
public abstract ComponentEnumerator
    GetEnumerator(Set visited);
}
}
```

The `ProcessComponent` class is abstract, and it leaves the `GetEnumerator(:Set)` method for subclasses to implement. For the `ProcessComposite` class, this code will look like:

```
public override ComponentEnumerator
    GetEnumerator(Set visited)
{
    return new CompositeEnumerator(
        this, _subprocesses, visited);
}
```

The `ProcessStep` class implementation of `GetEnumerator()` will be:

```
public override ComponentEnumerator
    GetEnumerator(Set visited)
{
    return new LeafEnumerator(this, visited);
}
```

Challenge 28.3

What pattern are you applying if you let classes in the `ProcessComponent` hierarchy implement `GetEnumerator()` to create instances of an appropriate enumerator class?

A solution appears on page 414.

With these small changes to the `ProcessComponent` hierarchy in place, we can now write code that enumerates a process composite. The object model of a typical Oozinoz process is shown in Figure 28.5.

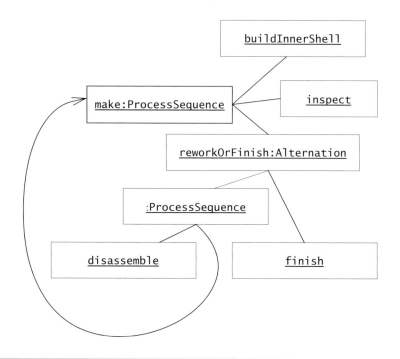

Figure 28.5   The process flow for making aerial shells is a cyclic composite.
Each leaf node in this diagram is an instance of ProcessStep.
The remaining nodes are instances of ProcessComposite.

The ShellProcess class in the Processes namespace has a static Make()
method that returns the object model shown in Figure 28.5. The following
short program enumerates all the nodes in this model:

```
using System;
using Enumerators;
using Processes;
public class ShowProcessEnumeration
{
    public static void Main()
    {
        foreach (ProcessComponent pc in ShellProcess.Make())
        {
            Console.WriteLine(pc);
        }
    }
}
```

Running this program prints the following:

```
Make an aerial shell
Build inner shell
Inspect
Rework inner shell, or complete shell
Rework
Disassemble
Finish: Attach lift, insert fusing, wrap
```

The names shown are those that the ShellProcess class gives to the process steps. Note that in the object model, the step after disassemble is make. The printout omits this, because the enumeration sees that it has already printed once (in the first line of output).

Adding Depth to a Composite Enumerator

The output of this program might be more clear if we indented each process step in accordance with its depth in the model. We can define the depth of a leaf enumerator to be 0, and note that the current depth of a composite enumerator is 1 plus the depth of its sub-enumerator. We can make the Depth() abstract in the ComponentEnumerator superclass as follows:

```
public abstract int Depth();
```

The code for a Depth() method for the LeafEnumerator class is:

```
public override int Depth()
{
    return 0;
}
```

The code for CompositeEnumerator.Depth() is:

```
public override int Depth()
{
    if (_subEnumerator != null)
    {
        return _subEnumerator.Depth() + 1;
    }
    return 0;
}
```

The following program produces more readable output:

```
using System;
using Enumerators;
using Processes;
public class ShowProcessEnumeration2
{
    public static void Main()
    {
        CompositeEnumerator e = (CompositeEnumerator)
            ShellProcess.Make().GetEnumerator();
        while (e.MoveNext())
        {
```

```
                    for (int i = 0; i < e.Depth(); i ++)
                    {
                        Console.Write("    ");
                    }
                    Console.WriteLine(e.Current);
                }
            }
        }
```

The output of this program is:

```
Make an aerial shell
    Build inner shell
    Inspect
    Rework inner shell, or complete shell
        Rework
            Disassemble
        Finish: Attach lift, insert fusing, wrap
```

Another improvement we can make to the ComponentEnumerator hierarchy is to allow for enumeration over just the leaves of a composite.

Enumerating Leaves

Suppose that we want to allow an enumeration to return only leaves. This can be useful if we are concerned with attributes that apply only to leaves, such as the time a process step takes. We can add a ReturnInterior property to the ComponentEnumerator class to record whether or not interior (non-leaf) nodes should be returned from the enumeration.

```
public bool ReturnInterior
{
    get
    {
        return _returnInterior;
    }
    set
    {
        _returnInterior = value;
    }
}
```

In the MoveNext() method of the CompositeEnumerator class, we'll need to pass this attribute down when we create a new enumeration for a composite node's child.

```
protected bool SubenumeratorNext()
{
    while (true)
    {
        //... as before
        ICompositeEnumerable c =
            (ICompositeEnumerable) _childEnumerator.Current;
        if (!_visited.Contains(c))
        {
            _subEnumerator = c.GetEnumerator(_visited);
            _subEnumerator.ReturnInterior = ReturnInterior;
        }
    }
}
```

We will also need to update the MoveNext() method of the CompositeEnu-merator class. The existing code is:

```
public override bool MoveNext()
{
    if (!_visited.Contains(_head))
    {
        _visited.Add(_head);
        _current = _head;
        return true;
    }
    return SubenumeratorNext();
}
```

Challenge 28.4

Update the MoveNext() method of the CompositeEnumerator class to respect the value of the ReturnInterior property.

A solution appears on page 415.

Creating an iterator (or "enumerator") for a new type of collection can be a significant design task. The resulting benefit is that your collection can become as easy to work with as any of the collection classes in the FCL.

Summary

The intent of the ITERATOR pattern is to let a client access the elements of a collection sequentially. The collection classes in the .NET FCL offer rich support for operating on collections, including support for iteration (or "enumeration"). If you create a new type of collection, you will often want to create an enumerator to go with it. Domain-specific composites are a common example of a new collection type. You can design a fairly generic enumerator for composites that you can then apply against a variety of composite hierarchies.

When you instantiate an enumerator, you should consider whether the collection can change while you are enumerating it. There is usually not much chance of this in a single-threaded application, but in a multi-threaded application, you may want to ensure that access to a collection is synchronized. To safely iterate in a multi-threaded application, you can synchronize access to a collection by locking on a mutex object. You can either block out all access while iterating or block access briefly while you make a clone of the collection. With a proper design, you can provide thread safety to the clients of your iterator code.

CHAPTER 29

VISITOR

To extend an existing class hierarchy, you normally simply add methods that provide the behavior you need. It can happen, though, that the behavior you need is not consistent with the thrust of the existing object model. It can also happen that you don't have access to the existing code. In such a case, it may be impossible to extend the hierarchy's behavior without modifying the hierarchy's classes. The VISITOR pattern, however, lets a hierarchy developer build in support for the prospect that another developer may want to extend the behavior of the hierarchy. The intent of VISITOR is to let you define a new operation for a hierarchy without changing the hierarchy classes.

VISITOR MECHANICS

The VISITOR pattern lets a small amount of forethought in developing a class hierarchy open a gateway to an unlimited variety of extensions that can be made by a developer who lacks access to the source code. The mechanics of the VISITOR pattern involve:

- In a class hierarchy, add an Accept() operation to some or all classes. Every implementation of this method will accept an argument whose type is an interface that you will create.

- Create an interface with a set of operations that share a common name (usually Visit), but that have different argument types. Declare one such operation for each class in the hierarchy for which you will allow extensions.

Figure 29.1 shows a class diagram of the MachineComponent hierarchy, modified to support VISITOR.

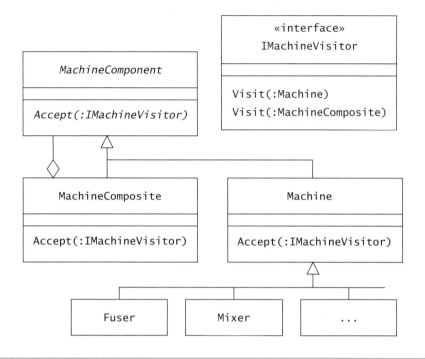

Figure 29.1   To prepare the MachineComponent hierarchy for VISITOR support, add the Accept() methods and MachineVisitor interface shown in this diagram.

Figure 29.1 doesn't explain how VISITOR works; the next section will do that. The figure just shows some of the groundwork that lets you apply VISITOR.

Note that not all the classes in the MachineComponent diagram implement an Accept() method. VISITOR does not require every class in the hierarchy to have its own implementation of the accepting method. As we shall see, though, it is important for each class that implements Accept() to appear as an argument in a Visit() method declared in the visitor interface.

The Accept() method in the MachineComponent class is abstract. Both subclasses implement this method with exactly the same code.

```
public override void Accept(MachineVisitor v)
{
    v.Visit(this);
}
```

You might think that since this method is identical in the Machine and MachineComponent classes, you could move the method up to the abstract MachineComponent class. However, a compiler will see a difference in these two "identical" methods.

Challenge 29.1

What difference will a C# compiler see between the `Accept()` methods in the `Machine` and `MachineComposite` classes?

A solution appears on page 414.

The `MachineVisitor` interface requires implementers to define methods for visiting machines and machine composites.

```
namespace Machines
{
    public interface IMachineVisitor
    {
        void Visit(Machine m);
        void Visit(MachineComposite c);
    }
}
```

The `Accept()` methods in the `MachineComponent`, together with the `IMachineVisitor` interface, invite developers to provide new operations to the hierarchy.

An Ordinary VISITOR

Suppose that you are working at the latest Oozinoz factory in Dublin, Ireland. The developers there have created an object model of the new factory's machine composition and have made this model accessible as the static `Dublin()` method of the `ExampleMachine` class. You'd like to be able to browse this structure in a tree view. Although you don't have access to the `Machine` hierarchy source code, the hierarchy does have VISITOR support built in, as shown in Figure 29.1. As a result, you can apply VISITOR to effectively add a new operation to `Machine` composites without altering any of the `Machine` composite code.

To create a browseable view of a machine composite, you need to create a `TreeView` control (from the `System.Windows.Forms` library). You can set the `TreeView` control's `Nodes` property to be a `TreeNode` composite that mirrors the machine composite. (The `TreeNode` class is also in the `System.Windows.Forms` library.) To create a `TreeNode` composite, you can create a visitor class that will traverse a machine composite, building the `TreeNode` composite as it goes. Suppose that you decide to call your new class `TreeNodeVisitor`.

The code for the `TreeNodeVisitor` class will need to keep one `TreeNode` object that represents the tree it's building, and another `TreeNode` object to mark the current position in the tree. The code for the `TreeNodeVisitor` class starts out as:

```csharp
using System;
using System.Windows.Forms; // for TreeNode
using Machines;
public class TreeNodeVisitor : IMachineVisitor
{
    private TreeNode _tree = null;
    private TreeNode _current = null;
    public TreeNode TreeNode
    {
        get
        {
            return _tree;
        }
    }
    public void Visit(Machine m)
    {
        //...
    }
    public void Visit(MachineComposite c)
    {
        //...
    }
}
```

When either of the `Visit()` methods executes, we need to create a TreeNode object to correspond to the visited object. Both `Visit()` methods will be able to use the following `AddNode()` method:

```csharp
protected TreeNode AddNode(MachineComponent m)
{
    TreeNode newNode = new TreeNode(m.ToString());
    if (_current == null)
    {
        _tree = newNode;
    }
    else
    {
        _current.Nodes.Add(newNode);
    }
    return newNode;
}
```

This code creates a new `TreeNode` object. If the _current pointer is `null`, it means that this is the very first `TreeNode` object, and so this object is the tree itself. Otherwise, the code just the adds new node to the current place in the tree.

When visiting a `Machine` object, we have only to add a `TreeNode` object for it.

```csharp
public void Visit(Machine m)
{
    AddNode(m);
}
```

When we visit a composite, we have to add a node for this composite itself and then change the _current pointer to be this node. This arranges for the children of the composite to be added to this node.

```
public void Visit(MachineComposite c)
{
    TreeNode oldCurrent = _current;
    _current = AddNode(c);
    foreach (MachineComponent mc in c.Children)
    {
        mc.Accept(this);
    }
    _current = oldCurrent;
}
```

After adding all the children, we need to reset the _current pointer to its former value, because we don't want any other visited nodes to add themselves to this composite.

Notice that the foreach loop in the Visit(:MachineComposite) method does not worry about whether a child component is an instance of Machine or an instance of MachineComposite. The Visit() method simply invokes the Accept() operation of each component. Which method executes as a result of this invocation depends on the type of the child. Figure 29.2 shows a typical sequence of method calls.

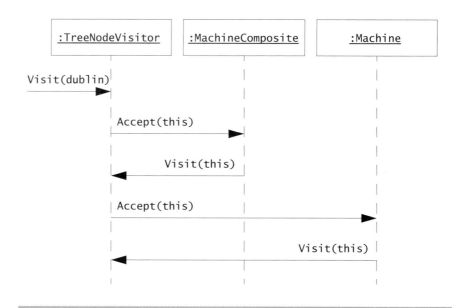

Figure 29.2   A `TreeNodeVisitor` object invokes an `Accept()` operation to determine which `Visit()` method to execute.

When the `Visit(:MachineComposite)` method executes, it invokes the `Accept()` operation on each of a composite's children. A child responds by invoking a `Visit()` operation on the `TreeNodeVisitor` object. As Figure 29.2 shows, the short trip from the `TreeNodeVisitor` object to the object that receives the `Accept()` invocation and back again picks up the type of the receiving object. This technique, known as *double dispatch*, ensures that the right `Visit()` method of the `TreeNodeVisitor` class executes.

With the VISITOR code in place, we can write a short program that displays a machine hierarchy in a browseable view:

```
using System;
using System.Windows.Forms;
using Machines;
using UserInterface;
public class ShowTreeNodeVisitor : Form
{
    public ShowTreeNodeVisitor()
    {
        TreeView view = new TreeView();
        view.Dock = DockStyle.Fill;
        view.Font = UI.NORMAL.Font;
        TreeNodeVisitor v = new TreeNodeVisitor();
        v.Visit(ExampleMachine.Dublin());
        view.Nodes.Add(v.TreeNode);
```

```
                Controls.Add(view);
                Text = "Show Tree Node View";
            }
            public static void Main()
            {
                Application.Run(new ShowTreeNodeVisitor());
            }
        }
```

Running this program creates the display shown in Figure 29.3.

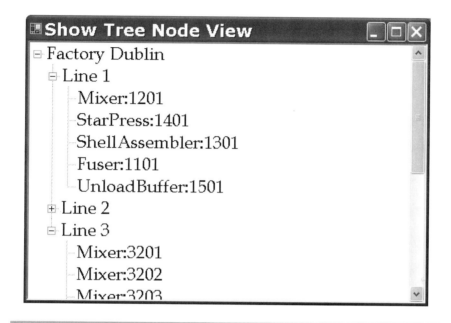

Figure 29.3   This GUI application presents the composition of machines at
the new factory in Dublin.

The double dispatching in VISITOR lets you create visitor classes with
methods that are specific to the different types in the visited hierarchy.

You can add almost any behavior through VISITOR, as you might if you
controlled the source code. As another example, consider a visitor that
finds all the machines (the leaf nodes) in a machine component.

```
        using System;
        using Machines;
        using Utilities;
        public class RakeVisitor : IMachineVisitor
        {
            protected Set _leaves;
            public Set GetLeaves(MachineComponent mc)
            {
                _leaves = new Set();
                mc.Accept(this);
                return _leaves;
```

```
        }
        public void Visit(Machine m)
        {
            // challenge!
        }
        public void Visit(MachineComposite mc)
        {
            // challenge!
        }
    }
```

Challenge 29.2

Complete the code of the RakeVisitor class to collect the leaves of a
machine component.

A solution appears on page 415.

A short program can find the leaves of a machine component and print
them out:

```
using System;
using Filters;
using Machines;
using Utilities;
public class ShowRakeVisitor
{
    public static void Main()
    {
        MachineComponent dublin = ExampleMachine.Dublin();
        ISimpleWriter w =
            new CommaListFilter(
                new WrapFilter(new ConsoleWriter(), 60));
        Set leaves = new RakeVisitor().GetLeaves(dublin);
        foreach (MachineComponent mc in leaves)
        {
            w.Write(mc.ID.ToString());
        }
        w.Close();
    }
}
```

This program uses a comma list filter and wrap filter to produce the following output:

```
3101, 2301, 1501, 2202, 2201, 1401, 2402, 2101, 1301, 1201,
3501, 3404, 1101, 3403, 3402, 3401, 3302, 3301, 2501, 3204,
3203, 3202, 3201, 2401, 3102
```

The TreeNodeVisitor and RakeVisitor classes each effectively add a new
behavior to the MachineComponent hierarchy, and these classes appear to
work correctly. However, there is some danger in writing visitors in that
they require an understanding of the hierarchy you are extending. A
change in the hierarchy may break your visitor, and you may misunder-

stand the mechanics of the hierarchy initially. In particular, you may have to handle cycles if the composite you are visiting does not prevent them.

Visitor Cycles

The `ProcessComponent` hierarchy that Oozinoz uses to model process flows is another composite structure that can benefit from building in support for Visitor. Unlike machine composites, it is natural for process flows to contain cycles, and visitors must take care not to cause infinite loops while traversing process composites. Figure 29.4 shows the `ProcessComponent` hierarchy.

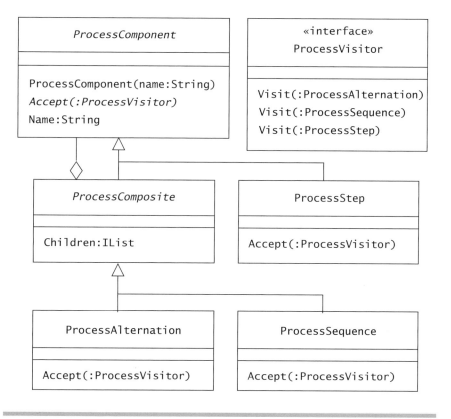

Figure 29.4   Like the `MachineComponent` hierarchy, the `ProcessComponent` hierarchy can build in support for Visitor.

Suppose that you want to print out a process component in a "pretty" or indented format. In Chapter 28, "Iterator," you used an iterator to print a process flow's steps. This printout looked like:

```
Make an aerial shell
    Build inner shell
    Inspect
    Rework inner shell, or complete shell
        Rework
            Disassemble
        Finish: Attach lift, insert fusing, wrap
```

Reworking a shell involves disassembling it and then making it again—
The step after "Disassemble" is "Make an aerial shell." The printout
doesn't show this step, because the iterator sees that the step has already
appeared once. However, it would be more informative to show the step
name and to indicate that the process enters a cycle at this point. It would
also be helpful to indicate which composites are alternations as opposed
to sequences.

To create a pretty printer for processes, you can create a visitor class that
initializes a StringBuilder object and that adds to this buffer as the visitor
visits the nodes in a process component. To indicate that a composite step
is an alternation, the visitor can prepend a question mark ("?") to an alternation step's name. To indicate that a step has occurred before, the visitor
can attach an ellipsis ("...") to the end of the step's name. With these
changes, the aerial shell process will print out as:

```
Make an aerial shell
    Build inner shell
    Inspect
    ?Rework inner shell, or complete shell
        Rework
            Disassemble
            Make an aerial shell...
        Finish: Attach lift, insert fusing, wrap
```

A process component visitor has to watch for cycles, but this is easily
achieved by using a Set object to keep track of the nodes the visitor has
already seen. The code for this class starts out as:

```csharp
using System;
using System.Text;
using Processes;
using Utilities;
public class PrettyVisitor : IProcessVisitor
{
    public static readonly string INDENT_STRING = "    ";
    private StringBuilder _buf;
    private int _depth;
    private Set _visited;

    public StringBuilder GetPretty(ProcessComponent pc)
    {
        _buf = new StringBuilder();
        _visited = new Set();
        _depth = 0;
        pc.Accept(this);
        return _buf;
    }
}
```

```
    protected void PrintIndentedString(String s)
    {
        for (int i = 0; i < _depth; i++)
        {
            _buf.Append(INDENT_STRING);
        }
        _buf.Append(s);
        _buf.Append("\n");
    }
    // ... Visit() methods ...
}
```

This class uses a `GetPretty()` method to initialize an instance's variables and to kick off the visitor algorithm. The `PrintIndentedString()` method handles the indentation of steps as the algorithm goes deeper and deeper into a composite. When visiting a `ProcessStep` object, the code simply prints the step's name.

```
public void Visit(ProcessStep s)
{
    PrintIndentedString(s.Name);
}
```

You might note from Figure 29.4 that the `ProcessComposite` class does not implement an `Accept()` method, but its subclasses do. Visiting a process alternation or process sequence requires nearly identical logic, as follows:

```
public void Visit(ProcessAlternation a)
{
    VisitComposite("?", a);
}
public void Visit(ProcessSequence s)
{
    VisitComposite("", s);
}
protected void VisitComposite(
    String prefix, ProcessComposite c)
{
    if (_visited.Contains(c))
    {
        PrintIndentedString(prefix + c.Name + "...");
    }
    else
    {
        _visited.Add(c);
        PrintIndentedString(prefix + c.Name);
        _depth++;
        foreach (ProcessComponent child in c.Children)
        {
            child.Accept(this);
        }
        _depth--;
    }
}
```

The difference between visiting an alternation and a sequence is that an alternation prints a question mark as a prefix. For either type of composite, if the algorithm has visited the node before, we print its name and an ellipsis. Otherwise, we add this node to a collection of visited nodes, print its prefix (a question mark or nothing), and "accept" the nodes, children. As is typical of the VISITOR pattern, the code uses polymorphism to decide if child nodes are instances of the ProcessStep, ProcessAlternation, or ProcessSequence classes.

A short program can now pretty print a process flow.

```
using System;
using Processes;
public class ShowPrettyVisitor
{
    public static void Main()
    {
        ProcessComponent p = ShellProcess.Make();
        PrettyVisitor v = new PrettyVisitor();
        Console.WriteLine(v.GetPretty(p));
    }
}
```

Running this program prints the following:

```
Make an aerial shell
    Build inner shell
    Inspect
    ?Rework inner shell, or complete shell
        Rework
            Disassemble
            Make an aerial shell...
    Finish: Attach lift, insert fusing, wrap
```

This output is more informative than the printout we achieved by just iterating over the process model. The one question mark that appears signals that this composite's steps are alternatives. Also, showing the Make step a second time, followed by an ellipsis, is more clear than simply omitting a repeated step.

The developers of the ProcessComponent hierarchy built in support for VISITOR by including Accept() methods in the hierarchy and by defining the IProcessVisitor interface. These developers are well aware of the need to avoid infinite loops while traversing process flows. As the PrettyVisitor class shows, the developers of the visitor also have to be aware of the potential for cycles in process components. It might help prevent errors if the ProcessComponent developers could provide some degree of cycle management support as part of their support of VISITOR.

Challenge 29.3

How can the `ProcessComponent` developers include cycle management support in the hierarchy's support for Visitor?

A solution appears on page 415.

Visitor Controversy

Visitor is a controversial pattern. Some developers consistently avoid applying it, while others defend its use and suggest ways to strengthen it, although these suggestions usually add complexity. The fact is that many design problems tend to accompany the Visitor pattern.

The fragility of Visitor shows up in the examples in this chapter. For instance, in the `MachineComponent` hierarchy, the hierarchy developers decided to differentiate between `Machine` nodes and `MachineComposite` nodes, but not to differentiate between `Machine` subclasses. If you need to distinguish between types of machines in your visitor, you will have to resort to using `is` or some other technique to tell which type of machine a `Visit()` method has received. You might argue that the hierarchy developers should have included all machine types as well as a catchall `Visit(:Machine)` method in the visitor interface. But new machine types come along all the time, so this does not appear to be any sturdier.

Another example of fragility showed up in the `ProcessComponent` hierarchy. The developers of the hierarchy are aware of the danger of cycles that lurks within process flow models. But can they convey their concerns to a visitor developer?

These problems may expose the fundamental problem with Visitor: Extending a hierarchy's behavior usually requires some expert knowledge of the hierarchy's design. If you lack that expertise, you may step in a trap such as not avoiding cycles in a process flow. If you do have expert knowledge of the hierarchy's mechanics, you may build in dangerous dependencies that will break if the hierarchy changes. The division of expertise and code control can make Visitor a dangerous pattern to apply.

The classic case where Visitor seems to work well without creating downstream problems is in computer language parsers. Parser developers often arrange for a parser to create an *abstract syntax tree*, a structure that organizes the input text according to the language's grammar. You may want to develop a variety of behaviors to accompany these trees, and the Visitor pattern is an effective approach for allowing this. In this classic case, there is usually little or no behavior in the visited hierarchy. Thus, all the responsibility for behavior design lies with visitors, avoiding the split of responsibility that this chapter's examples must endure.

Like any pattern, VISITOR is never necessary; if it were, it would automatically appear everywhere it was needed. For VISITOR, though, there are often alternatives that provide a sturdier design.

Challenge 29.4

List two alternatives to building VISITOR into the Oozinoz machine and process hierarchies.

A solution appears on page 416.

Summary

The VISITOR pattern lets you define a new operation for a hierarchy without changing the hierarchy classes. The mechanics for VISITOR include defining an interface for visitors and adding Accept() methods in the hierarchy that a visitor will call. The Accept() methods dispatch their calls back to the visitor in a double-dispatching scheme. This scheme arranges for the execution of a Visit() method that applies to the specific type of object from the hierarchy.

A visitor developer must be aware of some, if not all, the subtleties in the design of the visited hierarchy. In particular, visitors need to beware of cycles that may occur in the visited object model. This type of difficulty leads some developers to eschew VISITOR, regularly applying alternatives instead. Whether or not you use VISITOR should probably be a team decision that depends on your methodology and the specifics of your application.

APPENDIX A

DIRECTIONS

If you have read the book up to this point, congratulations! If you have worked through all the challenges, then I salute you! I feel confident that if you have read this book and worked the challenges, then you have developed a strong, working knowledge of design patterns. Now, where can you go from here?

Get the Most Out of This Book

If you have *not* worked through the challenges in this book... you are not alone! We are all busy and it is quite tempting to think about a challenge momentarily and then glance at the solution. That is certainly an ordinary experience, but you have the potential to become an extraordinary developer. Go back and rework the challenges, turning to the solutions only when you think you've got a correct answer or when you're completely stumped. Work through the challenges *now*—don't kid yourself that you'll somehow have more time later. By exercising your patterns knowledge on these challenges, you'll build the confidence you need to start applying patterns in your work.

In addition to working the challenges in this book, I suggest that you download the code from www.oozinoz.com and ensure that you can repeat the results of this book's examples on your own system. Knowing that you can get the code to run will give you more confidence than just working examples on paper. You may also want to set up new challenges for yourself. Perhaps you will want to combine decorator filters in a new way, or implement a data adapter that shows data from a familiar domain.

As you build fluency with design patterns, you should start to see that you understand classic examples of design patterns and you will begin to find ways to incorporate design patterns in your own code.

Understand the Classics

Design patterns often make a design stronger. This is not a new idea, so it is no surprise that many design patterns are built into the .NET FCL. If you can spot a design pattern in a body of code, then you can grasp the design yourself and communicate it to others that understand design patterns. For example, if a developer understands how DECORATOR works, then it is meaningful to explain that C# streams are decorators.

Here is a test of your understanding of some of the classic examples of design patterns that appear in C# and the FCL:

- How do GUI controls employ the OBSERVER pattern?
- Why do menus often use the COMMAND pattern?
- Why do drivers provide a good example of the BRIDGE pattern? Is each particular driver an instance of the ADAPTER pattern?
- What does it mean to say that C# streams employ the DECORATOR pattern?
- Why is the PROXY pattern fundamental to the design of ASP.NET?
- If sorting provides a good example of the TEMPLATE METHOD pattern, which step of the algorithm is left unspecified?

A good goal is to be able to answer these questions without referring to this book. It is also a good exercise to write down your answers, and to share your answers with a colleague.

Weave Patterns into Your Code

A primary purpose for learning design patterns is to become a better developer. Think about how to use patterns in the codebase that you work with most often. Here you have two choices: apply design patterns as you add new code, or apply design patterns through refactoring. If part of your code is complex and hard to maintain, you may be able to improve it by refactoring the code and employing a design pattern. Before diving into such a project, make sure that you have a customer for the result. Also be sure to create an automated test suite for the code that you are refactoring before you change the code.

Now, suppose that you understand the patterns you have studied and you're determined to employ them carefully and appropriately. How do you find an opportunity? Some opportunities arise fairly frequently. If you're looking for a chance to apply design patterns, consider the following:

- Does your codebase have any complex code that deals with the state of a system or the state of the application user? If so, you may be able to improve the code by applying the STATE pattern.

- Does your code combine the selection of a strategy with the execution of that strategy? If it does, you may be able to make the code better by using the STRATEGY pattern.

- Does your customer or analyst supply you with flowcharts that translate into code that is difficult to comprehend? If so, you can apply the INTERPRETER pattern, letting each node of the flowchart become an instance of a class in the interpreter hierarchy. You can thus provide a direct translation from the flow chart to the code.

- Does your code contain a weak composite that doesn't allow children to be composites themselves? You may be able to strengthen such code with the COMPOSITE pattern.

- Have you encountered relational integrity errors in your object model? You may be able to prevent them by applying the MEDIATOR pattern to centralize the modeling of object relations.

- Are there places in your code where clients are using information from a service to decide which class to instantiate? You may be able to improve and simplify such code by applying the FACTORY METHOD pattern.

By learning design patterns, you have developed a rich vocabulary of design ideas. If you are on the lookout for opportunities, it probably won't be long before you find a design that you can improve by applying a pattern.

Keep Learning

Somehow you had the opportunity, drive, and ambition to acquire and read this book. All I can say is, keep it up! I think the best advice for you as a developer is to decide how many hours a week you want to spend on your career. Take five hours off the top and pay yourself first. Spend that time away from the office, reading books and magazines or writing software related to any topic that interests you. Make this practice as regular as your office hours. Treat this aspect of your career seriously and you'll become a much better developer, and you'll probably find you enjoy your job more.

Now, suppose that you have given yourself plenty of time and you just need to set your direction. Before learning more about patterns, you may want to make sure that you understand the basics. If you haven't read *C# and the .NET Platform* [Troelsen] or *The Unified Modeling Language User Guide* [Booch], then let me highly recommend them. If you want to learn more about patterns, you have a lot of choices. For a walkthrough of real-istic examples of applying design patterns, I recommend *Pattern Hatching: Design Patterns Applied* [Vlissides]. If you want to add to your patterns vocabulary, my experience is that most shops would benefit from having a local expert on concurrency patterns. To learn about this important and often neglected aspect of development, I recommend reading *Concurrent Programming in Java* [Lea], at least until an equally excellent book on this topic appears for C#.

There are many directions that you can go; the most important practice is to keep going. Make learning a part of your career and pursue the topics that interest you most. Think of how strong you can become as a devel-oper, and become that strong. Keep up the good work!

Steve.Metsker@acm.org

SOLUTIONS

INTRODUCING INTERFACES

Solution 2.1   from page 10

An abstract class with no non-abstract methods is similar to an interface in terms of its utility. However, note the following:

- A class can implement any number of interfaces, but can subclass at most one abstract class.

- An abstract class can have non-abstract methods; all the methods of an interface are effectively abstract.

- An abstract class can declare and use variables; an interface cannot.

- An abstract class can have methods whose access is `public`, `internal`, `protected`, `protected internal`, or `private`. Interface members implicitly have `public` access, and no access modifiers (including `public`) are allowed on interface member declarations.

- An abstract class can define constructors; an interface cannot.

Solution 2.2   from page 13

The `IBorrower` interface requires a single member, the `BorrowReader()` method. The following code places the `IBorrower` interface inside the `DataLayer` namespace:

```
using System.Data;
namespace DataLayer
{
    public interface IBorrower
    {
        object BorrowReader(IDataReader reader);
    }
}
```

You can find this code and all the code for this book at www.oozinoz.com.

A class that borrows a reader using this design might looks as follows:

```
using System;
using System.Data;
using DataLayer;
public class ShowBorrowing2 : IBorrower
{
    public static void Main()
    {
        string sel = "SELECT * FROM ROCKET";
        DataServices2.LendReader2(
            sel, new ShowBorrowing2());
    }
    public object BorrowReader(IDataReader reader)
    {
        while (reader.Read())
        {
            Console.WriteLine(reader["Name"]);
        }
        return null;
    }
}
```

This code prints the same list of rocket names as its predecessor, the Show-Borrowing class.

Solution 2.3   from page 14

A short answer is as follows:

The delegate keyword introduces a new type, while the event keyword introduces a new member. An interface declaration specifies members, not types, and so events belong in interfaces while delegates do not.

A longer answer is:

The event keyword declares a special kind of field (an "event"), specifying its type (which must be a delegate type) and its name. C# limits access to events; clients cannot use all the behaviors of the event's type (its delegate type). Rather, clients may only use the += and -= behaviors that delegates provide. One effect of this limitation is that only the declaring class can invoke (or "fire") an event. But by simply containing a public event member, a class establishes part of the interface clients have to instances of the class. Because the presence of events establishes a standard, specific part of the interface to a class, it is reasonable to allow interfaces to include events.

Solution 2.4   from page 15

One solution is as follows:

```
public interface IAdvertisement2
{
    int ID { get; }
    string AdCopy { get; set; }
}
```

You can find this code in the `lib\ShowProperties` directory of the code available at www.oozinoz.com.

Here is a class that implements `IAdvertisement2`:

```
public class WebAd2 : IAdvertisement2
{
    private int _id;
    private string _adCopy = "";
    public WebAd2 (int id)
    {
        _id = id;
    }
    public int ID
    {
        get { return _id; }
    }
    public string AdCopy
    {
        get { return _adCopy; }
        set { _adCopy = value; }
    }
}
```

Notice that the `set` accessor must use the implicit parameter named `value`.

Solution 2.5 from page 16

The second and third statements are false in the challenge, and are corrected below. The second statement is false because an interface can contain events, not delegates. The third statement is false because it is allowable to define an interface with no members. The corrected statements and their locations in the *C# Language Specification* [Wiltamuth] are:

1. An interface defines a contract. (13, *Interfaces*)

2. Interfaces can contain methods, properties, **events**, and indexers. (13, *Interfaces*)

3. An interface declaration **may** declare **zero** or more members. (13.2, *Interface Members*)

4. All interface members implicitly have public access. (13.2, *Interface Members*)

5. It is a compile-time error for interface member declarations to include any modifiers. (13.2, *Interface Members*)

6. Like a non-abstract class, an abstract class must provide implementations of all members of the interfaces that are listed in

the base class list of the class. (13.4.5, *Abstract Classes and Interfaces*)

ADAPTER

Solution 3.1   from page 23

Your solution should look something like the diagram in Figure B.1.

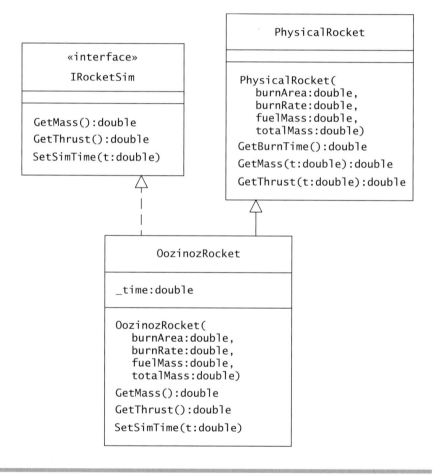

Figure B.1   The OozinozRocket class adapts the PhysicalRocket class to meet the needs declared in the IRocketSim interface.

Instances of the OozinozRocket class can function as either PhysicalRocket objects or as IRocketSim objects. The ADAPTER pattern lets you adapt the methods you have to the ones a client needs.

Solution 3.2   from page 23

The code for the completed class should be:

```
public class OozinozRocket : PhysicalRocket, IRocketSim
{
    private double _time;
    public OozinozRocket(
        double burnArea, double burnRate,
        double fuelMass, double totalMass)
        : base (burnArea, burnRate, fuelMass, totalMass)
    {
    }
    public double GetMass()
    {
        return GetMass(_time);
    }
    public double Thrust()
    {
        return GetThrust(_time);
    }
    public void SetSimTime (double time)
    {
        _time = time;
    }
}
```

You can find this code in the Fireworks library in the source code for this book.

Solution 3.3   from page 27

Figure B.2 shows a solution.

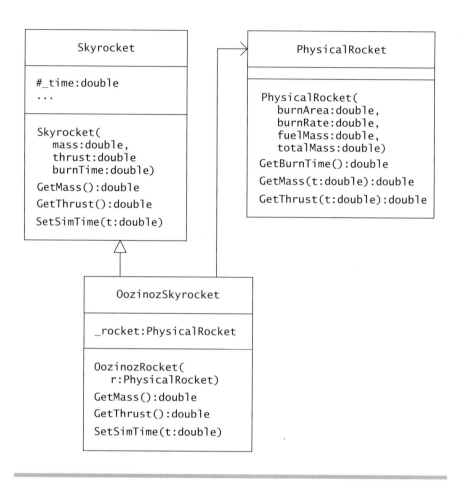

Figure B.2   An OozinozSkyrocket object is a Skyrocket object, but gets its
work done by forwarding calls to a PhysicalRocket object.

The OozinozSkyrocket class is an object adapter. It subclasses Skyrocket so
that an OozinozSkyrocket object can function where a Skyrocket object is
needed.

Solution 3.4   from page 27

Reasons why the object adapter design that OozinozSkyrocket class uses
may be more fragile than a class adapter approach include:

- There is no specification of the interface that OozinozSkyrocket
  class provides. As a result, the Skyrocket might change in ways
  that would create problems at runtime but go undetected at compile-time.

- The OozinozSkyrocket counts on being able to access the _time
  variable, although there is no guarantee that this variable will

always be declared as `protected`, and there is no guarantee about the meaning of this field in the `Skyrocket` class.

Solution 3.5   from page 32

Some good answers are:

- Having a class for each adapter, such as the `ListTable` class, allows adaptation that is specific to the data source. For example, we can augment `ListTable` with methods that allow specification of the order in which a list's objects' properties should appear.

- Moving adaptation logic out of the `DataGrid` class helps to keep the class from bloating with logic that pertains to each possible data source.

- Moving adaptation logic out of `DataGrid` opens the possibility of reusing the logic. For example, we might be able to arrange for a `TextBox` class to use the same adapters that `DataGrid` relies on.

- Specifying an `ITable` interface allows other developers to adapt new, unforeseen data sources to meet the needs of visual controls.

FACADE

Solution 4.1   from page 37

For isolating a developer from a toolkit's complexity, advantages of a facade include:

- Facades are usually easy to understand and use, while an IDE can be overwhelmingly complex itself.

- It is much easier to create a facade than to create an IDE.

- Facades don't generate code, so you don't wind up owning code that you don't want or don't understand.

Advantages of an IDE include:

- An IDE (and its wizards) can show both a simple, no-frills path to using a subsystem, while also allowing use of other features and customizations.

- An IDE is usually less restrictive than a facade in guessing or establishing what a "no-frills" use of a subsystem will be.

- An IDE can explore your environment—finding and testing database connections, for example—and help you generate code that works in your environment.

Solution 4.2   from page 44

Your diagram should look something like Figure B.3.

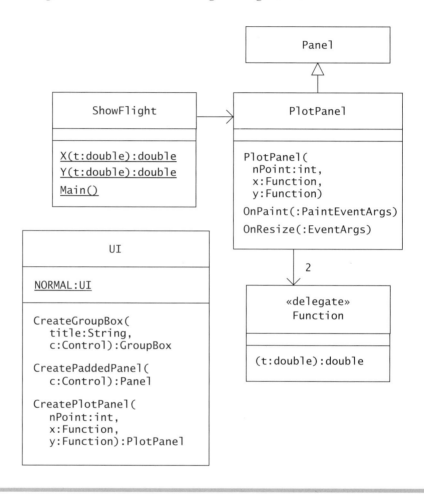

Figure B.3   This diagram shows a refactoring of the flight path application.

Note that all methods of UI are not static methods. Does your solution make these methods static? If not, why not?

The code for this book makes the UI methods non-static so that a UI subclass can override them, creating a different kit for building user interfaces. To make a standard user interface available, this design calls for a singleton NORMAL object that C# can deliver with the following line:

```
public static readonly UI NORMAL = new UI();
```

See Chapter 17, "Abstract Factory," for more information on building GUI kits.

Solution 4.3 from page 47

Some differences to note between demos and facades include:

- A demo is usually a standalone application, while a facade is usually not.
- A demo usually includes sample data; a facade does not.
- A facade is usually configurable, while a demo is not.
- A facade is intended for reuse, while a demo is not.
- A facade is intended for use in production; a demo is not.

Solution 4.4 from page 48

The MessageBox class is one of the few examples of a facade in the FCL. It is production-worthy, configurable, and designed for reuse. Above all else, the MessageBox class fulfills the intent of the FACADE pattern by providing a simple interface that makes it easy to display dialogs.

The MessageBox class is also a utility. Other than the instance methods it inherits from class Object, the MessageBox class has only static methods—overloads of the Show() method.

The MessageBox class does not provide examples or demos of how to use the class, but its associated help in Visual Studio does.

Solution 4.5 from page 48

Here are a few reasonable—but opposing—views regarding the paucity of facades in the .NET FCL.

- As a C# developer, you are well-advised to develop a thorough knowledge of the tools in the FCL. Facades necessarily limit the way you might apply any system. They would be a distraction and a potentially misleading element of the class libraries in which they might appear.
- A facade lies somewhere between the richness of a toolkit and the specificity of a particular application. Creating a facade requires some notion of the type of applications the facade will support. This predictability is impossible given the huge and diverse audience of the FCL.
- The scarcity of facades in the FCL is a weakness. Adding more facades would be a big help.

COMPOSITE

Solution 5.1   from page 50

Designing the Composite class to maintain a collection of Component objects lets a Composite object hold either Leaf objects or other Composite objects.

In other words, this design lets us model groups as collections of other groups. For example, we might want to define a user's system privileges as a collection of either specific privileges or other groups of privileges. As another example, we might want to be able to define a work process as a collection of process steps and other processes. Such definitions are much more flexible than defining a composite to be a collection of leaves.

Solution 5.2   from page 51

For the Machine class, GetMachineCount() should be something like:

```
public override int GetMachineCount()
{
    return 1;
}
```

The class diagram shows that MachineComposite uses a List object to track its components. To count the machines in a composite, you might write:

```
public override int GetMachineCount()
{
    int count = 0;
    foreach (MachineComponent mc in _components)
    {
        count += mc.GetMachineCount();
    }
    return count;
}
```

Solution 5.3   from page 53

Table B.1 provides reasonable definitions of machine composite behaviors.

Table B.1: Machine Composite Behaviors

Method	Class	Definition
GetMachineCount()	MachineComposite	Returns the sum of the counts for each component in components.
	Machine	Returns 1.
IsCompletelyUp()	MachineComposite	Returns true if all components are "completely up."
	Machine	Returns true if this machine is up.
StopAll()	MachineComposite	Tells all components to "stop all."
	Machine	Stops this machine.
GetOwners()	MachineComposite	Creates a set (not a list), adds the owners of all components, and returns the set.
	Machine	Returns this machine's owners.
GetMaterial()	MachineComposite	Returns a collection of all the material on components.
	Machine	Returns the material on this machine.

Solution 5.4   from page 56

The program prints the number "4."

There are in fact only three machines in the plant factory, but machine m is counted by both plant and bay. Both of these objects contain lists of machine components that refer to machine m.

The results could be worse. If, say, an engineer adds the plant object as a component of the bay composite, a call to GetMachineCount() will enter an infinite loop.

Solution 5.5   from page 58

A reasonable implementation of MachineComposite.IsTree() is:

```
public override bool IsTree(Hashtable visited)
{
    visited.Add(this.ID, this);
    foreach (MachineComponent mc in _components)
    {
        if (visited.Contains(mc.ID) || !mc.IsTree(visited))
        {
            return false;
        }
    }
    return true;
}
```

Solution 5.6   from page 60

Your solution should show the links in Figure B.4.

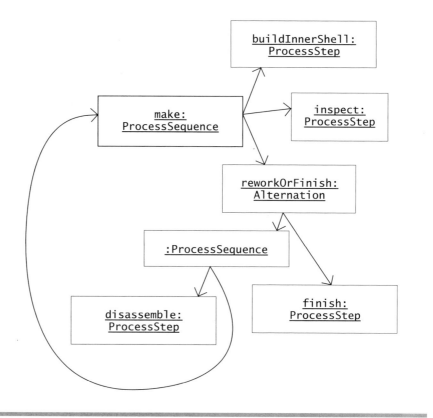

Figure B.4   The cycle inherent in manufacturing aerial shells shows up as a cycle in this object diagram.

BRIDGE

Solution 6.1   from page 66

To control various machines with a common interface, you can apply the ADAPTER pattern, creating an adapter class for each controller. Each adapter class can translate the standard interface calls into calls that existing controllers support.

Solution 6.2   from page 67

Your code should look something like the following:

```
public void Shutdown()
{
    StopProcess();
    ConveyOut();
    StopMachine();
}
```

Solution 6.3   from page 70

Figure B.5 shows a solution.

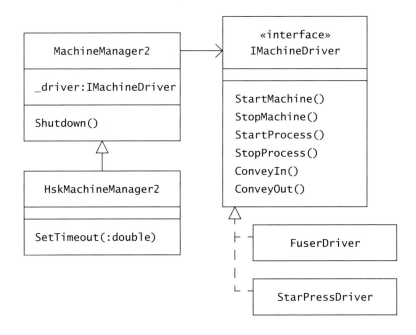

Figure B.5   This diagram shows an abstraction—a hierarchy of types of machine managers—separated from implementations of the abstract driver object the abstraction uses.

Solution 6.4   from page 71

Two arguments in favor of writing code specific to SQL Server are:

- We can't predict the future, so spending money now to prepare for eventualities that may never occur is a classic mistake. We have SQL Server now, and more speed means better response times, which is money in the bank today.

- By admitting that we're using SQL Server, we can use every feature available in the database, without worrying about whether the OLE DB layer supports it.

Two arguments in favor of using the OLE DB adapters and readers:

- If we write our code using OleDbDataAdapter objects, it will be easier to modify our code if we ever change database providers and start using, for example, Oracle. By locking the code into SQL Server, we diminish our ability to benefit from the competitive database market.

- Using OleDbDataAdapter will let us write experimental code that runs against Microsoft Access without relying on a test SQL Server database.

INTRODUCING RESPONSIBILITY

Solution 7.1   from page 76

Some problems with the given diagram are:

- The Rocket.Thrust() method returns a Rocket instead of some type of number or physical quantity.

- The LiquidRocket class has a GetLocation() method, although nothing in the diagram or in the problem domain suggests that we model rockets as having a location. Even if we did, there is no reason for liquid-fueled rockets to have a location while other Rocket objects do not.

- The IsLiquid() method may be an acceptable alternative to using the is operator, but then we'd expect the superclass to also have an IsLiquid() method that would return false.

- CheapRockets is plural, although class names are conventionally singular.

- The CheapRockets class implements IEnumerable, although we usually use collection classes to hold collections, rather than classes named after the objects they contain.

- A CheapRocket is an IEnumerable object composed of other IEnumerable objects. That design might apply to a composite enumerator, but it's hard to imagine how it applies to cheap rockets.

- We could model cheapness with attributes alone, so there is no justification for creating a class just for cheap rockets. The CheapRockets class also introduces a factoring that conflicts with factoring the rocket model as liquid or solid. For example, it is not clear how to model a cheap liquid rocket.

- The model shows that Firework is a subclass of LiquidRocket, declaring that all fireworks are liquid rockets, which is false.

- The model shows a direct relation between reservations and types of fireworks, although no such relation exists in the problem domain.

- The Reservation class has its own copy of _city, which it should get by delegation to a Location object.

Solution 7.2 from page 77

The value of this challenge is not to get the right answer, but rather to exercise your thinking about what makes up a good class. Consider whether your definition addresses the following points:

- A nuts-and-bolts description of a class is: "A class is a data structure that may contain data members (constants and fields), function members (methods, properties, events, indexers, operators, instance constructors, destructors and static constructors), and nested types. Class types support inheritance, a mechanism

whereby a derived class can extend and specialize a base class."
(From C# *Language Specification* [Wiltamuth].)

- A class establishes a collection of fields, which is to say it defines the attributes of an object. The attribute types are other classes, primitive data types (like bool and int), or interfaces.

- A class designer should be able to justify how a class's attributes are related.

- A class should have a cohesive purpose.

- The name of a class should reflect the meaning of the class, both as a collection of attributes and with respect to the class's behavior.

- A class must support all the behaviors it defines, as well as all those in superclasses, and all methods in interfaces that the class implements. (A decision to *not* support a superclass or interface method is occasionally justifiable.)

- A class should have a justifiable relationship to its superclass.

- The name of each of a class's methods should be a good commentary on what the method does.

Solution 7.3   from page 77

Two good observations are that the effects of invoking an operation may depend on the state of the receiving object and on the class of the receiving object.

An example of a method whose effect depends on an object's state appeared in Chapter 6, "Bridge," where the MachineManager2 class has a stopMachine() method. the effects of calling this method depend on which driver is in place for the MachineManager2 object.

When polymorphism is part of a design, the effect of invoking an operation can depend partially or entirely on the class of the receiving object. This principle appears in many patterns that lie ahead, especially FACTORY METHOD, STATE, STRATEGY, COMMAND, and INTERPRETER. For example, a hierarchy of strategy classes may all implement a getRecommended() method, employing different strategies to recommend a fireworks. It is easy to predict that getRecommended() will recommend a fireworks, but it is impossible to know which strategy will be employed without knowing the class of the object that receives the getRecommended() call.

Solution 7.4   from page 78

The code compiles with no problems. Access is defined at a class level, not an object level. So, for example, one Firework object can access another Firework object's private variables and methods.

Solution 7.5 from page 79

The problem is in the following statement:

```
m.Unload();
```

The compiler issues the following complaint:

```
Cannot access protected member 'Machine.Unload()' via a
qualifier of type 'Machine'; the qualifier must be of type
'Hopper' (or derived from it).
```

The `Hopper` class inherits the `Unload()` method and can invoke it, but only on instances of `Hopper` (or on instances of subclasses of `Hopper`).

Solution 7.6 from page 80

The code compiles without problems. Members with `internal` access are accessible within files in the same *assembly*. Although the `Bin` class is in a different namespace than the `Process` class, both classes compile into a single assembly, so the `Bin` class can access `internal` members of a `Process` object.

SINGLETON

Solution 8.1 from page 84

To prevent other developers from instantiating your class, create a single constructor with `private` access. Note that if you create other, non-private constructors, or create no constructors at all, other developers will likely be able to reinstantiate your class.

Solution 8.2 from page 84

Two reasons for lazy-initializing singletons are as follows:

- You might not have enough information to instantiate a singleton at static initialization time. For example, a `Factory` singleton might have to wait for the real factory's machines to establish communication channels.

- You might choose to lazy-initialize a singleton that requires resources, such as a database connection, especially if there is a chance that the containing application will not need the singleton in a particular session.

Solution 8.3 from page 86

Your solution should eliminate the possibility of confusion that can occur when two threads call the `recordWipMove()` method at approximately the same time.

```
public void RecordWipMove()
{
    lock (_classLock)
    {
        _wipMoves++;
    }
}
```

Is it possible that a thread might activate in the middle of an increment operation? Even if you're certain the answer is no, it's a good policy to carefully restrict access to a singleton's data in a multi-threaded application.

Solution 8.4   from page 87

OurBiggestRocket:	This class has an inappropriate name. You should model attributes such as "biggest" with class attributes, not with class names. If a developer *must* sustain this class, then perhaps it is a singleton.
TopSalesAssociate:	This class has the same problem as OurBiggestRocket.
Math:	This class is a *utility*, with all static methods and *no* instances. It is not a singleton.
System.Console:	This is also a utility.
TextWriter:	The Console class forwards Write() and Writeln() calls to its Out object. While the Out object is a Text-Writer object with unique responsibilities, it is not a unique instance of TextWriter, which is not a singleton class.
PrintSpooler:	If you really only have one printer in your company, then PrintSpooler might be a singleton.
PrinterManager:	At Oozinoz, you have lots of printers, and you can look up their addresses through the PrinterManager singleton.

OBSERVER

Solution 9.1 from page 93

One solution is shown in Figure B.6:

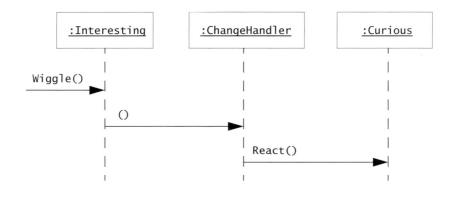

Figure B.6 An `Interesting` object's `Wiggle()` method invokes a delegate that calls a `Curious` object's `React()` method.

Solution 9.2   from page 99

One solution is shown in Figure B.7:

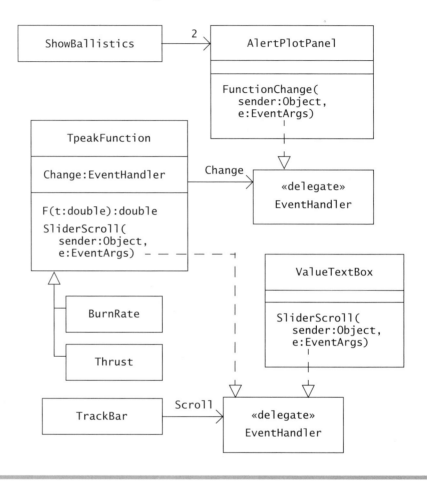

Figure B.7   This design calls for changes to propagate through the object model.

The primary design idea that Figure B.7 illustrates is the introduction of a new "Change" event in the `TpeakFunction2` class from which `Thrust2` and `BurnRate2` inherit. This event is of the same delegate type as the `TrackBar` class's `Scroll` event; the events are instances of the `EventHandler` delegate type.

The plot panels depend on the functions' `Change` events, and the functions depend on the slider's `Scroll` event (that is, the "trackbar's" `Scroll` event). When the slider moves, the functions update themselves and then invoke their `Change` events. Thus, the events flow through the application in the proper order. The design also replaces the TextBox component with a new subclass that registers for and reacts to slider events.

If you would like to see how this design looks in code, it is available in the ShowBallistics2 project.

Solution 9.3   from page 103

Figure B.8 shows a solution.

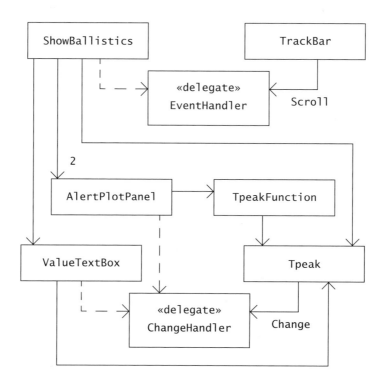

Figure B.8   This design has the application watch the slider, and the text box and plotting panels watch an object that holds the tPeak value.

A Tpeak object that holds a peak time value plays a central role in this design. The ShowBallistics application creates the Tpeak object and updates it whenever the slider moves. The display components (the text box and plotting panels) "listen to" the Tpeak object by instantiating the ChangeHandler delegate with a local method and adding this delegate instance to the Change event of the Tpeak object.

Solution 9.4   from page 106

Figure B.9 shows the calls that flow when a user moves the slider in the ballistics application.

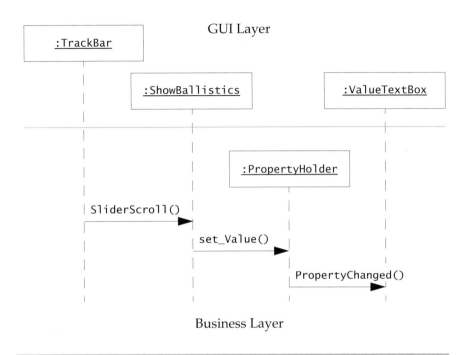

Figure B.9   MVC causes the path of change to loop through a business layer.

You have to use some judgment to complete this diagram. First, the TrackBar object does not actually invoke the SliderScroll() method. In fact, this object invokes its Scroll event and the event object invokes the application's SliderScroll() method through the delegate that the application instantiated and added to the event. You also have to decide how to label the method call that occurs when the code references a property. In fact, C# compilers generate set_XYZ() and get_XYZ() methods to correspond to an XYZ property. Finally, as with the TrackBar object, the PropertyHandler object does not call the ValueTextBox object's PropertyChanged() method directly, but rather invokes its Change event, and this event makes the PropertyChanged() call.

MEDIATOR

Solution 10.1 from page 112

Figure B.10 shows a solution.

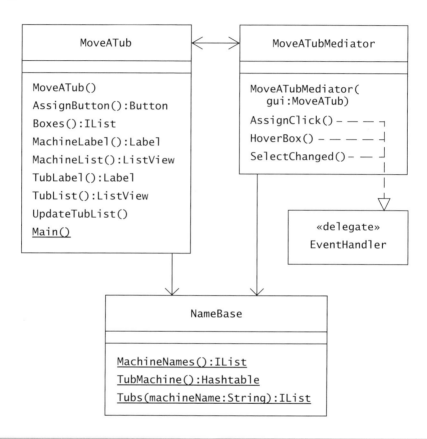

Figure B.10   The `MoveATub` class handles component-building and the
                `MoveATubMediator` class handles events.

In this design, the mediator class has what Martin Fowler calls "feature
envy" in *Refactoring* [Fowler]. The class seems more interested in the GUI
class than in itself, as the `SelectChanged()` method shows.

```
internal void SelectChanged(object sender, EventArgs e)
{
    //...
    _gui.AssignButton().Enabled =
        _gui.MachineList().SelectedItems.Count > 0 &&
        _gui.TubList().SelectedItems.Count > 0;
}
```

Some developers have a distaste for feature envy that will keep them from this type of design. You may find, though, that you like having one class for GUI component construction and layout, and a separate class for component interaction and the flow of use cases.

Solution 10.2   from page 113

Figure B.11 shows one solution.

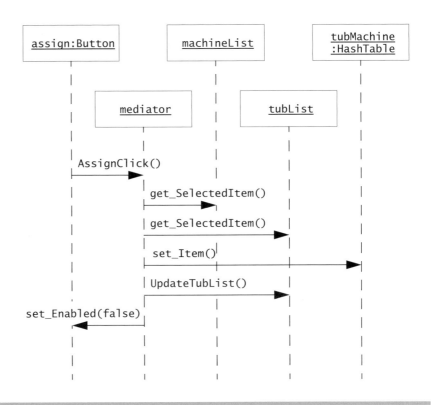

Figure B.11   This diagram highlights the central role of the mediator.

This solution takes liberties with the naming of messages in the sequence diagram. For example, references to a ListBox object's SelectedItem property appear as if they were method calls, as does the reference to the assign button's Enabled property. How you name messages in a sequence diagram is not as important as whether you feel that diagram will illustrate important points for another developer. The provided solution shows the role of the mediator as a dispatcher, receiving an event and taking responsibility for updating all objects affected by the event.

Solution 10.3 from page 117

Figure B.12 shows an updated object diagram.

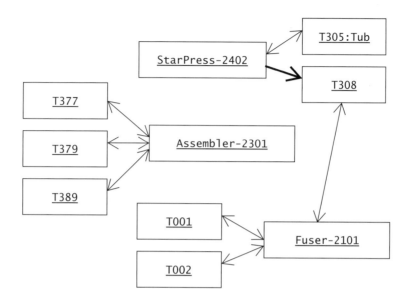

Figure B.12   Two machines think they contain tub T20308. The object model accepts a situation that neither a relational table nor reality will allow.

The problem that the developer's code introduces is that StarPress-2402 still thinks that it has tub T308. In a relational table, changing the machine attribute of a row automatically removes the tub from the prior machine. This automated removal does not occur when the relation is dispersed across a distributed object model. The proper modeling of the Tub/ Machine relation requires special logic that you can remove to a separate mediator object.

Solution 10.4 from page 120

The complete code for the TubMediator class should look something like:

```
public class TubMediator
{
    private Hashtable _tubMachine = new Hashtable();

    public Machine GetMachine(Tub t)
    {
        return (Machine) _tubMachine[t];
    }

    public IList GetTubs(Machine m)
    {
```

```
ArrayList al = new ArrayList();
IDictionaryEnumerator e =
    _tubMachine.GetEnumerator();
while (e.MoveNext())
{
    if(e.Value.Equals(m))
    {
        al.Add(e.Key);
    }
}
return al;
}
public void Set(Tub t, Machine m)
{
    _tubMachine[t] = m;
}
}
```

Solution 10.5   from page 121

- The FACADE pattern may help to refactor a large application.

- The BRIDGE pattern moves abstract operations to an interface.

- The OBSERVER pattern may appear as you refactor code to support an MVC architecture.

- The FLYWEIGHT pattern extricates the immutable part of an object so that this part can be shared.

- The BUILDER pattern moves the construction logic for an object outside the class to instantiate.

- The FACTORY METHOD pattern lets you reduce the amount of responsibility in a class hierarchy by moving an aspect of behavior to a parallel hierarchy.

- The STATE and STRATEGY patterns let you move state-specific and strategy-specific behavior into separate classes.

PROXY

Solution 11.1   from page 126

Problems with the design include:

- There is no clear requirement for the ability to show a temporary image while a large image loads. Most computers built since 2002 can load a full-screen image in less than a tenth of a second.

- Forwarding a subset of calls to an underlying PictureBox object is dangerous. The PictureBox class inherits over 50 (!) properties and over 30 methods from the Control class. To be a true proxy, the `PictureBoxProxy` object needs to forward most or all of these calls. Thorough forwarding would require many potentially erroneous methods, and this code would require maintenance as the `Control` class and its superclasses change over time.

- To create a slightly modified version of `PictureBox`, it is much easier to subclass the `PictureBox` class.

- You might question whether the "Absent" image and the desired image are in the right places in the design. It might make more sense to have the underlying `PictureBox` object leave its image null and have the `PictureBoxProxy` object control both the initial and desired image.

Solution 11.2   from page 127

There are many possible uses for a data reader proxy, including:

- Limiting access to specific fields (such as salaries or trade-secret information) in specific records

- Diverting requests to other data sources such as caches, other databases, or Web services

- Editing data from the database, such as upcasing rocket names

- Monitoring, logging, or simply counting data accesses

Solution 11.3   from page 131

One solution reads as follows:

```
using System;
using System.Data;
using DataLayer;
public class LimitingReader : DataReaderProxy
{
    public LimitingReader(IDataReader subject) :
        base (subject)
    {
    }
    public override object this [string name]
    {
        get
        {
            if (String.Compare(name, "apogee", true) == 0)
            {
                return 0;
            }
            else
            {
                return base [name];
            }
        }
    }
}
```

The constructor has no responsibility beyond passing the subject reader up to the superclass constructor. The indexer checks the name of the desired attribute and returns 0 if the name matches "apogee".

Note that there is a serious, but pluggable, hole in this design: Users of a LimitingReader object can acquire apogee information by using a numeric index. This problem is a reminder that part of the difficulty of PROXY is that you have to be aware of the behavior of every proxied method.

Solution 11.4   from page 136

One solution is:

```
using System;
class ShowClient
{
    static void Main()
    {
        Rocket r =
            new DataWebService().RocketHome("jsquirrel");
        Console.WriteLine(
            "Rocket {0}, Thrust: {1} Price: {2:C}",
            r.Name, r.Thrust, r.Price);
    }
}
```

CHAIN OF RESPONSIBILITY

Solution 12.1   from page 141

Some of the possible disadvantages of the CHAIN OF RESPONSIBILITY design that Oozinoz uses for finding a machine's responsible engineer include:

- We haven't specified how machines know their parent. In practice it may be difficult to ensure that parents are never null.

- The present design is light on details regarding how the system knows which engineers are presently in the factory and available. It's not clear how "real-time" this responsibility needs to be.

- It is conceivable that the search for a parent could enter an infinite loop.

Solution 12.2   from page 143

Your diagram should look similar to Figure B.13.

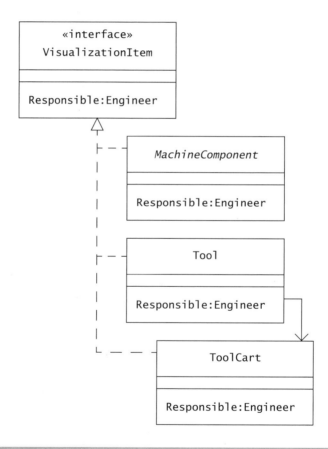

Figure B.13   Every `VisualizationItem` object can respond to a `Responsible` property request. Internally, a `VisualizationItem` object may forward the request to another object parent.

With this design, any client of any simulated item can simply ask the item for the responsible engineer. This approach relieves clients from the task

of determining which objects understand responsibility and puts the
onus on objects that implement the VisualizationItem interface.

Solution 12.3   from page 144

A) A MachineComponent object may have an explicitly assigned responsible person. If it doesn't, it passes the request to its parent.

```
public Engineer getResponsible()
{
    if (responsible != null)
    {
        return responsible;
    }
    if (parent != null)
    {
        return parent.getResponsible();
    }
    return null;
}
```

B) The code for Tool.Responsible reflects the statement that "Tools
are always assigned to tool carts."

```
public Engineer Responsible
{
    get
    {
        return _toolCart.Responsible;
    }
}
```

C) The ToolCart code reflects the statement that "Tool carts have a
responsible engineer."

```
public Engineer Responsible
{
    get
    {
        return _responsible;
    }
}
```

Solution 12.4   from page 145

Your solution should look something like Figure B.14.

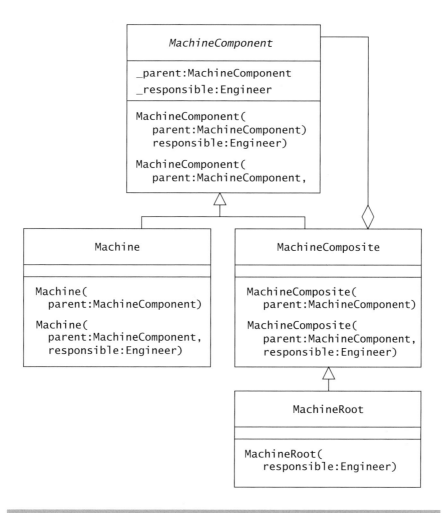

Figure B.14   The constructors in the MachineComponent hierarchy support
the rules that a MachineRoot object must have a responsible
engineer, and every MachineComponent object except a root
must have a parent.

Your constructors should allow Machine and MachineComposite objects to
be instantiated with or without an assigned engineer. Whenever a
MachineComponent object does not have an assigned engineer, it can get a
responsible engineer from its parent.

Solution 12.5   from page 146

Two examples where CHAIN OF RESPONSIBILITY might apply to objects that do not form a composite are:

- A chain of on-call engineers that follows a standard rotation. If the primary on-call engineer does not answer a production support page in a specific amount of time, the notification system pages the next engineer in the chain.

- When users enter information such as the date of an event, a chain of parsers can take turns trying to decode the user's text.

FLYWEIGHT

Solution 13.1   from page 148

An argument *for* the immutability of strings is:

In practice, strings are frequently shared among clients. If strings were mutable, many defects would occur as clients inadvertently affected each other. For example, a method that returns a customer's name as a string will typically retain its reference to the name. If the client, say, uppercases the string to use it in a hash table, the Customer *object's name would change as well, if not for the immutability of strings. In C#, you can produce an uppercase version of a string, but this must be a new object, not an altered version of the initial string. The immutability of strings makes them safe to share among multiple clients.*

An argument *against* the immutability of strings is:

The immutability of strings protects us from certain errors, but at a heavy price. First, developers are cut off from any ability to change a string, regardless of how we might justify this need. Second, adding special rules to a language makes the language harder to learn and use. C# is far, far more difficult to learn than the equally powerful Smalltalk language. Finally, no computer language can keep you from making errors. You'd be much better off if you could learn the language quickly, so that you'd have time to also learn how to set up and use a testing framework.

Solution 13.2   from page 149

You can move the immutable aspects of a substance, including its name, symbol, and atomic weight, into the Chemical class as Figure B.15 shows.

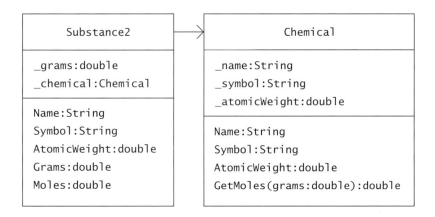

Figure B.15   The immutable part of the original Substance class is extracted into a separate class, Chemical.

The Substance2 class now maintains a reference to a Chemical object. As a result, the Substance2 class can still offer the same properties as the earlier Substance class. Internally, these properties rely on the Chemical class as the following Substance properties demonstrate:

```
public double AtomicWeight
{
    get
    {
        return _chemical.AtomicWeight;
    }
}
public double Grams
{
    get
    {
        return _grams;
    }
}
public double Moles
{
    get
    {
        return _grams / AtomicWeight;
    }
}
```

Solution 13.3   from page 151

A solution that might be tempting that you need to rule out is to make the Chemical constructor private. That will prevent the ChemicalFactory class from instantiating the Chemical class.

To help prevent developers from instantiating the Chemical class themselves, you can place Chemical and ChemicalFactory classes in the same assembly, and give the Chemical class's constructor internal access.

Solution 13.4   from page 153

Using a nested class is a more complex but more thorough approach to ensuring that only the ChemicalFactory2 class can instantiate new flyweights. The resulting code will look something like this:

```
using System;
using System.Collections;
namespace Chemicals
{
    public class ChemicalFactory2
    {
        private static Hashtable _chemicals =
            new Hashtable();
        private class ChemicalImpl : IChemical
        {
            private String _name;
            private String _symbol;
            private double _atomicWeight;

            internal ChemicalImpl (
                String name,
                String symbol,
                double atomicWeight)
            {
                _name = name;
                _symbol = symbol;
                _atomicWeight = atomicWeight;
            }
            public string Name
            {
                get { return _name; }
            }
            public string Symbol
            {
                get { return _symbol; }
            }
            public double AtomicWeight
            {
                get { return _atomicWeight; }
            }
        }
        static ChemicalFactory2 ()
        {
            _chemicals["carbon"] =
                new ChemicalImpl("Carbon", "C", 12);
```

```
            _chemicals["sulfur"] =
                new ChemicalImpl("Sulfur", "S", 32);
            _chemicals["saltpeter"] =
                new ChemicalImpl("Saltpeter", "KNO3", 101);
            //...
        }
        public static IChemical GetChemical(String name)
        {
            return (IChemical) _chemicals[name.ToLower()];
        }
    }
}
```

This code addresses the three challenges as follows:

- The ChemicalImpl nested class should be private so that only the ChemicalFactory2 class can use the class. Note that the nested class's access must be internal or public so that the containing class can instantiate the nested class. Even if you make the constructor public, no other class can use the constructor if the nested class itself is marked private.

- The ChemicalFactory2 constructor must be static to ensure that the class will build the list of chemicals exactly once.

- The GetChemical() method should look up chemicals by name in the class's hash table. The example code stores and looks up chemicals using the lowercase version of the chemical name.

INTRODUCING CONSTRUCTION

Solution 14.1   from page 157

Special rules regarding constructors include:

- If you do not supply a constructor for a class, C# will provide a default.

- You must use new to invoke a constructor.

- Constructor names must match the class name.

- The return type of a constructor is an instance of the class, whereas the return type of an ordinary method can be anything.

- Constructors cannot override a superclass constructor, so the new, virtual, override, abstract, and sealed keywords do not apply to constructor declarations.

- Constructors can invoke other constructors with :this() and :base().

Solution 14.2   from page 158

The following code will fail to compile:

```
using System;
public class Fuse
{
    private string _name;
    public Fuse(string name) { this._name = name; }
}
public class QuickFuse : Fuse
{
}
```

The compiler will issue an error something like:

```
No overload for method 'Fuse' takes 0 arguments
```

This error occurs when the compiler encounters the QuickFuse class and provides a default constructor for it. The default constructor has no arguments, and again, by default, invokes its superclass's constructor with no arguments. However, the presence of a Fuse() constructor that accepts a string parameter means that the compiler will no longer supply a default constructor. The default constructor for QuickFuse cannot invoke a superclass constructor with no arguments because this constructor no longer exists.

Solution 14.3   from page 159

The ShowStructs program prints the elements of the points and times arrays, but crashes when it tries to print an element of the strings array. The console output will look like:

```
{X=0,Y=0}
1/1/0001 12:00:00 AM

Unhandled Exception: System.NullReferenceException: Object
reference not set to an instance of an object.
   at ShowStructs.Main(String[] args)
   in c:\...\showstructs.cs:line 14
```

The program allocates the three arrays as follows:

```
Point[] points = new Point[1];
DateTime[] times = new DateTime[1];
String[] strings = new String[1];
```

When this code executes, it allocates all the space necessary and provides initial values for the structs, but not for the String object. Note that the compiler will detect and disallow the use of uninitialized values in a single struct. For example, the following lines will not compile:

```
Point p;
Console.WriteLine(p.X); // fails
```

The compiler will catch that the program uses Point p before p has a value. However, the compiler will not catch this same situation in an array of structs. The program thus prints the default values for a Point and DateTime struct. By comparison, the contents of strings[0] are nothing, not even null, so the program crashes when it refers to this element.

Solution 14.4   from page 159

A cautious answer is that the output depends on the implementation of ToString() in the Firework class. In fact, this method prints just a firework's name, so running ShowReflection produces:

```
Titan
```

The ShowReflection program works by first obtaining the Firework constructor that accepts a name, apogee, and price. The types of these arguments are String, Double, and Decimal, as the following code shows:

```
Type t = typeof(Firework);
ConstructorInfo c = t.GetConstructor(
    new Type[]{
        typeof(String),
        typeof(Double),
        typeof(Decimal)});
```

This code creates an object c that represents a Firework constructor. The following expression invokes this constructor, creating a new Firework object:

```
c.Invoke(new Object[]{"Titan", 6500, 31.95M})
```

Note that the Decimal type of a firework's price requires the suffix M on the literal value 31.95M. The ShowReflection program passes the results of the above invocation to Console.WriteLine(). This method invokes the object's ToString() method, which in the case of a Firework object, prints the firework's name.

BUILDER

Solution 15.1   from page 165

You can make the parser more flexible by letting the Regex object accept multiple blanks after a comma. To do so, change the construction of the Regex object as follows:

```
new Regex(", *")
```

Also, instead of just accepting blanks after a comma, you can allow any kind of whitespace by initializing the Regex object as follows:

```
new Regex(@",\s*")
```

The @",\s*" string requires a leading @ symbol so that the C# compiler will not interpret the backslash as an escape character. The \s characters specify whitespace, which is a "character class" in .NET regular expres-

sions. You can read more about regular expressions by searching
msdn.microsoft.com for "regular expression language elements."

Rather than making the regular expression more flexible, you might question the entire approach. In particular, you might want to press the travel
agencies to begin sending reservations in an XML format. You might
establish a set of tags to use and read them in with the `XmlTextReader`
class. Alternatively (and even more simply), you might establish a format
that a `SoapFormatter` object could accept.

Solution 15.2   from page 168

The `Build()` method of `UnforgivingBuilder` throws an exception if any
attribute is invalid; otherwise, it returns a valid `Reservation` object. Here
is one implementation:

```
public override Reservation Build()
{
    if (_date == DateTime.MinValue)
    {
        throw new BuilderException("Valid date not found");
    }
    if (_city == null)
    {
        throw new BuilderException("Valid city not found");
    }
    if (_headcount < MINHEAD)
    {
        throw new BuilderException(
            "Minimum headcount is " + MINHEAD);
    }
    if (_dollarsPerHead * _headcount < MINTOTAL)
    {
        throw new BuilderException(
            "Minimum total cost is " + MINTOTAL);
    }
    return new Reservation(
        _date,
        _headcount,
        _city,
        _dollarsPerHead,
        _hasSite);
}
```

The code checks that the date is not `DateTime.MinValue`. Since structs cannot be null, we need a way to indicate that a value has not been set. This
code adopts the convention of using the minimal value for a struct to
indicate the lack of a known value.

The code checks that _date and _city values are set, and checks that
headcount and dollars/head values are acceptable. The `Reservation-
Builder` superclass defines the constants MINHEAD and MINTOTAL.

If the builder encounters no problems, it returns a valid `Reservation`
object.

Solution 15.3 from page 169

As before, the code must throw an exception if the reservation fails to specify a city or date as there is no way to guess these values. Regarding missing values for headcount or dollars/head:

1. If the reservation request specifies no headcount and no dollars/head, set the headcount to the minimum and set dollars/head to the minimum total divided by the headcount.

2. If there is no headcount but there is a dollars/head value, set the headcount to be at least the minimum attendance and at least enough to generate enough money for the event.

3. If there is a headcount but no dollars/head value, set the dollars/head value to be high enough to generate the minimum take.

Solution 15.4 from page 169

One solution is as follows:

```
public override Reservation Build()
{
    bool noHeadcount = (_headcount == 0);
    bool noDollarsPerHead = (_dollarsPerHead == 0M);
    //
    if (noHeadcount && noDollarsPerHead)
    {
        _headcount = MINHEAD;
        _dollarsPerHead = MINTOTAL / _headcount;
    }
    else if (noHeadcount)
    {
        _headcount =
            (int) Math.Ceiling(
                (double)(MINTOTAL / _dollarsPerHead));
        _headcount = Math.Max(_headcount, MINHEAD);
    }
    else if (noDollarsPerHead)
    {
        _dollarsPerHead = MINTOTAL / _headcount;
    }
    //
    Check();
    return new Reservation(
        _date,
        _headcount,
        _city,
        _dollarsPerHead,
        _hasSite);
}
```

This code relies on a Check() method that is similar to the Build() method of the UnforgivingBuilder class:

```
    protected void Check()
    {
        if (_date == DateTime.MinValue)
        {
            throw new BuilderException("Valid date not found");
        }
        if (_city == null)
        {
            throw new BuilderException("Valid city not found");
        }
        if (_headcount < MINHEAD)
        {
            throw new BuilderException(
                "Minimum headcount is " + MINHEAD);
        }
        if (_dollarsPerHead * _headcount < MINTOTAL)
        {
            throw new BuilderException(
                "Minimum total cost is " + MINTOTAL);
        }
    }
}
```

FACTORY METHOD

Solution 16.1   from page 173

One solution is:

```
using System;
using System.Collections;
namespace Utilities
{   public class Set
    {
        private Hashtable h = new Hashtable();
        public IEnumerator GetEnumerator()
        {
            return h.Keys.GetEnumerator();
        }
        public void Add(Object o)
        {
            h[o] = null;
        }
    }
}
```

With this code in place, you can use a foreach statement with a Set object.
For example:

```
using System;
using Utilities;
public class ShowSet
{
    public static void Main()
    {
        Set set = new Set();
        set.Add("Shooter");
        set.Add("Orbit");
        set.Add("Shooter");
        set.Add("Biggie");
        foreach (string s in set)
        {
            Console.WriteLine(s);
        }
    }
}
```

This program demonstrates the use of a foreach loop with a Set object. Running it prints out the following:

```
Biggie
Orbit
Shooter
```

Solution 16.2   from page 173

There are many possible answers, but ToString() is probably the most commonly used method that creates a new object. For example, the following code creates a new String object:

```
String s = DateTime.Now.ToString();
```

The creation of strings often happens behind the scenes. Consider:

```
Console.WriteLine(DateTime.Now);
```

This code creates a String object from the DateTime object, ultimately by calling the ToString() method of DateTime structure.

Another frequently used method that creates a new object is Clone(), a method that usually returns a shallow copy of the receiving object.

Solution 16.3   from page 175

Figure B.16 shows that the two credit check classes implement the ICreditCheck interface. The factory class provides a method that returns an ICreditCheck object. The client that calls CreateCreditCheck() does not know the precise class of the object it receives.

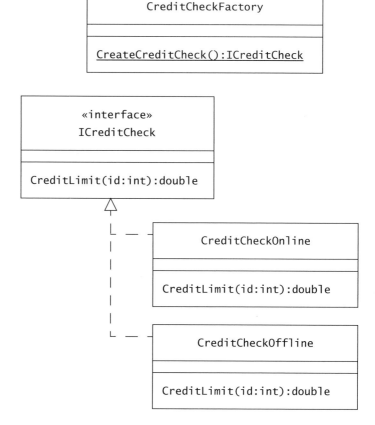

Figure B.16   Two classes implement the ICreditCheck interface. The
              decision of which class to instantiate lies with the service
              provider rather than with the client that needs a credit check.

The CreateCreditCheck() method is a static method, so clients need not
instantiate the CreditCheckFactory class to get an ICreditCheck object.
You can make this class abstract or give it a private constructor if you
want to actively prevent other developers from instantiating it.

Solution 16.4   from page 175

If you take the leap of faith that the static method IsAgencyUp() accurately
reflects reality, the code for CreateCreditCheck() is simple.

```
public static ICreditCheck CreateCreditCheck()
{
    if (IsAgencyUp())
    {
        return new CreditCheckOnline();
    }
    else
    {
        return new CreditCheckOffline();
    }
}
```

Solution 16.5   from page 177

Figure B.17 shows a reasonable diagram for the Machine/MachinePlanner parallel hierarchy.

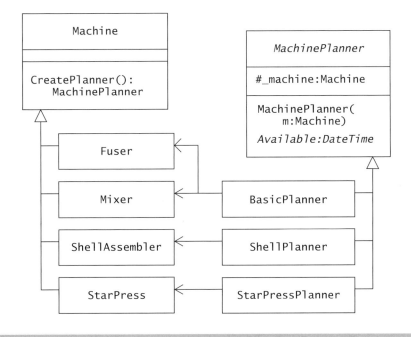

Figure B.17   Planning logic is now in a separate hierarchy. Each subclass of Machine knows which planner to instantiate in respond to a CreatePlanner() call.

This diagram indicates that subclasses of MachinePlanner must implement the Available property. The diagram also indicates that classes in the MachinePlanner hierarchy accept a Machine object in their constructors. This allows the planner to interrogate the object it is planning for, regarding criteria such as the machine's location and the amount of material it is currently processing.

Solution 16.6   from page 177

A `CreatePlanner()` method for the `Machine` class might look like:

```
public virtual MachinePlanner CreatePlanner()
{
    return new BasicPlanner(this);
}
```

The `Fuser` and `Mixer` classes can rely on inheriting this method, while the `ShellAssembler` and `StarPress` class will need to override it. For the Star-Press class, the `CreatePlanner()` method might be:

```
public override MachinePlanner CreatePlanner()
{
    return new StarPressPlanner(this);
}
```

These methods show the FACTORY METHOD pattern at work. When we need a planner object, we call the `CreatePlanner()` message of the machine we want to plan for. The specific planner we receive depends on the machine.

ABSTRACT FACTORY

Solution 17.1   from page 183

One solution is as follows:

```
public class BetaUI : UI
{
    public BetaUI ()
    {
        Font f = Font;
        _font = new Font(f, f.Style ^ FontStyle.Italic);
    }
    public override Button CreateButtonOk()
    {
        Button b = base.CreateButtonOk();
        b.Image = GetImage("cherry-large.gif");
        return b;
    }
    public override Button CreateButtonCancel()
    {
        Button b = base.CreateButtonCancel();
        b.Image = GetImage("cherry-large-down.gif");
        return b;
    }
}
```

This code takes the approach of using the base class methods as much as possible.

Solution 17.2   from page 184

One solution for producing a more resilient design would be to specify the expected creation methods and standard GUI properties in an interface, as Figure B.18 shows.

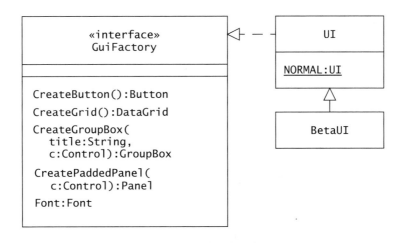

Figure B.18   This design of abstract factories for GUI controls reduces the dependency of subclasses on method modifiers in the UI class.

Solution 17.3   from page 187

Figure B.19 shows a solution to providing concrete classes in Credit.Canada that implement the interfaces and abstract class in Credit.

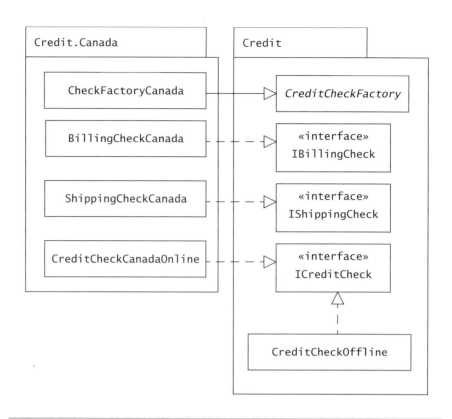

Figure B.19   The `Credit.Canada` package provides a family of concrete
              classes that conducts a variety of checks for Canadian calls.

One subtlety is that you need only one concrete class for offline credit
checking, since at Oozinoz, offline checking is the same for calls from the
U.S. and Canada.

Solution 17.4   from page 189

Here is one solution:

```
using System;
using Credit;
namespace Credit.Canada
{
    public class CheckFactoryCanada : CreditCheckFactory
    {
        public override IBillingCheck CreateBillingCheck()
        {
            return new BillingCheckCanada();
        }
        public override ICreditCheck CreateCreditCheck()
        {
            if (IsAgencyUp())
            {
```

```
                return new CreditCheckCanadaOnline();
            }
            else
            {
                return new CreditCheckOffline();
            }
        }
        public override IShippingCheck CreateShippingCheck()
        {
            return new ShippingCheckCanada();
        }
    }
}
```

Your solution should:

- Have `Create-` methods for any method inherited from the abstract `CreditCheckFactory` class

- Have the proper interface for the return type of each `Create` method

- Return a `CreditCheckOffline` object if the agency is down

Solution 17.5   from page 189

An example justification is:

> *Placing country-specific classes in separate namespaces helps developers at Oozinoz to organize software and development efforts. By placing the classes for each country in a separate namespace, we keep country-specific packages independent of each other. We can be confident, for example, that U.S.-specific classes have no impact on Canada-specific classes. We can also add support for new countries easily. For example, when we start doing business with Mexico, we can create a new namespace that provides the check services we need in a way that makes sense in that country. This has the further advantage of letting us assign the* `Credit.Mexico` *package to a developer who has expertise in working with services and data from Mexico.*

An argument against:

> *Although this separation is nice in theory, it's overwrought in practice. We'd rather have one namespace with all classes in it, at least until we expand to nine or ten countries. Spreading these classes over multiple namespaces winds up causing three (or more) times the configuration management work when a change that cuts across all of these namespaces needs to be implemented.*

PROTOTYPE

Solution 18.1   from page 193

Advantages of this design include:

- We can create new factories without creating a new class; we might even create a new GUI kit at runtime.

- We can produce a new factory by copying one and making slight adjustments. For example, we can make the GUI kit for a beta release identical to the normal kit except for font differences. The PROTOTYPE approach lets a new factory's buttons and other controls "inherit" values such as colors from a predecessor factory.

Disadvantages include:

- The PROTOTYPE approach lets us change values such as colors and fonts for each factory, but does not allow us to produce new kits that have different behavior. For example, the current `BetaUI` class overrides the `ListView()` method to rotate the list's images. We can't duplicate that functionality with PROTOTYPE.

- The motivation for stopping the proliferation of user interface kit classes is not clear—why is this proliferation a problem? We have to put the kit initialization software somewhere, presumably on static methods on the proposed `UIKit` class. This approach doesn't really cut down on the amount of code we have to manage.

What's the right answer? In a situation like this, it may help to experiment: Write code that follows both designs and evaluate how the design looks in practice. There will be times, though, when team members fundamentally disagree about which direction to take. This is a good thing—it shows that you are surfacing and discussing design. If you never disagree, you are likely not hammering out the best design. For those times when you do disagree, even after thoughtful discussion, you may need an architect, a lead designer, or a neutral third party to break ties.

Solution 18.2   from page 194

One way to summarize the function of `MemberwiseClone()` is "new object, same fields."

The `MemberwiseClone()` method creates a new object with the same class and attribute types as the original. The new object also receives all the same field values as the original. If these fields are base types, such as integers, the values are copied. But if the fields are references, the *references* are copied.

The object that the MemberwiseClone() method creates is a *shallow copy*; it shares any subordinate objects with the original. A *deep copy* would include complete copies of all of the parent object's attributes.

Suppose that a Machine object has a numeric ID and a Location attribute, where Location is another class. Then the results of calling Memberwise-Clone() on a Machine object will be a new Machine object with a copy of the ID and with a reference to the same Location object as the original. The copy and original will share the Location object, which is almost surely not the desired result. Calling MemberwiseClone() is often only the first step in creating a valid copy.

Solution 18.3   from page 194

The suggested code will leave just three objects, as Figure B.20 shows.

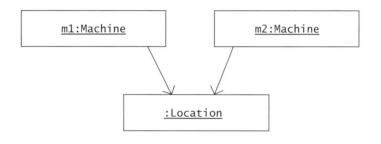

Figure B.20   An insufficient design for cloning can create an incomplete copy that shares some objects with its prototype.

The current version of the Clone() method for MachineSimulator calls base.Memberwiseclone(), which class Object implements. This method creates a new object with the same fields. Primitive types, such as the int instance fields in a MachineSimulator, are copied. In addition, object references, such as the Location field in MachineSimulator, are copied. Note that the *reference* is copied, not the object. This means that Object.MemberwiseClone() produces the situation that Figure B.20 shows.

The code in the challenge changes the bay and coordinates of the second machine's location. However, since there is really only one Location object, this modification changes the location of both simulations. Thus, the println() statement displays 2 as the value of m1.location.bay.

Solution 18.4   from page 196

A reasonable solution is as follows:

```
using System;
using System.Windows.Forms;
namespace UserInterface
{
    public class OzGroupBox : GroupBox
    {
        public OzGroupBox Copy()
        {
            return (OzGroupBox) this.MemberwiseClone();
        }
        public OzGroupBox Copy2()
        {
            OzGroupBox gb = new OzGroupBox();
            gb.BackColor = BackColor;
            gb.Dock = Dock;
            gb.Font = Font;
            gb.ForeColor = ForeColor;
            return gb;
        }
    }
}
```

Both the Copy() method and the Copy2() method relieve clients of OzGroupBox from invoking a constructor and thus support the PROTOTYPE idea. However, the manual approach of Copy2() may be much safer. This approach relies on knowing which attributes are important to copy, but it avoids copying attributes that you may know nothing about.

MEMENTO

Solution 19.1   from page 203

Here is one implementation of the Pop() for FactoryModel:

```
public void Pop()
{
    if (_mementos.Count > 1)
    {
        _mementos.Pop(); // pop the current state
        if (RebuildEvent != null) RebuildEvent();
    }
}
```

This code is careful to ignore Pop() requests if the stack is down to its initial state with a single memento. The top of the stack is always the current state, so the Pop() code has only to pop the stack to expose the previous memento.

When you write a createMemento() method, you should convince yourself (or your colleagues) that the method returns all the information necessary to reconstruct the receiving object. In this example, a machine simulator can reconstruct itself from a clone, and a factory simulator can reconstruct itself from a list of machine simulator clones.

Solution 19.2   from page 206

The `HandleUndo()` method rebuilds the picture boxes in the panel that shows the following machines:

```
protected void HandleUndo()
{
    MachinePanel().Controls.Clear();
    foreach (Point p in _factoryModel.Locations)
    {
        MachinePanel().Controls.Add(CreatePictureBox(p));
    }
    UndoButton().Enabled = _factoryModel.MementoCount > 1;
}
```

This code also ensures that if the factory model contains just the initial, empty list of machines, the user cannot request a further undo.

Solution 19.3   from page 206

Storing a memento as an object assumes that the application will still be running when the user wants to restore the original object. Reasons that will force you to save a memento to persistent storage include:

- The ability to restore an object's state has to survive a system crash

- You anticipate the user will exit the system and will want to resume work later

- You need to reconstruct an object on another computer

Solution 19.4   from page 208

One solution is:

```
internal void Restore(object sender, System.EventArgs e)
{
    OpenFileDialog d = new OpenFileDialog();
    if (d.ShowDialog() == DialogResult.OK)
    {
        using (FileStream fs =
            File.Open(d.FileName, FileMode.Open))
        {
            IList list = (IList)
                (new SoapFormatter().Deserialize(fs));
            _factoryModel.Push(list);
        }
    }
}
```

This code is almost a mirror of the Save() method, although the Restore() method must cast the deserialized value and must ask the factory model to push the recovered location list.

Solution 19.5   from page 209

The meaning of *encapsulation* is to limit access to an object's state and operations. Saving an object (such as a collection of factory location points) in textual form exposes the object's data and allows anyone with a text editor to change the object's state. Thus, saving an object as a SOAP-formatted string violates encapsulation, at least in theory.

Violation of encapsulation through persistent storage may be a concern in practice, depending on your application. To address this threat, you might limit access to the data (as is common in a relational database). In other cases, you might encrypt the data (as is common when transmitting sensitive HTML text). The point here is not whether the words *encapsulation* and *memento* apply to a design so much as the real importance of ensuring data integrity while supporting the data's storage and transmission.

INTRODUCING OPERATIONS

Solution 20.1   from page 214

CHAIN OF RESPONSIBILITY distributes an operation across a chain of objects. Each method implements the operation's service directly or forwards calls to the next object in the chain.

Solution 20.2   from page 214

A complete list of C# method modifiers is:

```
new public protected internal private static virtual sealed
override abstract extern
```

Although some developers might be tempted to explore using all these modifiers in a single method definition, several rules limit the ability to use them in combination. Section 10.5 of the *C# Language Specification* [Wiltamuth] lists these limitations.

Solution 20.3   from page 215

No. If you were to somehow change the return value of Bitmap.MemberwiseClone(), the code wouldn't compile. The MemberwiseClone() signature matches the signature of Object.MemberwiseClone(), so the return type must match as well.

Solution 20.4   from page 217

1. A delegate declaration	b. defines a class that derives from the class `System.Delegate`.
2. A delegate instance	f. encapsulates one or more methods.
3. The expression on the right side of the += operator	c. creates a delegate instance.
4. `Click`	a. is an instance variable whose type is `System.EventHandler`.
5. The `System.EventHandler` delegate	e. specifies the parameters and return type, but no name for the method.
6. The `LoadImage()` method	d. must have the same parameters and return type as `System.EventHandler`.

Solution 20.5   from page 218

One argument *for* leaving exception declarations out of method headers is:

> *We should first note that Java does not require methods to declare all the exceptions that might be thrown. Any method might, for example, encounter a null pointer and throw an undeclared exception. It's impractical (as Java admits) to force programmers to declare all possible exceptions. Applications need a strategy for handling all exceptions. Requiring developers to declare certain types of exceptions is no substitute for architecting in an exception-handling policy.*

On the other hand:

> *Programmers need all the help they can get. It's true than an application architecture needs to have a solid exception-handling strategy. It's also clearly impractical to force developers to declare in every method the possibility of pervasive problems such as null pointers. But for some errors, such as problems in opening a file, requiring the caller of a method to handle possible exceptions is a useful reminder. C# throws out the baby with the bathwater by removing any declaration of possible exceptions from method headers.*

Solution 20.6   from page 219

The figure shows one algorithm (the procedure to determine if an object model is a tree), two operations (which appear as two signatures in the MachineComponent class), and four methods.

TEMPLATE METHOD

Solution 21.1   from page 226

Your completed program should look something like the following:

```
using System;
using System.Collections;
using Fireworks;
public class ShowComparator
{
    public static void Main()
    {
        Rocket r1 = new Rocket(
            "Mach-it",  1.1, 22.95m, 1000, 70);
        Rocket r2 = new Rocket(
            "Pocket",   0.3,  4.95m,  150, 20);
        Rocket r3 = new Rocket(
            "Sock-it",  0.8, 11.95m,  320, 25);
        Rocket r4 = new Rocket(
            "Sprocket", 1.5, 22.95m,  270, 40);
        Rocket[] rockets = new Rocket[] { r1, r2, r3, r4 };
        Array.Sort(rockets, new ApogeeCompare());
        foreach (Rocket r in rockets)
        {
            Console.WriteLine(r);
        }
    }
    private class ApogeeCompare : IComparer
    {
        public int Compare(Object o1, Object o2)
        {
            Rocket r1 = (Rocket)o1;
            Rocket r2 = (Rocket)o2;
            return r1.Apogee.CompareTo(r2.Apogee);
        }
    }
}
```

Solution 21.2   from page 229

The code for MarkMoldIncomplete() passes the information about an incomplete mold to the material manager. One solution is:

```
            using System;
            using Aster;
            using BusinessCore;
            public class OzAsterStarPress : AsterStarPress
            {
                public override void MarkMoldIncomplete(int id)
                {
                    GetManager().SetMoldIncomplete(id);
                }
                public MaterialManager GetManager()
                {
                    return MaterialManager.GetManager();
                }
            }
```

Solution 21.3   from page 230

What you want is a hook. You might phrase your request something like:

> *I wonder if you could be so kind as to add a call in your*
> ShutDown() *method, after discharging the paste and before*
> *flushing? If you call it something like* CollectPaste(), *I can*
> *use it to save the paste that we reuse here at Oozinoz.*

The developers are likely to negotiate with you concerning the name of the method. The point is that by requesting a hook in a TEMPLATE METHOD, you can make your code much stronger than you can by working around an inadequacy in the existing code.

Solution 21.4   from page 232

The GetPlanner() method in the Machine class should take advantage of the abstract CreatePlanner() method.

```
            public MachinePlanner GetPlanner()
            {
                if (_planner == null)
                {
                    _planner = CreatePlanner();
                }
                return _planner;
            }
```

This code requires that you add a _planner attribute to the Machine class. After adding this attribute and the GetPlanner() method in Machine, you can delete the attribute and method in the subclasses.

This refactoring creates an instance of TEMPLATE METHOD. The GetPlanner() method lazy-initializes the planner variable, relying on the CreatePlanner() step that subclasses supply.

STATE

Solution 22.1   from page 236

As the state machine shows, when the door is open, touching the "one-touch" button will take the door to the StayOpen state, and a second touch will start the door closing.

Solution 22.2   from page 239

Your code should look something like:

```
public void Complete()
{
    if (_state == OPENING)
    {
        SetState(OPEN);
    }
    else if (_state == CLOSING)
    {
        SetState(CLOSED);
    }
}
public void Timeout()
{
    SetState(CLOSING);
}
```

Solution 22.3   from page 244

Your code should look something like:

```
namespace Carousel
{
    public class DoorClosing : DoorState
    {
        public DoorClosing(Door2 door) : base (door)
        {
        }

        public override void Touch()
        {
            _door.SetState(_door.OPENING);
        }

        public override void Complete()
        {
            _door.SetState(_door.CLOSED);
        }
    }
}
```

Solution 22.4   from page 245

Figure B.21 shows a reasonable diagram.

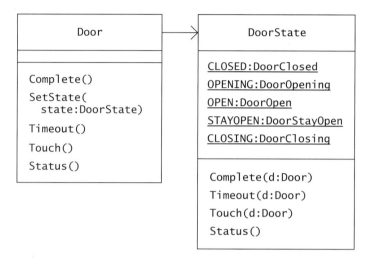

Figure B.21   This design lets DoorState objects be constants. The DoorState
state transition methods update the state of a Door object they
receive as a parameter.

STRATEGY

Solution 23.1   from page 250

Figure B.22 shows one solution.

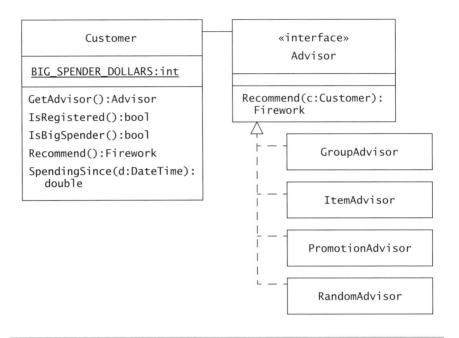

Figure B.22   The advertising policy at Oozinoz includes four strategies that
appear as four implementations of the Advisor interface.

Solution 23.2   from page 252

The GroupAdvisor and ItemAdvisor classes are instances of ADAPTER, providing the interface a client expects using the services of a class with a different interface.

Solution 23.3   from page 255

Your code should look something like:

```
public Firework GetRecommended()
{
    return GetAdvisor().Recommend(this);
}
```

Once the advisor is known, polymorphism does all the work.

Solution 23.4   from page 255

The presence of multiple, similar singletons is reminiscent of the
FLYWEIGHT pattern that organizes a group of similar, shareable, immutable objects. To this point, *Design Patterns* mentions that "STRATEGY objects
often make good flyweights." On the other hand, the intent of FLYWEIGHT
is to use sharing to support large numbers of fine-grained objects efficiently. It's a bit of a stretch to imagine that you'll ever have "large numbers" of alternative strategies.

Solution 23.5 <span></span> from page 256

Is a reusable sort routine an example of TEMPLATE METHOD or an example of STRATEGY?

For STRATEGY:

> TEMPLATE METHOD, *according to the original* Design Patterns *book, lets "subclasses" redefine certain steps of an algorithm. But the* Array.Sort() *method doesn't work with subclasses; it requires a* Comparator *instance. Each instance of* Comparator *provides a new method, and thus a new algorithm and a new strategy. The* Sort() *method is a good example of* STRATEGY.

For TEMPLATE METHOD:

> *There are many sorting algorithms, but* Collections.sort() *employs only one (QuickSort). Changing the algorithm would mean changing to, say, a heap sort or a bubble sort. The intent of* STRATEGY *is to let you plug in different algorithms. That doesn't happen here. The intent of* TEMPLATE METHOD *is to let you plug a step into an algorithm. That is precisely how the* Sort() *method works.*

COMMAND

Solution 24.1 <span></span> from page 258

Your code should look something like the following:

```
using System;
using System.Windows.Forms;
public class ShowCommand : Form
{
    public ShowCommand()
    {
        MenuItem exitItem = new MenuItem();
        exitItem.Text = "Exit";
        exitItem.Click += new EventHandler(ExitApp);

        MenuItem fileItem = new MenuItem();
        fileItem.Text = "File";
        fileItem.MenuItems.Add(exitItem);

        Menu = new MainMenu();
        Menu.MenuItems.Add(fileItem);
        Text = "Show Command";
    }

    static void Main()
    {
```

```
            Application.Run(new ShowCommand());
        }

        private void ExitApp(object o, EventArgs e)
        {
            Application.Exit();
        }
    }
```

The ExitApp() method matches the signature that the EventHandler delegate type requires and achieves the desired result of exiting the application.

Solution 24.2   from page 261

The completed program command should looks something like:

```
using System;
delegate void Command();
class ShowTimerCommand
{
    static void Main()
    {
        Console.WriteLine(TimeThis(new Command(Snooze)));
    }
    static void Snooze()
    {
        System.Threading.Thread.Sleep(2000);
    }
    static TimeSpan TimeThis(Command c)
    {
        DateTime t1 = DateTime.Now;
        c();
        return DateTime.Now.Subtract(t1);
    }
}
```

Running the ShowTimerCommand program will produce a result something like:

```
00:00:02.0028800
```

This is the approximate time it takes a method to "sleep" for 2,000 milliseconds.

Solution 24.3   from page 263

Your code should look something like:

```
public virtual void ShutDown()
{
    if (InProcess())
    {
        StopProcessing();
        if (MoldIncomplete != null)
        {
            MoldIncomplete(this);
        }
    }
    UsherInputMolds();
    DischargePaste();
    Flush();
}
```

Note that the value of the MoldIncomplete delegate variable is null until a client adds a delegate instance to it (with +=).

Solution 24.4   from page 263

In FACTORY METHOD, a client knows *when* to create a new object, but doesn't know what kind of object to create. FACTORY METHOD moves object creation to a method that isolates a client from knowing which class to instantiate. This principle also occurs in ABSTRACT FACTORY.

Solution 24.5   from page 264

The intent of the MEMENTO pattern is to provide storage and restoration of an object's state. Typically, you can add a new memento to a stack with each execution of a command, popping and reapplying these mementos when a user needs to undo commands.

INTERPRETER

Solution 25.1   from page 274

The Execute() method of the ForCommand class should look something like the following code:

```
private void Execute(MachineComponent mc)
{
    Machine m = mc as Machine;
    if (m != null)
    {
        _variable.Assign(new Constant(m));
        _body.Execute();
        return;
    }
    MachineComposite comp = mc as MachineComposite;
    foreach (MachineComponent child in comp.Children)
    {
        Execute(child);
    }
}
```

The Execute() code walks through a machine composite. When it encounters a leaf node—a machine—the code assigns the variable to the machine and executes the ForMachine object's body command.

Is it nonintuitive that nothing forces the _body command to use the same variable the loop sets? If so, note that C# for and foreach loops work this same way. You may get used to seeing a variable that is set in a foreach loop and used in the loop's body, but nothing forces the body to use the variable.

Solution 25.2   from page 278

One solution is:

```
public override void Execute()
{
    if (_term.Eval() != null)
    {
        _body.Execute();
    }
    else
    {
        _elseBody.Execute();
    }
}
```

Solution 25.3   from page 278

One way to write WhileCommand.cs is:

```
using System;
namespace RobotInterpreter2
{
    public class WhileCommand : Command
    {
        protected Term _term;
        protected Command _body;

        public WhileCommand(Term term, Command body)
        {
            _term = term;
```

```
                    _body = body;
                }

                public override void Execute()
                {
                    while (_term.Eval() != null)
                    {
                        _body.Execute();
                    }
                }
            }
        }
    }
```

Solution 25.4   from page 279

One answer is:

> *The intent of the* INTERPRETER *pattern is to let you compose executable objects from a hierarchy of classes that provides various interpretations of a common operation. The intent of* COMMAND *is merely to encapsulate a request in an object.*

Can an interpreter object function as a command? Sure! The question of which pattern applies depends on your intent. Are you creating a toolkit for composing executable objects, or are you encapsulating a request in an object?

INTRODUCING EXTENSIONS

Solution 26.1   from page 285

In mathematics, a circle is certainly a special case of an ellipse. However, in OO programming, an ellipse has certain behaviors that a circle does not. For example, an ellipse may be twice as wide as it is tall—a circle can't do that. If that behavior is important to your program, then a Circle object won't function as an Ellipse object and will represent a violation of LSP.

Solution 26.2   from page 286

The expression tub.Location.IsUp() might lead to programming errors if there are any subtleties around the value of a tub object's Location property. For example, the Location property might be null or might be a Robot object if the tub is in transit. If Location is null, then evaluating tub.Location.IsUp() will throw an exception. If Location is a Robot object, the problem may be even worse as we try to use a robot to collect a tub from itself. These potential problems are manageable, but do we want the ensuing code to be in the method that uses the tub.Location.IsUp() expression? No. The necessary code may already be in the Tub class! If not, it belongs there, to prevent us from having to recode around the same subtleties in other methods that interact with tubs.

Solution 26.3   from page 287

One example is:

```
public static String getZip(String address)
{
    return address.Substring(address.Length - 5);
}
```

There are a few smells here, including "Primitive Obsession," using a string to contain several attributes.

Solution 26.4   from page 288

One set of solutions is shown in the completed Table 26.1:

Table 26.1: Extending Behavior with Design Patterns

Example	Pattern at Play
A fireworks simulation designer establishes an interface that defines the behaviors your object must possess to participate in the simulation	ADAPTER
A toolkit lets you compose executable objects at runtime	INTERPRETER
A superclass has a method that requires subclasses to fill in a missing step	TEMPLATE METHOD
An object lets you extend its behavior by accepting a method encapsulated in an object and invoking that method at an appropriate moment	COMMAND
A code generator inserts behavior that provides the illusion that an object executing on another machine is local	PROXY
A design lets you register for callbacks that will be issued when an object changes	OBSERVER
A design lets you define abstract operations that depend on a well-defined interface and lets you add new drivers that fulfill the interface	BRIDGE

DECORATOR

Solution 27.1 from page 298

One solution is:

```
using System;
namespace Filters
{
    public class RandomCaseFilter : OozinozFilter
    {
        protected Random ran = new Random();
        public RandomCaseFilter(ISimpleWriter writer) :
            base (writer)
        {
        }
        public override void Write(char c)
        {
            _writer.Write(ran.NextDouble() > .5
                ? Char.ToLower(c)
                : Char.ToUpper(c));
        }
    }
}
```

Random text can be eye-catching. Consider the following program:

```
using System;
using Filters;
public class ShowRandom
{
    public static void Main()
    {
        ISimpleWriter w = new RandomCaseFilter(
            new ConsoleWriter());
        w.Write(
            "buy two packs now and get a " +
            "zippie pocket rocket -- free!");
        w.WriteLine();
        w.Close();
    }
}
```

This program uses the ConsoleWriter class developed later in this chapter. Running the program prints something like:

```
bUy tWO pAcks NOw ANd geT A ZiPpIE PoCkEt RocKeT -- frEe!
```

Solution 27.2 from page 300

One solution is:

```
using System;
namespace Filters
{
    public class ConsoleWriter : ISimpleWriter
    {
        public void Write(char c)
        {
            Console.Write(c);
        }
        public void Write(string s)
        {
            Console.Write(s);
        }
        public void WriteLine()
        {
            Console.WriteLine();
        }
        public void Close()
        {
        }
    }
}
```

Solution 27.3   from page 306

One solution is:

```
using System;
namespace Functions
{
    public class Exp : Frapper
    {
        public Exp(Frapper f) : base (f)
        {
        }
        public override double F(double t)
        {
            return Math.Exp(_sources[0].F(t));
        }
    }
}
```

Solution 27.4   from page 308

One solution is:

```
using System;
using System.Windows.Forms;
using Functions;
using UserInterface;

public class ShowBrightness
{
    public static void Main()
    {
        Frapper brightness =
            new Arithmetic(
```

```
            '*',
            new Exp(
                new Arithmetic(
                    '*', new Constant(-4), new T())),
            new Sin(
                new Arithmetic(
                    '*', new Constant(Math.PI), new T()))));
        PlotPanel2 p =
            new PlotPanel2(100, new T(), brightness);
        Panel p2 = UI.NORMAL.CreatePaddedPanel(p);
        GroupBox gb = UI.NORMAL.CreateGroupBox(
            "Brightness vs. Total Burn Time", p2);
        gb.Font = UI.NORMAL.Font;
        Form f = new Form();
        f.DockPadding.All = 10;
        f.Text = "Brightness";
        f.Controls.Add(gb);
        Application.Run(f);
    }
}
```

ITERATOR

Solution 28.1 from page 314

The `DisplayUpMachines()` routine launches a new thread that can wake up at any time, although the `Sleep()` call helps to ensure that `NewMachineComesUp()` executes while `DisplayUpMachines()` is sleeping. The output indicates that in the given run, the `DisplayUpMachines()` method retains control through two iterations, printing the list from index 0 to 1.

```
Mixer:1201
ShellAssembler:1301
```

At this point, the second thread wakes up and places "`Fuser:1101`" at the beginning of the list, bumping all the other machine names down one slot. In particular, "`ShellAssembler:1301`" moves from index 1 to index 2.

When the primary thread regains control, the `DisplayUpMachines()` method prints the remainder of the list, from index 2 to the end.

```
ShellAssembler:1301
StarPress:1401
UnloadBuffer:1501
```

Solution 28.2 from page 316

An argument against the use of `Sychronized()` methods is:

> *The* `Synchronized()` *methods either misfire completely (if you iterate with a* for *loop) or crash the plane, unless you build in*

the logic to catch the exception InvalidOperationException *that gets thrown.*

An argument against a locking-based approach is:

Designs that provide thread-safe iteration rely on cooperation between threads that may access the collection. The whole point of the Synchronized() *methods is to catch the case where threads aren't cooperating.*

Neither the Synchronized() methods nor the locking support built into C# can make multi-threaded development easy and fool-proof. For an excellent source on concurrent programming, read *Concurrent Programming in Java* [Lea].

Solution 28.3   from page 323

As Chapter 16, "FACTORY METHOD," described, iterators provide a classic example of the FACTORY METHOD pattern. A client that wants an enumerator for an instance of a ProcessComponent knows when to create the iterator, but the receiving class knows which class to instantiate.

Solution 28.4   from page 327

One solution is:

```
public override bool MoveNext()
{
    if (!_visited.Contains(_head))
    {
        _visited.Add(_head);
        if (ReturnInterior)
        {
            _current = _head;
            return true;
        }
    }
    return SubiteratorNext();
}
```

VISITOR

Solution 29.1   from page 331

The difference is in the type of the this object. The Accept() method calls the Visit() method of a MachineVisitor object. The Accept() method in the Machine class will look up a Visit() method with the signature visit(:Machine), while the Accept() method in the MachineComposite class will look up a method with the signature visit(:MachineComposite).

Solution 29.2   from page 336

A solution is:

```
using System;
using Machines;
using Utilities;
public class RakeVisitor : IMachineVisitor
{
    protected Set _leaves;
    public Set GetLeaves(MachineComponent mc)
    {
        _leaves = new Set();
        mc.Accept(this);
        return _leaves;
    }
    public void Visit(Machine m)
    {
        _leaves.Add(m);
    }
    public void Visit(MachineComposite mc)
    {
        foreach (MachineComponent child in mc.Children)
        {
            child.Accept(this);
        }
    }
}
```

Solution 29.3   from page 341

One solution is to add a Set argument to all the Accept() and Visit() methods so that the set of visited nodes gets passed around. The Accept() method for the ProcessAlternation, ProcessSequence, and ProcessStep subclasses would be:

```
public void Accept(IProcessVisitor v, Set visited)
{
    v.Visit(this, visited);
}
```

Now visitor developers must create classes with Visit() methods that accept the visited set. This is a significant hint that using the set is a good idea, although the visitor developer retains responsibility for populating the set.

Solution 29.4   from page 342

Alternatives to applying VISITOR include:

- Add the behavior you need to the original hierarchy. You can achieve this if you are in good communication with the hierarchy

developers, or if you are in a shop that does not recognize code
ownership.

- You can let a class that must operate on a machine or process
  structure just traverse the structure. If you need to know the type
  of, say, a composite's child, you can use the is operator, or you
  might build in Boolean functions such as IsLeaf() and IsCompos-
  ite().

- If the behavior you want to add is of a significantly different
  thrust than the existing behavior, you can create a parallel hierarchy. For example, the MachinePlanner class in Chapter 16,
  "Factory Method," places a machine's planning behavior in a
  separate hierarchy.

OOZINOZ SOURCE

The primary benefit of learning about design patterns is that understanding them will help you improve your code. You can make your code smaller, simpler, more elegant, easier to maintain, and more powerful through the application of design patterns. For design patterns to pay off, you need to see design patterns manifest in working code, and you must become comfortable building and rebuilding design patterns into a codebase. It can be helpful to start with working examples, and toward that end this book includes many examples that show the use of design patterns in C# code. Building the Oozinoz source and walking through the code examples that support this book's text will help you to begin using design patterns in your own code.

Acquiring and Using the Source

To get the source code that goes with this book, go to www.oozinoz.com, download the source code zip file, and unzip its contents, placing the code anywhere you like.

The Oozinoz source code is free. You may use it as you wish, with the sole restriction that you may not claim that you wrote it. On the other hand, neither I nor the publisher of this book warrants the code to be useful for any particular purpose.

Building the Oozinoz Code

If you do not have an environment for developing C# and .NET program, you need to acquire one and gain some expertise in using it, so that you are able to write, compile, and execute your own programs. You can purchase a development tool, such as Microsoft's Visual Studio, or you can work with open source tools.

If you have Microsoft's Visual Studio .NET, you can build the Oozinoz software, creating class libraries and executable programs by using the `oozinoz.sln` "solution" file. Just double click on this file and build the solution.

If you are working without Visual Studio, you can build the Oozinoz code with NAnt, so long as you have a `csc` compiler. NAnt is a free build tool that you can download from http://nant.sourceforge.net. If you are comfortable using open-source software, then you should find it easy to install NAnt. If you are new to open source, you may have some learning curve to climb, for example, to learn how to modify your "path." It's well worth gaining this expertise, and NAnt is about as easy to learn as anything you'll encounter in open source software. Once you have NAnt running, go to (that is, `cd` to) the top-level `oozinoz` directory. This directory contains a `nant.build` file. Type `nant`, and NAnt will build all the class libraries and program executables, placing them in the `bin` directory.

Helping the Oozinoz Code Find Files

It can be difficult to write code for a C# program that finds an external file, such as a JPEG or GIF image file. Suppose that an Oozinoz executable file is stored in a `bin` directory, and an image that the program needs is in an `..\images` directory. How can a program find an image in the `images` directory? You might try:

```
Image i = Image.FromFile(@"..\images\someimage.gif");
```

This approach sometimes fails because C# will interpret the path as relative to the directory from which the user launched the program. The user's current directory can be anything. The relative path approach as shown will work only if the user happens to be in the directory where the code (the `exe` or `dll`) file resides. What we need is a path relative to the location of the executable code.

To find the directory in which a program or class library is executing, you can use the `Location` property of the `Assembly` class from the `System.Reflection` namespace. This property tells where the code is executing, regardless of the user's current directory. Using this location, you can build a relative path to determine the path to, say, an `images` directory. This approach almost always works. The `GetFileName()` method of the `FileFinder` class in the Oozinoz `Utilities` class library takes exactly this approach, but augments it with two other strategies.

One problem with finding files is that some programs and utilities will move or copy a class library before executing it. For example, the Active Server Pages example in the PROXY chapter involves copying class libraries (`dll` files) to a new location. To allow for such cases, the `GetFileName()` method looks for an `oozinoz` environment variable that points to the top-

level oozinoz directory. For example, you might define OOZINOZ as
e:\samples\oozinoz, if that's where you put the source code. For remote
proxy examples to work, it is important for you to define the OOZINOZ
variable.

The GetFileName() method actually checks the OOZINOZ variable before
looking for files in paths relative to the executing assembly. If both of
these approaches fail, the GetFileName() method looks for the Oozinoz
code to be in the top-level directory of the current disk, such as c:\oozi-
noz.

The FileFinder class employs an arsenal of techniques for finding image,
database, and text files that support the code examples. Can you be sure
that at least one of these techniques is working on your machine? Yes! You
should confirm that the code is working by running NUnit against the
Oozinoz test library.

Testing the Code with NUnit

The Oozinoz libraries include a Testing.dll class library that is designed
for use with NUnit. NUnit is a free automated testing framework. You
can download NUnit from http://nunit.org. If you know JUnit, you will
probably find NUnit easy to learn. If you're not familiar with either JUnit
or NUnit, the best way to learn how to use these tools is to learn from a
friend or peer. Barring that, you can work through the online documentation for these tools, or find a book on the topic. There is more of a learning
curve than with, say, NAnt, but learning to use an automated testing
framework will equip you with a skill that you will use for years to come.

A difficulty associated with using NUnit is that as the framework executes, it moves the Testing.dll file, making it difficult for Oozinoz programs to find external files, such as the Oozinoz database. To address this
difficulty, you should define an OOZINOZ environment variable that points
to the top-level oozinoz directory. Define this variable and build the Oozinoz code. Run NUnit, open the oozinoz\bin\Testing.dll file, run the test,
and look for a green bar.

Finding Files Yourself

It can be difficult to find a particular file that corresponds to code that you
see in the book. Often, the easiest way to find, say, a particular application
is to search the source tree for the application's name. The code is organized so that you should be able to find files by browsing the oozinoz

directory tree. Table C.1 shows the subdirectories of oozinoz and explains their contents.

Table C.1: Names and Contents of Subdirectories of the **oozinoz** Directory

Directory Name	Directory Contents
app	Contains subdirectories for "applications"—C# files that build into executable programs.
bin	Contains all executable programs and dynamic link libraries that result from a build. Both the provided Visual Studio solution and nant.build file direct their output to the bin directory.
config	Contains files that support various applications.
db	Contains the (rather tiny) Oozinoz Microsoft Access database.
images	Contains images that various Oozinoz applications use.
lib	Contains subdirectories for libraries—C# files that build into a dynamic link library.
nunit	Contains the essential class library of the NUnit automated testing framework.

Summary

Your investment in learning design patterns will begin to bear fruit as you change the way you write and refactor code. You may be able to apply design patterns in your own code immediately, but it sometimes helps to peruse another developer's working code. Getting the Oozinoz code working on your machine is a useful exercise, as is learning to use the open source tools NAnt and NUnit. Learning these tools and getting the Oozinoz code (or anyone else's code) to run can be hard work, but that hard work will pay off by increasing skills that you can use as new technologies come along.

UML AT A GLANCE

This appendix briefly explains the features of the Unified Modeling Language (UML) that this book uses. UML provides conventional notation that this book applies to illustrate the design of OO systems. While UML is not overly complex, you can easily underestimate the richness of the features that UML provides. For a rapid introduction to most of the features of UML, read *UML Distilled* [Fowler]. For a more thorough review, read *The Unified Modeling Language User Guide* [Booch]. By learning to use standard nomenclatures and notations, we learn to communicate at a design level, making us all more productive.

Classes

Figure D.1 applies some of the UML features for illustrating classes.

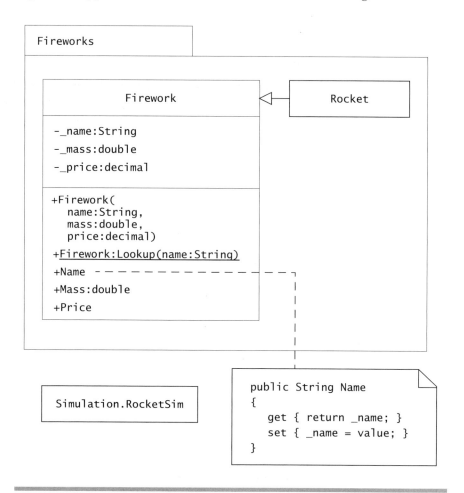

Figure D.1   The Fireworks package includes the Firework and Rocket classes.

Notes on class diagrams:

- Draw a class by placing the name of a class centered in a rectangle. Figure D.1 shows three classes: Firework, Rocket, and RocketSim.

- There is no requirement in UML that a diagram shows everything about a portrayed element, such as all the methods of a class or the complete contents of a package.

- Indicate a package by placing the name of the package in a rectangle, left-aligned with a larger box that may show classes and other types. In Oozinoz code, a package corresponds to both a namespace and a class library. For example, the classes in Figure Figure D.1 are in the `Fireworks` namespace and are compiled into the `fireworks.dll` class library.

- When showing a class outside a package diagram, you may prepend the class's namespace and a dot to the class's name. For example, Figure D.1 shows that the `RocketSim` class is in the `Simulation` namespace.

- You can show a class's instance variables in a rectangle beneath the class name. The `Firework` class has the instance variables `_name`, `_mass`, and `_price`. Follow the variable's name by a colon and the variable's type. In Oozinoz code, instance variables conventionally begin with an underscore, to help distinguish them from other variables.

- You may indicate that an instance variable or a method is private by preceding it with a minus sign (-). A plus sign (+) indicates that a variable or method is public, and a pound sign (#) indicates that a variable or method is protected.

- You can show a class's methods and C# properties in a second rectangle beneath the class's name. Show a property as a method with no parentheses. You may show the type of a property by following it with a colon and its type.

- When a method accepts parameters, you may show them, as the `Lookup()` method does.

- Variables in method signatures usually appear as the name of the variable, a colon, and the type of the variable. You may omit or abbreviate the variable name if its type implies the variable's role.

- Indicate that a method is static by underlining it, as the `Lookup()` method shows.

- Make notes by drawing a dog-eared rectangle. The text in notes may contain comments, constraints, or code. Attach notes to other diagram elements with a dashed line. Notes can appear in any UML diagram.

Class Relationships

Figure D.2 shows a few of the UML's features for modeling class relationships.

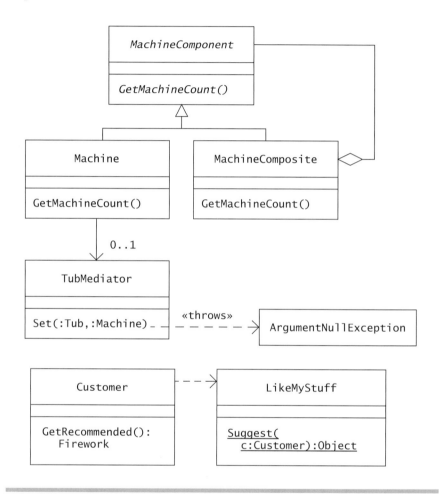

Figure D.2   A MachineComposite object contains either Machine objects or other composites. The Customer class depends on the LikeMyStuff class without instantiating it.

Notes on class relationship notation:

- Show a class name (or method) name in italics to indicate that the class (or method) is abstract.

- Use a closed, hollow arrowhead to point to a class's superclass.

- Use a line between classes to indicate that instances of the classes are connected in some way. Most commonly, a line on a class diagram means that one class has an instance variable that refers to the other class. The `Machine` class, for example, uses an instance variable to retain a reference to a `TubMediator` object.

- Use a diamond to show that instances of a class contain a collection of instances of another class.

- An open arrowhead indicates navigability. Use one to emphasize that a class has a reference to another class and that the pointed to class does not have a back reference.

- A multiplicity indicator, such as 0..1, indicates how many connections may appear between objects. Use an asterisk (*) to indicate that zero or more instances of an object of a class may be connected to objects of an associated class.

- When a method may throw an exception, you can show this with a dashed arrow pointing from the method to the exception class. Label the arrow with a «`throws`» stereotype.

- Use a dashed arrow between classes to show a dependency that does not use an object reference. For example, the `Customer` class relies on a static method from the `LikeMyStuff` recommendation engine.

Interfaces

Figure D.3 shows the basic features for illustrating interfaces.

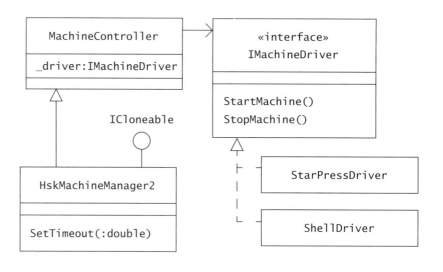

Figure D.3   You can indicate an interface with either an «interface» stereotype or with a lollipop.

Notes on interfaces:

- You can draw an interface by placing the text «interface» and the name of the interface in a rectangle, as Figure D.3 shows. You can show that a class implements an interface with a dashed line and a closed, hollow arrowhead.

- You can also show that a class implements an interface by showing a line and circle (a "lollipop"), plus the name of the interface.

- Interfaces and their methods are always abstract in C#. Oddly enough, interfaces and their methods do *not* appear in italics, unlike abstract classes and abstract methods in classes.

Delegates and Events

At the time of this writing, UML does not provide a notation for C# delegates and events. This book models its notations for delegates after UML interfaces, as Figure D.4 shows.

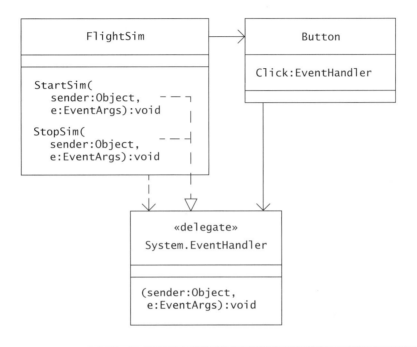

Figure D.4   You can model a delegate type with notation similar to the notation for modeling interfaces.

Notes on delegates and events:

- You can draw a delegate type by placing the text «delegate» and the name of the delegate type in a rectangle, as Figure D.4 shows.

- Place the delegate type's parameters and return type in a second rectangle beneath the delegate type name. Show the parameters in parentheses, separated from the return type with a colon.

- Use a dashed line and a closed, hollow arrowhead to indicate that a method matches a delegate type (that is, has the same parameter types and return value as a delegate type).

- You can show that a class maintains a variable whose type is a delegate type in the same way that you show other instance vari-

ables. Figure D.4 shows that the Button class maintains a Click
variable whose type is the EventHandler delegate type.

- In C# code, you can mark an instance variable such as the Click
  variable in Figure D.4 as an "event" by modifying the declaration
  with the event keyword. This modification reduces the public
  interface of the delegate instance.

- Use a dashed arrow to show that a class depends on a delegate.

Objects

An object diagram illustrates specific instances of classes, as Figure D.5
shows.

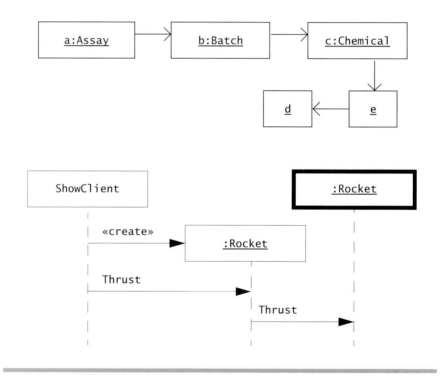

Figure D.5   Depictions of objects indicate the objects' names and/or types.
             A sequence diagram shows a succession of method calls.

Notes on object diagrams:

- You can show an object by giving its name and type, separated by
  a colon. You may optionally show just the name, or just a colon

and the type. In any case, underline the name and/or type of the object.

- Use a line between objects to indicate that one object has a reference to another. You can use an open arrowhead to emphasize the direction of the reference.

- You can show a sequence of objects sending messages to other objects, as the lower part of Figure D.5 shows. The order of messages is top to bottom, and the dashed lines indicate the existence of the object over time.

- Use the «create» stereotype to show that one object creates another. Figure D.5 shows the ShowClient class creating a local Rocket object.

- Draw a darker, thicker box around an object to indicate that it is active in another thread, process, or computer. Figure D.5 shows a local Rocket object forwarding a request for its Thrust property to a Rocket object running on a server.

States

Figure D.6 shows a UML statechart diagram.

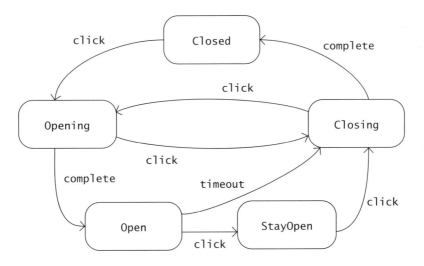

Figure D.6   A statechart diagram shows transitions from state to state.

Notes on illustrating states:

- Show a state in a rectangle with rounded corners.

- Show state transitions with open arrows.

- A statechart does not need to map directly to a class or object diagram, though you may arrange for a direct translation, as Figure 22.3 shows.

GLOSSARY

ABSTRACT CLASS	A class that cannot be instantiated, either because it contains *abstract methods* or because it is declared to be abstract.
ABSTRACT METHOD	A declaration of an operation that concrete subclasses must implement.
ABSTRACT SYNTAX TREE	A structure, created by a parser, that organizes input text according to a language's grammar.
ABSTRACTION	A class that depends on abstract methods that are implemented in subclasses or in implementations of an interface.
ACTIVE SERVER PAGES (ASP)	A set of technologies from Microsoft for building Web services.
AERIAL SHELL	A firework that is fired from a *mortar* and that explodes mid-flight, ejecting and igniting stars.
ALGORITHM	A well-defined computational procedure that takes a set of values as input and produces a value as output.
APOGEE	The greatest height that a fired or flying *firework* achieves.
ASSAY	An analysis, usually of a chemical mixture.
ASP.NET	The ASP technologies upgraded to work in the *.NET FRAMEWORK*
BUSINESS OBJECT	An object that models an entity or process in a business.
CAROUSEL	A large, smart rack that accepts material through a doorway and stores it.
CLIENT	An object that uses or needs to use another object's methods.
COMPOSITE	A group of objects in which some objects may contain others, so that some objects represent groups and others represent individual items, or *leaves*.

COMMON OBJECT REQUEST BROKER ARCHITECTURE (CORBA)	A standard design (common architecture) for facilitating (brokering) object requests that pass between systems.
CONCRETE CLASS	A class that can be instantiated; compare to *abstract class*.
CONSOLIDATION LANGUAGE	A computer language, such as C#, that absorbs the strengths and discards the weaknesses of its predecessors.
CONSTRUCTOR	In C#, a special method whose name matches the class name used to instantiate the class.
CONTEXT-FREE LANGUAGE	A *language* that can be described with a *grammar*.
CONTROL	A *graphical user interface* element, such as a button or text box.
CYCLE	A *path* in which a node (or object) appears twice.
DEEP COPY	A complete copy of an object in which the new object's attributes are complete copies of the original object's attributes.
DELEGATE	A *delegate type* or an instance of a delegate type.
DELEGATE TYPE	In C#, a declaration of a name for the type and signature (the return type and parameter types) of methods that can be used to instantiate the type.
DESIGN PATTERN	A *pattern*—a way to pursue an intent—that operates at about a class level.
DIRECTED GRAPH	a *graph* in which edges have a direction—they point.
DOUBLE DISPATCH	A design in which a class B object dispatches a request to a class A object and the class A object immediately dispatches a request back to the class B object with additional information about the class A object's type.
DRIVER	An object that operates a computer system (such as a database) or an external device (such as a line plotter) according to a well-specified interface.
DUD	A *firework* that does not work correctly, particularly a firework that is designed to explode but doesn't.
ENCAPSULATION	A design that limits, through a specified interface, access to an object's data and operations.

EVENT	In C#, a keyword that limits client access to otherwise public members of a *delegate type* variable. Also, a delegate type variable (such as `Click`) marked with the `event` keyword.
EXTENSIBLE MARKUP LANGUAGE (XML)	A textual language that relies on tags (or markup) to contain information about the text and that specifically separates classes or types of documents from their instances.
FIREWORK	An combustible composition that may burn, fly, or explode, providing entertaining visual and aural effects.
FRAMEWORK CLASS LIBRARIES (FCL)	The collection of packages of reusable classes that Microsoft supplies as part of the .NET Framework.
GRAMMAR	A set of composition rules.
GRAPH	A collection of nodes and edges.
GRAPH THEORY	A mathematical conception of nodes and edges. When applied to an object model, a graph's nodes are usually objects, and a graph's edges are usually object references.
GRAPHICAL USER INTERFACE (GUI)	A layer of software in an application that lets a human interact with (graphical depictions of) buttons, menus, sliders, text areas, and other components.
HOOK	A provision that a developer places in code to give other developers a chance to insert code at a specific spot in a procedure.
HOPPER	A container that dispenses chemicals, usually into a machine.
IMMUTABLE	Unchangeable; specifically, an object with values that cannot change.
IMPLEMENTATION	The C# statements that make up the bodies of a class's methods.
INTEGRATED DEVELOPMENT ENVIRONMENT (IDE)	A software tool collection that combines support for code editing and debugging with other tools for creating new software.
INTERFACE	The collection of methods and fields that a class permits objects of other classes to access. Also, a C# interface that defines the methods that an implementing class must provide.
INTERPRETER	An object composed from a composition hierarchy in which each class represents a composition rule that determines how the class implements (or "interprets") an operation that occurs throughout the hierarchy.

KIT	A class with `Create-` methods that return instances of a family of objects. See Chapter 17, "Abstract Factory."
LANGUAGE	Usually a set of strings, but generally a set of objects that follows a pattern established by a collection of rules. These rules typically include composition rules (a *grammar*), and may include other rules (such as the rule that identifiers must be declared before they are used). A language that can be fully described with a grammar is a *context-free* language.
LAW OF DEMETER (LOD)	A principle of object-oriented design that maintains that an object's method should send messages only to: argument objects, the object itself, or the object's attributes.
LAYER	A group of classes with similar responsibilities, often collected in a single class library, and usually with well-defined dependencies on other layers.
LAZY-INITIALIZE	To instantiate an object when it is first needed.
LEAF	An individual item within a *composite*.
LISKOV SUBSTITUTION PRINCIPLE (LSP)	A principle of object-oriented design that maintains that an instance of a class should function as an instance of its superclass.
LOCK	An exclusive resource that represents possession of an object by a thread.
LOOSE COUPLING	A comparatively small and well-defined amount of responsibility that interacting objects bear for each other.
MESSAGE	Usually a method call, but generally a portrayal of communication between objects, as in a sequence diagram.
METHOD	An *implementation* of an *operation*.
METHOD LOOKUP	The algorithm for deciding which definition of a method to use when a client calls an object's method.
MODEL/VIEW/ CONTROLLER (MVC)	A design that separates an interesting object (the model) from user interface elements that portray it (the view and controller.)
MOLE	A number (Avogadro's number) defined as the number of atoms in 12 grams of carbon 12. The beauty of this number is that it lets you apply chemical equations while working with measurable quantities of chemical batches. If you know that the molecular weight of a chemical is mw, then mw grams of the chemical will contain one mole of the chemical.
MORTAR	A tube from which an aerial shell is fired.

MUTEX	An object shared by threads that contend for control of the object's *lock*. The word "mutex" is a contraction of the words "mutual exclusion."
NAMESPACE	A name for a group of related types that often corresponds to the name of a class library.
NANT	A free build tool that you can download from http://nant.sourceforge.net.
.NET FRAMEWORK	A suite of products, primarily from Microsoft, for developing and operating systems with tiered, object-oriented architectures.
N-TIER	A type of system that assigns layers of responsibility to objects running on different computers.
OOZINOZ	A fictional fireworks company that takes its name from the sound of an audience at an exhibition.
OPERATION	A specification of a service that can be requested from an instance of a class.
PARALLEL HIERARCHY	A pair of class hierarchies in which each class in one hierarchy has a corresponding class in the other hierarchy.
PARAMETRIC EQUATIONS	Equations that define a group of variables (such as x and y) in terms of a standard parameter (such as t).
PARSER	An object that can recognize elements of a *language* and decompose their structure, according to a set of rules, into a form suitable for further processing.
PATH	In an object model, a series of objects such that each object in the series has a reference to the next object in the series.
PATTERN	A way of doing something; a way of pursuing an intent.
PERSISTENT STORAGE	Storage of information on a device, such as a disk, that retains information even when powered down.
POLYMORPHISM	The principle that method invocation depends on both the operation invoked and the class of the invocation receiver.
POSTORDER TRAVERSAL	An iteration over a tree or other composite object in which a node is returned after its descendants.
PREORDER TRAVERSAL	An iteration over a tree or other composite object in which a node is returned before its descendants.
PROPERTY	In C#, a class member similar to a method but oriented to get or set a specific characteristic of the class suggested by the property name, and accessed without parameters or parentheses.

RANDOM CASE	A STRiNG like thIS wHOSE ChARActErs MAY bE uPPeR OR LOwER caSe, AT RANdom.
REFACTOR	Change code to improve its internal structure without changing its external behavior.
REFLECTION	The ability to work with types and type members as objects.
RELATION	The way in which objects stand with regard to each other. In an object model, the subset of all possible references from objects of one type to objects of a second type.
ROMAN CANDLE	A stationary tube that contains a mixture of explosive charges, sparks, and stars.
ROOT	In a *tree*, a distinguished node or object that has no parent.
SEQUENCE DIAGRAM	A drawing that shows a flow of messages between objects.
SESSION	The event of a user running a program, conducting transactions within the program, and exiting.
SHALLOW COPY	As opposed to *deep copy*, a shallow copy limits the depth to which it copies an object's attributes, letting the new object share subordinate objects with the original.
SHELL	See AERIAL SHELL.
SIGNATURE	A combination of the name of a method and the number and types of formal parameters to the method. Also, in *delegate types*, the return and parameter types of a method, but not the method name.
SIMPLE OBJECT ACCESS PROTOCOL (SOAP)	A standard for encoding a method call in a textual (specifically, an XML) form.
STAR	A compressed pellet of an explosive mixture, usually part of an aerial shell or Roman candle.
STAR PRESS	A machine that molds chemical paste into fireworks stars.
STATE	A combination of the current values of an object's attributes.
STATIC METHOD	A method that is bound to a class and that can be invoked against the class or against an object whose declared type is the class.
STRATEGY	A plan or approach for achieving an aim given certain input conditions.
STREAM	A serial collection of bytes or characters, such as those that appear in a document.

STRUCTURED QUERY LANGUAGE (SQL)	A computer language for querying relational databases.
TIER	A layer that executes on a computer.
TITLE CASE	A String Like This Whose Characters Are Uppercase If They Follow Whitespace.
TREE	An object model that contains no *cycles*.
UNIFIED MODELING LANGUAGE (UML)	A notation for illustrating design ideas.
UNIFORM RESOURCE LOCATOR (URL)	A pointer to a resource on the World Wide Web.
VISUAL STUDIO	A tool that facilitates software development in C# and other languages.
WIZARD	A series of dialogs that walk a user through a task.
WORK IN PROCESS (WIP)	Partially manufactured goods in a factory.

BIBLIOGRAPHY

Albahari, Ben, Peter Drayton, and Brad Merrill. 2002. C# Essentials, Second Edition. Sebastopol, CA: O'Reilly & Associates.

Alexander, Christopher, Sara Ishikawa, and Murray Silverstein. 1977. A Pattern Language: Towns, Buildings, Construction. Oxford, England: Oxford University Press.

Alexander, Christopher. 1979. The Timeless Way of Building. Oxford, England: Oxford University Press.

Booch, Grady, James Rumbaugh, and Ivar Jacobsen. 1999. The Unified Modeling Language User Guide. Boston, MA: Addison-Wesley.

Cormen, Thomas H., Charles E. Leiserson, and Ronald L. Rivest. 1990. Introduction to Algorithms. Cambridge, MA: The MIT Press.

Cunningham, Ward, ed. The Portland Patterns Repository. Available online at www.c2.com.

Drayton, Peter, Ben Albahari, and Ted Neward. 2002. C# in a Nutshell. Sebastopol, CA: O'Reilly & Associates.

Fowler, Martin and Kendall Scott. 2000. *UML Distilled, 2d ed*. Boston, MA: Addison-Wesley.

Fowler, Martin. 1999. Refactoring. Boston, MA: Addison-Wesley.

Gamma, Erich, Richard Helm, Ralph Johnson, and John Vlissides. Design Patterns. 1995. Boston, MA: Addison-Wesley.

Honderich, Ted, ed. 1995. The Oxford Companion to Philosophy. New York, NY: Oxford University Press.

Lea, Doug. 2000. Concurrent Programming in Java, Second Edition. Boston, MA: Addison-Wesley.

Liberty, Jesse. Programming C#. 2001. Sebastopol, CA: O'Reilly & Associates.

Lieberherr, Karl J. and Ian Holland. 1989. Assuring Good Style for Object-Oriented Programs. Washington, D.C. IEEE Software.

Liskov, Barbara. May, 1987. Data Abstraction and Hierarchy. SIGPLAN Notices, volume 23, number 5.

Metsker, Steven J. 2001. Building Parsers with Java. Boston, MA: Addison-Wesley.

Petzold, Charles. 2002. Programming Microsoft Windows with C#. Redmond, WA: Microsoft Press.

Riordan, Rebecca M. 2002. Microsoft ADO.NET Step by Step. Redmond, WA: Microsoft Press.

Russell, Michael S. 2000. The Chemistry of Fireworks. Cambridge, UK: Royal Society of Chemistry.

Sontag, Susan. 1979. Illness as Metaphor. New York, NY: Random House.

Troelsen, Andrew. 2001. C# and the .NET Platform. Berkeley, CA: Apress.

Vlissides, John. 1998. Pattern Hatching/Design Patterns Applied. Boston, MA: Addison-Wesley.

Weast, Robert C., ed. 1983. *CRC Handbook of Chemistry and Physics, 63rd ed*. Boca Raton, FL: CRC Press.

Wiltamuth, Scott and Anders Hejlsberg. C# Language Specification. Available online at http://msdn.microsoft.com/.

Wolczko, Mario and Randall B. Smith. 1996. Prototype-Based Application Construction Using SELF 4.0. Available online at www.cs.ucsb.edu/oocsb/self/.

Index

A

Abs class, 304
Abstract classes, 347, 349
  defined, 431
  and interfaces, 9–10
ABSTRACT FACTORY pattern, 160, 179–190, 191
  abstract factories and factory method, 185–189
  defined, 179, 190
  GUI kits, 179–184
  namespaces and abstract factories, 189
  abstract keyword, and constructor declarations, 381
Abstract methods, 69–71, 223, 426
  defined, 431
Abstract syntax tree, 341
  defined, 431
Abstraction, 17, 65–72, 214, 359
  defined, 71, 431
Accept() method, 342, 414–415
  MachineComponent class, 330, 333
  ProcessComponent hierarchy, 340
Access modifiers, 151, 153
  in C#, 78
  function of, 80
Active server pages (ASP), 132, 418
  defined, 431
ADAPTER pattern, 5, 17, 19, 19–33, 70, 226, 351, 410
  usefulness of, 33

Add or Remove Programs, Control Panel, 133
AddNode() method, 332
Add/Remove Windows Components, 133
Administrative Tools, Control Panel, 133
ADO.NET, 35–36
Advisor interface, 250
Aerial shells, 38, 58, 61, 176, 324, 358
  defined, 431
  process flow for making, 59
Alexander, Christopher, 1
Algorithms, 218–219, 220–221, 223–224
  defined, 218, 431
Anchoring a chain, 144–146
Apogee, 130, 132, 225–226, 374
  defined, 431
  app subdirectory, oozinoz directory, 420
Architectural patterns, intent of, 1–2
Argument-free delegate, 102
Arithmetic class, code for, 304–5
Array class, 224
ArrayList class, 224
ArrayList collection, 14
ASP.NET, 132, 137, 344
  central benefit of, 137
  defined, 431
Assay class, 53
Assay, defined, 53, 431
AssignButton() method, 111
AssignTub() method, 89
Aster star press, 227–229